To

Melania

with

love

Henrietta

5/18/05

PEACE

OTHER MRI PRESS PUBLICATIONS
Music as Culture 2d
Chaka, An opera in two chants
Intercultural Music Vols 2-5
Intercultural Musicology Vols 1-4

MRI Press

...is still one of the most challenging books in ethnomusicology. In contrast to other works that approach music out of its context, the authors discuss music as a social and cultural product, and as part of human behavior. It is consistently provocative and enlightening, addressing issues that have become part of mainstream ethnomusicological research such as aesthetics, cognition, and performance. It also explores theories and discusses fieldwork methodology, illustrating these with examples from the authors' fieldwork in Malta, Madagascar, the United States, and other places...

Laura Larco, University of Maryland, College Park
From a review of *Music as Culture* at Amazon.com 17 July 2000
***

...The implications of this bi-cultural reality subsequently becomes the subject of *Intercultural Music I* [and]...illustrate how one aspect of a research insight can generate ideas that could make the research proceed into other areas thereby widening the intellectual horizon...

Ezenwa-Ohaeto, *Pan Africa* 1997: 2,1
From a review *of Intercultural Music Volume 1*
***

...This is the second volume in the important initiative that seeks to address—and thereby—integrate both the concept and practice of "intercultural music" within our contemporary discourse on music. Readers wishing to gain a background understanding of intercultural music and its related terms such as interculturalism, intercultural composition, and intercultural musicology should consult the introduction to the first volume (1995)...The range of articles and issues are contributed by individuals from different fields and disciplines who offer their perspectives on what intercultural music means to them...

Daniel Avorgbedor, *Intercultural Musicology* 2001: 21, 3
From a review of *Intercultural Music Volume 2*
***

...Publication of a CD recording of Akin Euba's *Chaka* thus marks a special moment in African art music composition. First heard at the University of Ife in 1970...This 1998 recording, the first of its kind, features a revised version of the work. While no recording can ever substitute for a live performance, the present document affords us the opportunity to hear and imagine the musical drama. It exemplifies Euba's way with voice, his conception of various characters, and his vision of this most artificial of genres. Most importantly, perhaps, *Chaka* on CD makes it easier for students, younger composers, and the music-loving public to gauge what is possible in the realm of modern African operatic composition...

Kofi Agawu, *Research in African Literatures* 2001:32,2
From a review of *Chaka*

Around the World in 80 Years

MUSIC RESEARCH INSTITUTE
MRI PRESS
POINT RICHMOND

A MEMOIR

by HENRIETTA YURCHENCO
A MUSICAL ODYSSEY

Published by the Music Research Institute, MRI Press
© 2002 by the Music Research Institute
All rights reserved. Published 2002
English version. Printed in the United States of America

Publisher:

MRI Press
P. O. Box 70362
Point Richmond, CA 94807-0362
e-mail: cynkim@attbi.com

Library of Congress Control Number 2002110387
Yurchenco, Henrietta, author.
    Music, Ethnomusicology, Folk Music, Anthropology. .
    345 p. 6" X 9" — (Worlds without Boundaries: Biographies in Music)
    Includes photographs, index and author's bibliography/discography and list of
    field collections
    ISBN 0-9627473-5-1
    1. Around the World in 80 Years. A MEMOIR A Musical Odyssey.
        Title.

Layout/typesetting/ and indexing, Lisa M. Kimberlin
Cover color, Gloria M. Perrino
Proofreader, Carolyn H. Baker.
Proofreader for Discography, Lyuba Birinbaum

Printed by Van Volumes, Three Rivers, Massachusetts USA

To My Family

To the Memory of:

DR. DANIEL RUBIN DE LA BORBOLLA, friend and mentor

DR. MANUEL GAMIO, friend and mentor

WALDEEN, friend, dancer, poet

PAUL KRESH, writer

JAMES LESTER, beloved nephew

Publisher's note

MRI's first book series, *Intercultural Music*, now in its fifth volume, is published for the Centre for Intercultural Music Arts based at the Institute of Education, University of London, U.K.

This memoir inaugurates *Worlds without Boundaries: MRI Biographies in Music* in the form of autobiographies, biographies, and memoirs. All too often, the subjects portrayed are not seen in the context of their time and era. These books will focus on those who chose music as their life's work and who I believe have made major contributions to the arts that have yet to be fully realized. Often they work outside the mainstream and perhaps are not in sync with their time, or simply have a different vision of what music is all about. Hence, this series is meant to capture the essence of individuals who exemplify the maverick, the visionary, the outspoken, and the risk taker.

Dr. Cynthia Tse Kimberlin
Publisher/Editor, MRI Press
Point Richmond, California USA

Prologue

This extraordinary woman of slight frame,
    has gone places and recorded music that the
outside world' didn't know existed, and then come back
to New York City and put it on the radio for anyone and
everyone to listen to. Hooray for Henrietta Yurchenco and
the First Amendment to the U.S. Constitution!

Pete Seeger

April 12 2002

Preface

When I was 19, I decided I was not to be a concert pianist. I figured the world would not even notice my defection. Certainly it didn't need another pianist who forgot the key she was in, and suffered attacks of nerves. Rather than fight them, I decided to back out gracefully, admit defeat, and try something else. I became an ethnomusicologist. This was not a conscious decision on my part; it just evolved little by little, over many years. This is the story of how it happened...

***

Contents

★ ★ ★

Mexico

Seri

Yaqui

Tarahumara

cora

Huichol

Purepecha

Mixteco   Teotzil
Zapoteco   Tzeltal
Mis   Tojolabal

Guatemala

MEXICO

BELIZE

Chajúl (Ixil)

ˈrabinal
(Quiche)

HONDURAS

EL SALVADOR

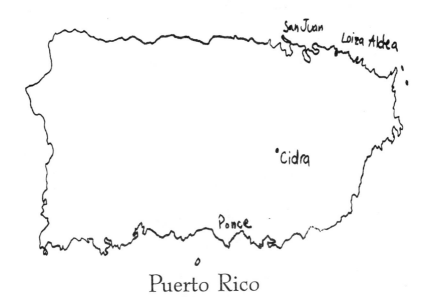

Puerto Rico

Provinces of Spain and
Baleraic Islands

Chapter One - New Haven
1916-36

I was born on March 22, 1916, in New Haven, Connecticut, during the worst snowstorm of the year. My mother gave birth at home, the way most poor children came into the world in those days. She always attributed my pale complexion to the blizzard that raged that day, and her eyes would sparkle each time she recounted the story of my birth.

My mother (known as Rivka in Yiddish and Rebecca in English), born in the Ukrainian town of Nemirov, came of a middle-class family. Her father, a small merchant, one of the few positions permitted Jews in Czarist Russia, was respected by his Christian neighbors for his honesty and industry, especially the Grand Duchess, the owner of Nemirov, his best customer. Even as a child my mother was headstrong and demanding. Unlike most "stetl" girls she insisted on learning to read and write Yiddish, just like the yeshiva *bucher* (boys) in her community, and she got her way. Besides her native Ukrainian and Russian, she also spoke Polish and Slovak, learned from itinerant peasants who worked in nearby fields. She always spoke affectionately of her family and the easy childhood she enjoyed, yet, at the tender age of 16, she left home and immigrated to America.

Mom proudly describes herself, arriving at New York's Ellis Island in 1911, as "properly dressed and corseted", the visible signs of a respectable woman. She had traveled all the way from Russia by herself, a lovely young woman, a little over five feet tall, with pale skin, brown hair, gray-blue eyes, and fashionably plump. Her parents had provided her with a few necessary items, a feather bed, a samovar and some Russian crystal with which to start her life in the New World. Unfortunately, the samovar and the crystal disappeared, pawned or sold during hard times. The feather bed ended up as soft pillows, the last of which lies on my bed to this very day.

Despite the first years as a seamstress in a sweatshop working ten hours a day, my mother, like most Eastern European Jews, was happy to be in America. She would listen to her Italian and Irish neighbors describe wistfully life in the Old Country, and dreams of some day returning home to buy their own businesses with money earned in America. For a Jew from the "Pale of Settlement," home brought back memories of pogroms and discrimination, and no wish to see it again. For Mom, the New World offered free lending libraries, concerts of classical music, museums, and the freedom to go anywhere she liked without restriction.

Although homebound all her married life, she admired the bold women of her generation -- Margaret Sanger, the Suffragists, free souls like Isadora Duncan, and shared her husband's radical political views. She was indeed fortunate, the only member of her immediate family to come to America, and the only one saved from the Holocaust.

Mom used to describe the natural beauty of the Ukraine in glowing terms: "I tell you, Yentl (Henrietta in English), you never saw such wheat, it grew taller than your father. The apples were as big as grapefruits, the cauliflower and cabbage that big," she would say, drawing huge circles in the air to indicate their size. We children would scoff at her: "Oh, Mom, cabbages don't grow that big." But she wasn't exaggerating after all. I've never been to the Ukraine and can't vouch for what grew there in my mother's time, but many years later I saw such enormous vegetables and fruits at the Carmel market in Israel.

The rest of my mother's family, her mother and father, sisters and brothers, fled revolution-torn Russia in 1919, following the main road from Nemirov to the city of Rovno, Poland. There they thrived and lived in relative peace with their Christian neighbors -- or so we thought. Even before Hitler's rise to power in 1933, their letters began to speak of rising anti-Semitism; within a few years there was real alarm. They begged my mother to bring them to America. But in the bleak years of the Depression neither she nor her relatives in New Haven could help them. Besides, who in late 1920s believed that Jews were in any particular danger, and was it any different from the past?

When the war began in 1939, my mother heard no more from Poland, the war had brought a complete news blackout. Years later, after my parents' death, we discovered the horrible truth. Early in the war, probably 1942, her entire family -- sisters, spouses and children were lined up in the town square, tortured and shot to death. Only her youngest brother, in a summer boys' camp, escaped the massacre. Eluding the Nazis, he fled from Poland to Tashkent in Soviet Asia but died there in a freak accident. On Victory day, all Tashkent went on a wild binge to celebrate the war's end. My uncle, in a drunken stupor, fell into the river and drowned!

I've been told that I inherited my strong temperament from my paternal grandmother; an old photograph of my grandmother depicts a tall, slender, authoritative woman dressed in a conventional, high collared black silk dress. I don't remember her at all, but I do recall my aunts' off-hand remarks that Minnie had a "waspish" temper and could be mean and bossy. They never forgave her for abandoning my father (known

3

as Itzok in Yiddish and Edward in English) and his brother (Nathaniel) while she and her three daughters came to America. To leave two small boys with relatives was unforgivable even though common practice at the time. My father never forgot how ill-treated the two brothers were.

When it was their turn to come, the two boys left their birthplace, Brest Litovsk, and traveled together across Europe, met at each railroad connection by Jewish agencies until they reached Amsterdam. and then across the Atlantic in steerage. Years later, he would say wryly: "Well, *tochter* (daughter), I came on a better boat than the Pilgrims." But to a boy hardly in his teens, such inconveniences counted for nothing. My father believed he was going to a land of freedom with limitless opportunities.

My father seldom spoke of his mother, and then only to regret her short-sightedness. He had wanted to be a carpenter, a respectable occupation, but low on the social scale. Perhaps she envisioned him as a doctor or lawyer (every Jewish mother's dream), or some other elevated career. But they never materialized. Pop never went to college, never became a doctor, not even a carpenter. One day, while working as a carpenter's apprentice he injured his hand. His mother put her foot down: "You don't do that kind of work," she said. "So I never learned a trade," my gentle father would say ruefully. "I went into business, and failed miserably."

Like many immigrants, Pop wanted to be a "real" American, shed his old speech, mannerisms and habits from the "old country." He enthusiastically endorsed every new invention, every new processed food, anything that would make life easier. To him a real American was practical, progressive, always looking for new solutions to old problems.

Pop was captivated by America's romantic legends. As a boy he admired the macho image of Wild Bill Hickok and Buffalo Bill. In the "old country" peasants tilled their piece of land for a lifetime, seldom venturing further than the nearest village. Here in America, life could be full of adventure. Even notorious gunmen, like Jesse James and Billy the Kid (who killed 21 people, one for each year of his life), were symbols of democracy. After all, hadn't they fought bankers and railroad barons? Besides, where else but in America could a poor and uneducated boy rise above his circumstances to become a millionaire?

In reality, he rubbed shoulders not with bankers and robber barons but with other poor immigrants like himself. They shared the same tenement -- Italians, the Irish, Slavs -- worked at low-paying jobs, their children went to the same public schools and played together in the street; they lived in peace with each other. Sure, there was anti-Semitism, but no killing All in all, it was a better life than the one left behind.

My father was a quiet, gentle man who loved his wife and children above everything in the world. It was he who sprawled on the floor playing games with us, who cradled us when we were ill. When my mother's patience was exhausted from our childish scrapping, she would threaten: "Wait until your father comes home. He'll give you a good spanking." Never! He couldn't bear to lay a hand on us; at most we'd receive a mild rebuke: "Children, I can't believe you would do such a thing!" And those words hurt more than a thrashing; we tried not to anger or disappoint him.

Pop was too gentle a man to succeed in the hard world of business. He went broke in the 1920s, after two failed attempts to run a grocery store in the poor Black section of town. They lived on credit, and seldom paid their debts. After Pop's death in 1959, his nephew recalled him as a young man: "He was a lively guy, a gay blade who loved a good time." I imagine "a good time" meant gambling at pinochle, excursions to Savin Rock (New Haven's Coney Island), and picnics at the seashore. Certainly my father was not a drinking man, nor a woman-chaser. He was a high-minded idealist concerned with arts and politics. I still treasure a photograph taken in 1912. Seated on the grass, he and his brother Nathan are reading the *Socialist Call*, the leading pre-World War I radical newspaper.

Mom and Pop will always remain in my memory as the rarest of human beings -- warm, loving, understanding. The welcome mat was always at the door for strangers, down- and-outers, whoever needed friendship or companionship. Though we had political differences with my mother and father's relatives, we kept in close contact with them. The Veners and the Kippermans, my mother's aunts, were small-business people who concentrated on living from day to day, keeping their heads above water. My parents thought them indifferent to other people's misery. "Here we are," Mom would say, "in a terrible Depression, the whole world falling apart, and my Aunt Emma talks only about Shirley Temple," an exaggeration, but perhaps they survived bad times better than we did. We lived with our bitterness much of the time; they sought relief from it. Our favorite was Cousin Barney, who was my sister's age. We adored him, and spent many happy hours in his company. We lost contact with Barney for many years, but at a recent family reunion, now with his wife Ruth, he said: "Your house was so warm and loving; Rivka and Eddie, how can I ever forget them?"

I was six years old, my sister Ruth three, when my brother was born. The day before, my mother had hung the family laundry to dry on the clothesline suspended from the back porch; the next morning she was in labor. Ruth and I crouched under the kitchen table, comforting each other as Mom's screams from the bedroom door announced the birth of Nathan, named after my father's brother who had died of influenza during the war. (He later added a middle name, Hale, in honor of the American revolutionary hero.) My brother's birth was the cause of great rejoicing: Like other Jewish women, my mother had yearned for a boy-child, and happily he appeared on the third try. Nate grew up to be a handsome man, somewhat resembling Paul Newman. Socially active his entire life, he died before he was 70 years old, leaving behind his devoted wife, Rebecca, and four beautiful and talented children, Emily, Martha, Loren and Daniel.

I vaguely remember the flat on Garden Street where Nate was born. The big, cast-iron coal stove in the kitchen/dining room barely heated the adjoining bedrooms, but it provided the perfect temperature for cooking and baking. On the back porch we had a wooden, aluminum-lined icebox, which the ice-man filled with a block of ice every other day during the summer. The ice was used to cool the lemonade and homemade root beer Pop made. It also helped me endure hours of piano practice in the summertime: My mother would wrap a chunk of ice in a washcloth and place it on a plate next to the piano. It was not as effective as the air-conditioning I enjoy now, but it kept my hands and brow cooled as I played!

In the wintertime, dairy products were stored outside on the porch. Many foods we consumed during the winter were preserved in the fall, and had to last until the next summer when fresh fruits and vegetables were available again. This was a time of great fun; we all pitched in, peeling, cutting and sorting, while Mom and Pop stirred the pots of bubbling strawberry, gooseberry and (my favorite) plum jam, green tomatoes, apple sauce,

7

peaches, the half-sour pickles we all loved, and anything else cheap and plentiful. When everything was ready -- the Mason jars sterilized, filled, tightly sealed with wax, snapped shut with metal clamps and neatly arranged on pantry shelves -- my father would say with an air of exhaustion: "Rivka, why do you bother? You can buy everything ready-made in the grocery store." Scornfully, my mother would reply: "Sure, sure, but not as good as mine!" That would silence him -- until the next year.

One of our joys was my mother's cooking; she was an even better baker, and Pop was her able assistant. To this day, my sister and I prepare those favorite family dishes: delicate cheese *blintzes* sautéed in butter; aromatic cabbage borscht served with fresh dill and sour cream; *olipses,* cabbage leaves stuffed with meat. I make *mandelbrot,* pastry bars of ground almonds, and my sister makes the more complicated *strudel.* My parents would collaborate on the *strudel*-sumptuous morsels of thin, almost transparent pastry filled with nutmeats, sweet jam, raisins, apples and honey. Potato *latkes* and the Thanksgiving pumpkin pies were my father's specialties, and I have yet to taste better ones. The *latkes,* thin and crisp, were topped with sour cream (although many people prefer them with apple sauce). We children would crowd around the stove, plates in hand, waiting in turn for each *latke* to come off the hot griddle, to be eaten instantly.

Years later, when I was married and living in New York, I asked my mother to send me the recipe for her rich, buttery coffee cakes. Mom knew the ingredients from long usage, but had never measured them exactly, a handful of this, a pinch of that, a finger-length of something else. They spent an entire day measuring every ingredient, and finally sent me the recipe, along with Pop's usual comment to buy coffee cake at the bakery to

8

save myself fuss and bother. As you can imagine, I ignored his advice, and to this day make those wonderful cakes.

Our neighbors were a grand mix of Italian and Irish immigrants. Poverty had brought them together, as prosperity later pulled them apart. Neighbors always helped out in times of illness, to run an errand or babysit during emergencies. In the next building lived a distant relative of my father, who had married an English servant girl and brought her to America. I remember her for the pies she baked, with a delicate, flaky pastry. But most of all, she was a wonderful story-teller. While my parents went off to their meetings or choral rehearsals, she would entertain us with English folk tales from her youth -- scary stories of ghosts, the living dead, fairies, and the half-human female creatures with seaweed hair that live at the bottom of lakes and rivers. We would shiver and cling to each other in terror while begging for another story, and then another, until the adults' return would shatter the spell of enchantment she had woven around us.

The back yard was our favorite play area. On the paved area, we played hopscotch and cruised around on roller skates. In the unpaved part stood a huge apple tree, which became the center of our universe; we spent hours climbing its branches or reading books while propped against its huge trunk. With help from the adults, we built a playhouse near the tree and filled it with junk from around the neighborhood -- discarded furniture, lamps and threadbare rugs. We made tables out of orange crates donated by the grocery store, and covered them with worn-out tablecloths and the neighbors' cast-off chipped dishes. The playhouse was girls' territory, and generally we chased the boys away; after all, we were not about to tolerate their sloppiness. When we felt magnanimous we'd invite them in, but not for long. We played house, acting all the parts, and yelled at our "children" just the way our parents (sometimes) yelled at us.

In the 1920s we owned a car, one of those open cars popular at the time, and rode around with the top open to the sky. If we got caught in the rain, we would attach glass shields over the sides. My father was an excellent driver. Sometimes we'd go on picnics to Wharton Brook, a park of tangled woods we children loved to explore. We would saunter along trails, cool our bare feet in the fresh water, pick blueberries and, before leaving, always fill bottles with pure mountain spring water to take home.

When the car broke down and could no longer be fixed, we took the trolley to Lighthouse Point, a public beach on Long Island Sound. The ride cost us five cents; we'd rent a locker for our clothes for ten cents, and eat our picnic lunch in the tree-lined shade near the beach. The big treat of the day was an ice cream cone for each of us. We would enviously eye the children eating in restaurants and buying souvenirs for sale along the beach. But we had a wonderful time diving in the waves, floating on our backs and swimming far out into the Sound. I can still hear my mother's warning cries: "Come back, you're over your head, you'll drown if you don't watch out!" But we were good swimmers and never suffered anything worse than a rash from the slimy red jellyfish that lined the water's edge.

Mom was the strength of the family, although Pop bore the brunt of earning a living. When there were no more jobs, no more household treasures to sell, no money left from insurance policies (paid in small premiums over many years and cashed in for a pittance), and we children were still too young to work, Mom would swallow her pride and ask her relatives for help. The occasional ten dollars her relatives doled out fed our family of five for an entire week. I never figured out how she did it but she, like other poor women, knew how to cut corners. When our shoes wore out she had them resoled; shoes were thrown out only when we outgrew them or the uppers cracked, exposing our feet to the elements. To ready them for the next day's wear, she would spend the evening at the shoemaker's shop, waiting patiently while he repaired each pair. She enjoyed those trips away from home, the only time she was off-duty; it was her time to relax, relieved from household drudgery and the constant care of three little ones. Neighbors must have joined her at the shoe shop for a little socializing, because she always returned with a fresh supply of local news and the latest from the "old country."

Like other homebound women, Mom supplemented Pop's meager earnings with domestic work. Some families took in boarders, but in our cramped tenement quarters we had no room for anyone else; my sister and I shared the same room and the same bed for much of our childhood. She earned a little extra money by feeding an old peddler his mid-day meal and, in addition, received a bonus: fresh vegetables and fruits he sold from his horse-drawn wagon.

Under such circumstances, we learned to be self-sufficient at an early age, and not to ask for what couldn't be given, neither money nor special attention. We had few toys; I never owned so much as a doll. When we had nothing to do and would complain, Mom would order us out of the house with a few choice words: "Go bang your head against the wall!" She had no time for our boredom what with mountains of unwashed clothes, food shopping, cooking and cleaning. In those days before supermarkets, a half-day was needed to gather supplies from the grocery, butcher, fish market and produce store. We learned to entertain ourselves, play with neighborhood kids, and invent games of our own. When we learned to read and write we formed literary and art clubs with our school chums, wrote stories and

11

painted birthday cards. Only at night, when chores were done, did we have our parents' undivided attention.

In the early years, life revolved around our parents and their friends. Everyone would sit around the kitchen table near the coal stove (the living room was reserved for strangers), having cake and tea, served Russian-style, in a glass. Holding a cube of sugar between the teeth, the adults would sip the hot tea, letting the sugar dissolve slowly and sweetly in the mouth. Sometimes they would even substitute raspberry or strawberry jam for sugar. Only people from the "old country" did this; the rest of us drank out of cups, and were contemptuous of this arcane habit. "Mom," we would say irritably, "you're not in Russia anymore, so why don't you drink like the rest of us?" (Poor Mom, she finally gave in, not because she preferred our way, but to avoid embarrassing us in front of our American-born friends -- although I would occasionally catch her sipping tea through a sugar cube on the sly.) As the evening wore on, the cake would gradually disappear (except for a few pieces she hid away). Later, when our guests had all gone home, she would take stock of the empty plates, shaking her head in mock distress, and say: "Look at that, I spend the whole day baking and in one minute it's all gone." But I can only imagine how despondent she would have been had her guests refused second and third helpings!

Although my family's social life was fueled by political talk, we children were always glad when the adults wearied of serious stuff and told stories. On long winter nights, friends from Latvia, Estonia, Russia and the Ukraine would regale us with tales of shtetl life and the odd people who lived there, especially the men and boys who spent a lifetime studying Torah, and the women who not only kept house and brought up the children, but earned a living in the marketplace -- just so their menfolk could study undisturbed. This way of living was incomprehensible to us, brought up in America. My mother would boast proudly that her family was different; her father earned a living, and never let his wife work. I never forgot my father's description of the chief Hassidic rabbi of his village: "He wore a beautiful fur hat and a sable-lined coat," he said, " and rode through the village streets in a fine coach drawn by two horses, like a king. The Duke who owned our village never tangled with him, and always bowed to him when they met on the street."

Stories we liked best were the hair-raising adventures of the Russian revolution. Sasha, a 6'4" Russian compatriot, was the best story-teller of the lot. Night after night, he regaled us with vivid descriptions of daring encounters with the White (Czarist) Army, and how he defeated them single-handedly. "I had two sabers in my hands," he would recount, "and seated on my horse I cut them down, one at a time, as they came near. You see that scar on my face?" he'd challenge us. "Once they got me, but never again." One day we decided to look into his past. Imagine our astonishment when we discovered his real age: He had been only 11 or 12 years old during the Revolution! Those stories were pure inventions, hatched from his fertile imagination. But we didn't care if they were true or not; they entertained us. Finally, as we grew older, the enchantment wore off.

We children were never formally taught Yiddish; we picked it up from the daily talk around the dining table. Mostly, we retained Mom's peppery proverbs and curses (beloved by Jews), remembered from her own childhood. These one-liners defined a wide range of opinions about the world and the people who daily crossed her path. We were told, for example, to watch out for certain people because "m'schlut yidden" (they hit Jews). When things went wrong, "Ah klug auf Columbus" (a curse on

13

Columbus). With no known solution or person to blame, what better person than Columbus, conveniently out of reach. My mother had no time or patience for fantasies. Thus, a foolish solution for a serious problem elicited *"Wird helfen wie a toiten bankus"* (it will help like a dead leech), recalling the medieval treatment for disease. The comment *"arois gevorfen de gelt"* (money thrown away) had less do with money than with time and effort wasted stupidly. She also had an equivalent for the American "drop dead": *"Ich hob dir en bud"* (I have you in the bath) which makes no sense in translation, but somehow we knew what it meant. And someone considered crazy beyond redemption was said to be *"meshuga auf toit"* (crazy to the death). Practically every year was a bad year for one reason or another, so the expletive *"a schwarz yuhr"* (a black year) was in perennial use. And the curse *"Soll sie vaksin vie a zsbile mit en kopf en drerd"* (May he grow like an onion with his head in the ground) was cast on whomever was on Mom's hit list of the moment.

The colorful array of characters -- *shlemiels, shlemazls, mishagoyim, ganoivin* (crooks) and shlepper, words now in common usage in American English -- were, in my childhood, exclusive to Jews. Nicknames were often derived from quirks of character or physical attributes; unlike Anglo-Saxon custom, such imperfections were frankly acknowledged. A fool was openly called a *nar*; an ugly girl was a *meeskeit*; someone with a long nose was dubbed *di nuz*; a relative with poor eyesight was referred to as the *blinde* (blind one). For my vinegary temper, I was called a *shlang* (snake), and it stuck to me for years. My sister fared better: she was called the *brenn* (one who burns), referring to her youthful energy. No one was exempt--the rich, the poor, the young, the old, the greenhorn, the old settler, the professor, the dunce. Each person was stamped with a label that identified him or her, a caricature, to be sure, but true to life.

14

I never received any religious instruction. My father was a confirmed atheist. Every month he received a journal, published by the 4H Society, which promoted atheism. Many of the articles were tracts disproving Bible stories. "Children," Pop would say, "how can you believe that the whale swallowed Jonah and then spit him up as good as new? Do you really believe that Moses spoke to God, and that the burning bush didn't burn out? You see, children, all those stories are fairy tales and not to be believed." Years later, I was to cherish these wonderful stories, not as reality but as myth.

Despite my father's atheism, my mother would go to the synagogue on Yom Kippur and Rosh Hashanah, the Jewish New Year. For my sister and me, those autumn holidays were our favorite season. We'd briefly attend services and then join our friends at various parties and gatherings. In the days when Pop had a job and we could afford a few luxuries, we bought new clothes, especially for the holidays.

My mother followed my father's beliefs. In my childhood I remember her preparations for Passover, the house cleaning, the special Passover dishes brought out from storage. One year they disappeared, never to be seen again. We children dared not admit to our Jewish friends that we had no real *Seder* on Passover, just a regular dinner. One year, we nagged Mom so much that finally she asked the old peddler to conduct a legitimate ceremony. What a wonderful time we had that night! We sat through the whole long reading of the *Haggadah* and its numerous rituals without even fidgeting; we hunted for the hidden matzos, and were deeply awed when the traditional glass of wine was placed outside the door for the prophet Elijah. Would he really come?, we asked. After the *Seder*, seeing that the glass was still full, we regretfully concluded that Elijah had drunk too much before reaching our door, but had taken a few drops just to be fair.

15

Later my father said, "Children, I could have conducted the *Seder* as good as the old man. But he never did, that remark was meant to impress us with his knowledge.

At the center of our home life was politics. An admirer of American dissenters Robert LaFollette and Norman Thomas, in the early 1930s, my father joined fraternal organizations connected to the Communist Party. The works of Marx, Engels and Lenin began to be quoted at home, not their economic theories, which we hardly understood, but the slogans which summed up their goals: "From each according to his ability, to each according to his needs" and "the dictatorship of the proletariat" were accepted without question. But the bedrock of communist doctrine was support for the Soviet Union, accepted on faith, never to be questioned just as the virginity of Mary is accepted by Catholics. In my "wisdom" at age 16, I considered it a waste of time to talk with anyone not a communist.

On May Day and other occasions we kids would participate in the parades organized by the Communist Party. Proudly we'd march down New Haven streets, carrying banners and singing revolutionary songs like the "Internationale" and "Avanti Populi," the Italian communist anthem. Our neighbor, the plump Mrs. Katz, was always there, urging the few curious spectators to join the marchers. "Come on in," she'd shout with a sweeping wave of her hand. "Come on in, cost no money," (the "n" pronounced like the Spanish ñ). Workers, farmers, close your ranks!" There were few workers and no farmers among us, only intellectuals, housewives and the elite of the party -- painters, printers and carpenters.

Two of my cousins, sons of Pop's sister Pauline, were Trotskyites and would argue heatedly with my father. "I tell you," my cousin Sam used to shout, "hundreds of thousands of writers, scientists, poets, musicians are daily being shipped off to Siberia, tortured and killed in prisons for any criticism of the regime!" "Don't say that!" my father would shout back. "You are liars, counter-revolutionaries who want to destroy to Soviet Union!" The rest of the family would hover nearby, trying to calm the troubled waters.

Discussions at the dining table were often loud and volatile. To interrupt, to outshout someone was legitimate, how else could you make the point? In moments of calm deliberation, we acknowledged listening to other opinions was a mark of civilized behavior; but in the heat of the argument, who listened? Opinions on political and social matters were never censured within the family circle, although we were warned about expressing them in public. In this way I learned how to voice my opinions early. But I also learned the value of silent revolt. I committed my first act of rebellion at the age of 10 by refusing to recite the Lord's Prayer in school assembly. Without making a fuss, I just did what I thought was right for me. I was applying the lessons of my parents: Better quiet rebellion than angry, self-righteous confrontation, and it has served me throughout my life.

Over time Pop's 19th century humane idealism was replaced by a rigid, implacable dogma -- and he didn't even realize it. When I returned from Mexico in 1946,1 told him I could no longer support the Soviets. His sorrowful answer still rings in my ears: "*tochter*, I never believed that I would ever hear you say such a thing." Yet, barely ten years later, he was to learn from Khrushchev's report to the Supreme Soviet Council the shocking truth about the Stalin years. That revelation dealt a crushing blow to my parents' lives. All their friends had been of the Left, and were the source of a rich social life. Old friends disappeared, and no new ones took their place. Gone were the choruses they had sung with, gone the protest meetings, and gone the yearly May Day celebrations. Worst of all, my parents felt their ideals betrayed: They had been so loyal, so steadfast in their belief -- and now it had all come to nothing.

Besides politics there was music. Both my parents were passionate music lovers. My mother's love for music began as a young girl in Russia, when she and her friends would steal into the gardens of the Grand Duchess to listen to concerts given in the palace. Hiding in the shadows under huge, open windows, she heard for the first time music she would love the rest of her life, and pass on to her children. She sang folk songs in a high lovely soprano and we learned them from her. My father, also an avid lover of classical music, played the mandolin as a young man. It was a sorry day when he had to sell his mandolin; he never replaced it, even when times got better. Until we bought a piano in 1926 and my lessons began, the phonograph was the center of our musical life. I cut my musical teeth on popular operatic arias and overtures, Bach, Mozart and Beethoven played by Fritz Kreisler and Mischa Elman on the violin, and Ignaz Paderewski on the piano. The fine concerts at New Haven's Woolsey Hall were out of our reach. The early Victor Red Seal and Columbia recordings on breakable '78s were my father's pride and joy, and he bought them whenever a few extra coins jingled in his pocket.

From early on my sister, brother and I were also immersed in literature. As we grew older we read such classics as *Alice in Wonderland*, works by the humorist Dorothy Parker ("If all the girls at the Yale Prom were laid end to end, I wouldn't be surprised!"), and the poetry of Edward Lear; our favorite character was the cat in a pea-green boat, and we reveled in its logic turned-on-its-head. In *Alice*, the tea-party was a favorite chapter; it tickled our sense of the absurd. We'd roll those smart

18

lines around our tongues ("much of a muchness"); we loved the curious characters, so serious in their lunatic behavior, and found the far-fetched logic of conversation an antidote to adult stuffiness and dullness. We repeated with glee the words of the Knave of Hearts during his trial accused of stealing some tarts:

> 'Give the evidence,' said the King. 'Where shall I
> begin?' asked the White Rabbit. And the King
> answered solemnly, 'Begin at the beginning, and
> go on until the end. Then stop.'

Those lines would send us into convulsions of laughter. I attribute my later interest in Dadaism and Surrealism to my reading of Lewis Carroll.

My sister Ruth must have felt slighted by the special attention I received with my piano lessons. Yet my parents were very aware of each of us as separate and distinct personalities. I always considered my sister very beautiful and intelligent. She was always at the head of her class and brought home the best grades. She loved theater and showed real talent, but never developed those talents, regretfully bowing to the necessity of earning a living in those difficult years. In later years, I enjoyed listening to Ruthie argue a political or social point with David Lester, her brilliant scientist husband. Marshaling her facts and standing her ground in rebuttals, she could tear his arguments to shreds. He would say with genuine pride and respect, "Ruthie, you would have made a hell of a lawyer!"

She and I sometimes acted in amateur plays like *Waiting for Lefty* by Clifford Odets. We read Dreiser, and Jack London, and writers on the social problems of the 1930s. But we were also introduced to the great Russian and French writers, especially the work of Sholom Aleichem, the great Jewish scholar. As younger children, since our parents couldn't afford summer camp, we spent summers at the library. We'd bring home armfuls of mystery and spy stories written for girls, and read into the night until Mom shouted warnings that we would go blind from so much reading. Then we'd turn out the lights and go to sleep.

When I started to take lessons on our new second-hand upright piano, music in my home assumed a tangible form; we could hear it live in our own living room. I took lessons from my cousin, Fanny Kipperman, and shortly after I began she informed my parents: "Henrietta is very talented." From then on, my musical education became a top concern of the family. My practice hours were carefully monitored. I was shooed away from the kitchen if I tried to help my mother: "Leave the dishes alone, I'll do them. You go and play the piano." It is a miracle to me how I ever learned to cook or sew, but I did although I cannot remember how I circumvented my mother's opposition. My friends were politely told to wait until I was through practicing before being allowed into the house. I gave that piano a real workout, and after a number of years it fell apart; some of the notes didn't sound, strings broke, it went out of tune as fast as it was tuned. With no money to buy another one I practiced on my friends' pianos when they weren't at home. My musical talent occasionally brought me invitations from the wealthy members of the family. I still have the vivid memory of a visit to the home of Lillian Perlmutter, a cousin who lived at Woodmont, a resort on the Connecticut shore (Lillian became a sculptor, and later married Joseph Hirschhorn, the wealthy art collector.) One day, when I was about 11 or 12, Lillian took me to the shore for a swim and later introduced me to her friends, the only time I was to see the '20s generation in the flesh. My cousin's circle was not as wealthy as the Long Island set memorialized in F. Scott Fitzgerald's novel, *The Great Gatsby*, but they were a reasonable facsimile. To my childish eyes they looked so chic, so sophisticated, so modern! Corsets -- the abomination of my mother's generation -- were nowhere to be seen. All the women wore the new fashion of the time: short (above the knee), straight shifts, pastel-colored silk stockings and pointed high-heeled shoes. They wore headbands around their short, marcelled hair, looking just like the "flappers" in the John Held cartoons of that time. They all smoked cigarettes in long holders, and drank gin (available from any neighborhood bootlegger during Prohibition). The men were equally elegant, wearing white pants (known as "ducks"), V-neck sweaters, blue or white blazers and two-toned shoes. All afternoon they hung around the piano, singing the latest songs, like "Baby Face" and "What Is This Thing Called Love?". Huddled in a corner of their big living room couch, I watched them dance the Fox Trot and the Charleston. How I wished I would grow up fast so I could be like them!

Playing my pieces was easy; I learned everything in record time, mostly after just a few days of practice. Fanny gave my mother instructions that I was to play only what she assigned. (Later on I realized how short-changed I had been; it kept me from improvising and learning to read at sight, abilities necessary for a pianist's career.) I was a good and obedient pupil, but I chafed under Fanny's rigidity. To fool my mother, I would quickly learn and memorize my lesson and then read a book placed on a chair nearby, reading as I played. One day my mother caught me and raised a storm: "If you do that again I'll stop your lessons!" I dared not try that anymore. Soon Fanny passed me on to her own teacher, Reuven Kosakoff, a composer and pianist who had studied in Germany under the great Artur Schnabel.

I was about 11 when my serious musical studies began. How I dreamed of going to study in Germany, the mecca for so many

American music students. How I dreamed that I would sail away on a big ship, play in international competitions and win all the prizes! But alas, it was never to be.

The years of study with Reuven were truly magical. He taught me to be a musician -- to think about music, to understand its form, and to extract warmth and tonal variety from a basically percussive instrument. Perfect playing was expected of me; everything had to be just right. Sometimes we'd spend the whole lesson on two phrases, playing them over and over until I struck the right mood. No work was finished until technique and musical understanding were perfectly synchronized.

My weekly walk to Reuven's house, especially in the early spring, was the high point of my adolescent years. In early April the maple, chestnut and elm trees that lined the streets were already covered with tiny new-green leaves, pale and transparent. With music books under my arm, my soul soared. In a few minutes I would enter the house, sit down at the Steinway with my beloved teacher at my side, and play what I had learned during the week. How I treasured those hours, the miracle of playing, my fingers dancing on the keys in long cascades of perfectly matched notes! Each year I worked on a new program -- Beethoven, Mozart and Haydn sonatas; works of Schubert, Chopin, Brahms and Schumann; and the moderns, like Debussy, Ravel and Bartok (whom I was to meet in 1940 in New York, just as he arrived fleeing from the Nazis).

From the beginning I had an affinity for dissonant modern harmony. To my ears, it was fresh and stimulating. Reuven introduced me to the piano works of Bartok and Schoenberg, radical composers of that time, and I literally swooned with delight. Nothing has ever sounded foreign to me since then. Most Western musicians struggle to overcome their aversion for music not their own; I had no such problem. When I was 18 I gave my first full-length concert, at the small but beautiful auditorium of the New Haven Medical Society, and Reuven and his family paid the rental and program printing costs. The concert was a complete success: I started with the Bach Italian Concierto, conquered my nerves after the first movement, and sailed through the rest of a very difficult program without a hitch. It was a moment of triumph; I was on top of the world.

But that concert was the end of my career as a pianist. The next year, overcome by nervousness, I backed out of Reuven's student recital. My sister remembers, although I don't, that I cried for three whole days. Even though I continued to play for a number of years, I never recovered the momentum. I was locked into my fear of blackout, of paralysis on stage, which was beyond my control. Having given up the idea of a concert career, I felt a sense of relief: No longer would I have to suffer the nervous attack, which preceded every performance. On the other hand, my heart was heavy; I loved the instrument, the music I played, the skills I had acquired. Music had become my life, the core of my being, the source of my joy pleasure. I realized I must put it on hold, and do something else, but I also knew it would have to be something in the field of music.

My membership in the John Reed Club, the Communist Party's intellectual wing, was my doorway to the world beyond home and school. I was still in high school at the time, bored with classes that offered little for my curious mind. At the club, surrounded by Yale University students from all over the world, I was exposed for the first time to modern literature, the arts, theater and music that shaped my tastes and attitudes for many years to come.

That education, however, came wrapped in Marxist doctrine. Accordingly, all art was propaganda of the ruling class, and the duty of the artist was to create a new art for the revolution, a position I soon questioned. My final departure from Marxism, however, came in the 1940s when the Soviet Central Committee denounced Prokofiev and Shostakovich for writing "decadent capitalist" music. I was not about to recognize a bunch of politicos as musical experts. In retrospect, it is ironic that Nazi and Communist official art became two sides of the same coin, both monuments to banality and mediocrity. I brushed the cobwebs from my mind, and learned to think without the Marxist crutch.

Besides its left politics, the John Reed Club was the citadel of the new Bohemia, successor to the Jazz Age. Although long over we still bore the marks of that giddy era -- bobbed hair and short skirts -- smoked and drank in public, but hard times made us a sober generation. How could we enjoy the luxuries of the 1920s like champagne, sports cars, raccoon coats and life in Paris when we could hardly pay the rent?

It was hope and love that sustained me. My first tentative love affairs are not worth a mention, for they began as quickly as they ended until I met Chenk. Basil ("Chenk") Yurchenco was a student at the Yale Art School and a fellow club member. Born in Argentina of Russian parents, he was a lively, creative man and I fell in love for the first time in my life. We became lovers shortly after meeting, and married a few years later in New York.

Suddenly Chenk opened my eyes to a new and exciting world, and I became his eager student. Together we saw avant-garde films like Cocteau's "Beauty and the Beast" and Luis Buñel's "The Andalusian Dog". We went to exhibits of cubist, Dadaist and surrealist painting at the Yale Gallery. Even in those days, long before he became an architect, Chenk was fascinated by the new architecture of Frank Lloyd Wright, Le Corbusier of France, and Walter Gropius and Marcel Breuer of

Germany' Bauhaus (with whom he would study years later at Harvard).

Part of my education was watching Chenk paint in his studio. I came to love the smell of paint, the sized canvases and ornate frames that he collected from junk shops around town. I went shopping with him and learned to distinguish good brushes and paints from bad. Most of all, I learned about technique, brush strokes, color, line and the way it came together on the canvas. He loved music, but a concert also provided him with an opportunity to draw caricatures of performers and audience. To this day, I admire the wit and humor of those wonderfully clever drawings, and wish he had never abandoned painting for architecture. The few paintings and drawings I have occupy choice positions on the walls of my apartment.

Every once in a while we would see the new productions at New Haven's Schubert Theater. For many years the Schubert was the principal try-out theater in the country. Failure in New Haven meant never reaching Broadway. The popular saying "Bombed in New Haven, banned in Boston" indicated two strikes against you; the first, for displeasing a seasoned theatrical audience, and the second, for offending the prudish Victorian sensibilities of "Boston Brahmins". Besides the theater Chenk introduced me to the ballet; I saw the first performance in America of the famous "Ballet Russe de Monte Carlo". There are no words to describe the impact that Stravinsky's *Petruschka*, De Falla's *El Sombrero de Tres Picos* had on my young impressionable mind. For weeks afterwards I was haunted by all I had seen and heard; dance, sets, costumes, the best from Europe, all come to our shores.

In 1934, Chenk moved to New York to work for the Federal Art Project, an agency of the WPA (Works Progress

Administration). It was understood that I would join him the following year. Meanwhile, I attended the Yale School of Music, the tuition paid for by a wealthy friend of Chenk's. I signed up for all the usual courses, continued lessons with Reuven, and taught at a local music school. But I was impatient to join Chenk in New York, and glad when the term ended. It was time to leave provincial New Haven, to breathe fresh air, to spread my wings and fly. I packed my few possessions, bid a tearful farewell to my parents, and boarded the train for New York City. It was June of 1936, and I was just 20 years old.

***

Chapter Two – New York City 1

1930s-1940s

Before the Great Depression plunged us into poverty, my father bought a car, an open touring car, the kind popular in those years. The greatest adventure for the family was an occasional trip to New York. Nothing impressed me more than the huge apartment houses along Riverside Drive and the uniformed doormen standing like sentinels at each entrance. To live in such a place became my secret dream. One day I would live there, I promised myself. I imagined myself smartly dressed in the latest fashion, strolling in the park with my sprightly French poodle; later my maid would serve me my breakfast in the dining room overlooking the Hudson River, with the majestic Palisades in full view.

Well, my life didn't turn out that way. I never developed a taste for such luxuries. But some of my childish dreams did come true. Today I have breakfast in the dining alcove of my 12th-floor apartment, not on Riverside Drive but downtown Chelsea; it also overlooks the Hudson River but I have no servants and no poodle. But who cares? I see magnificent sunsets, streaks of red, purple, and orange, watch luxurious cruise ships, guided by little red tugs, glide by on their way to West Side docks. Though my work subsequently took me to the most remote corners of the world, New York has remained my home.

Chenk met me at Grand Central Station that happy June day in 1936, and took me to his tiny apartment on Manhattan's east side, our home for a year. The day we married, we took the subway to City Hall, paid $2.00 for the license and $2.00 each for witnesses provided by the marriage bureau, and were pronounced man and wife. I would have loved a formal wedding surrounded by friends and family, but not Chenk, he hated ceremonies of any kind.

Then I found a piano teacher. I took one lesson and quit. I had become so used to Kosakoff's analytical approach no one else satisfied me. Soon I stopped playing altogether but continued my musical education at the Mannes School in Manhattan. That was the end of my formal training. From then on I became involved in the life of the city, a booming metropolis despite the Depression bread lines, soup kitchens, shantytowns and bank failures. We fervently believed if we fought for a common purpose, we could bring justice and freedom to the world. To promote the idea we went to demonstrations, shouted slogans on picket lines and protest marches, and spent evenings at countless "cause" parties. We were the greatest partygoers of all time -- for a noble purpose.

Because of Chenk, my first New York acquaintances were painters and sculptors. Many had lived in Paris during the 1920s art movement (surrealism, Dadaism abstractionism) and returned home after the 1929 stock market crash, broke, and with no prospects of earning a living. The Roosevelt Administration came to their rescue, established the Federal Arts Project, and hired them to supply artwork for schools and other public buildings. With private patrons in short supply, they were glad to get the work even though paid a pittance, hardly enough to keep body and soul together. Our friends mainly lived in cold-water lofts in downtown Manhattan, ate sparingly, but never succumbed to despair or lost faith in themselves. Saturday mornings we would see them at the 57th Street art galleries, weekends we gathered at cafeterias around

Union Square to argue about art and politics into the wee hours of the night. There was gentle Ruth Gikow; Byron Browne, the blond Aryan from Yonkers with a thick New York accent; the hearty German, Hannes Von Wight; tall, handsome Philip Guston; elegant Bourgogne Diller, and Max Spivacke, looking like the actor Jean Gabin in turtleneck sweater and cigarette dangling from his lower lip.

Stuart Davis and Arshile Gorky were the most respected of all the artists, and stories about them were legion. I vividly remember Arshile at a party on east 8th Street standing alone on the terrace overlooking the 9th Street gardens. "For God's sake, Arshile," someone called out, "come on in, we're going to eat." "No," he said, "I'm so lonely. You eat without me." We always wondered how anyone could be lonely, surrounded by a bevy of admirers. Years later, when I learned of his suicide, that incident came to mind.

But about art, Gorky was a severe and uncompromising critic. Once, it is told, a young painter asked him for a critique of her work. It was one of those depressing social scene paintings typical of the time. Sadly, he commented: "This, my dear, is poor painting for poor people." To her question about whether to paint or "function" (i.e., be active politically) he replied, "Function, function." For Arshile, the sacrifice of art for politics stirred nothing but his contempt.

I can't remember when it happened but one day I received a call about a demonstration of the Artists Union (yes, painters had organized just like industrial workers) at the Museum of Modern Art; I chased down to 53rd Street to see many of our friends carrying signs and yelling slogans demanding their work be exhibited on a par with Europeans. The police swooped down and arrested as many as fit into the "Black Maria" (police wagon). When the desk sergeant at the police station asked for their names, they gave those of their favorite painters -- Rembrandt, Picasso, Matisse, Cezanne and Leonardo da Vinci. The poor cops must have been completely bewildered, but the painters had the time of their lives. I think they were fined some insignificant sum for disturbing the peace, but the story made the papers and the Museum changed its policy of discriminating against American painters.

My life was about to change; soon I was to be an actor in the affairs of the city rather than a spectator. I got a job at WNYC, the municipally owned radio station atop the Municipal Building in lower Manhattan. As Federal Arts Project supervisor of the abstract murals then being installed at the station, Chenk got wind of a job opening. He introduced me to Isaac Brimberg, the station's chief engineer and strategist who introduced me to the director Morris Novik, an appointee of then Mayor La Guardia. I was 23 at the time, had never been inside a radio station, and didn't know a microphone from a screwdriver. But I must have impressed them, because I was hired soon afterward. Perhaps Novik, determined to change the station's unimaginative programming, welcomed my youth and self-confidence. I never disappointed him; during the two years on staff I produced the first programs of world folk and tribal music ever presented on New York airways, initiated the first two American Music Festivals, which even after my departure, continued for decades. I was in the center of all that was new and exciting in New York's musical scene in the pre-World War II years. Although I quickly acquired a reputation for weird programming, I was always supported by the mayor and station administration. Shortly after I was hired and had begun my folk music broadcasts, Novik called me into his office. Dick Pack, our publicity man, was there, too. "Chenk (my name at WNYC) how would you like to program a ten-day festival of American music to run between Lincoln's and Washington's birthdays? Dick thinks you could do the job." I must have glowed, I was so excited. "Sure," I blurted out, "I'd love to do it." Novik said, "You plan all the folk, jazz and classical music, and Dick will schedule the pop music from our recordings." The project was big and bold; we held concerts in our studios and remote broadcasts in the city's leading concert halls. Morris and the Mayor contacted the best orchestras and choruses, and I rounded up composers and their organizations. I'm sure that every composer who had ever written a note on paper asked for time on the Festival program. After all, WNYC was the one place in the city where an unknown composer could get a hearing. I can still see the young Leonard Bernstein, tearing down the hallway to play his piano sonata on the League of Composers program hosted by Aaron Copeland. Roy Harris, Henry Brant, Paul Bowles, Norman Della Joio, David Diamond, Morton Gould and Vernon Dukelsky (known as Vernon Duke in the pop field) all played their works. Elie Siegmeister brought his American Chorus, and Earl Robinson, whose "Ballad for Americans" was making history, sang "I Dreamed I Saw Joe Hill Last Night" -- his eulogy to the IWW leader executed in Utah in 1916 by anti-labor officials.

Although I had relative freedom to explore music, it did not extend to politics. Nevertheless, I decided to take the risk and program a scene from Mark Blitzstein's controversial leftist musical play "No For An Answer". Novik, uneasy about the possible censorship by the watch-dog City Council said, "Go see Blitzstein, ask him to go easy on the politics, but be diplomatic. We don't want him to accuse us of censoring him." I explained the station's position to Mark at his apartment in the Village. He laughed, "Okay, I'll steer away from politics." He was true to his word. For the broadcast he had excerpted a romantic scene from the play. Listening to it from the control room, I suddenly

31

froze: A love duet was in progress! My God, I thought, they sound as if they're doing it right in the studio! I hadn't counted on sex, only politics. At that time, suggestive lyrics, as in the blues, were absolutely forbidden; it was an unspoken law. I waited for the axe to fall; sure some puritanical busybody would call, protesting loudly our moral turpitude, the waste of taxpayers' money, etc. Finally the long afternoon passed without a single complaint. To this day, I am convinced nobody was listening to WNYC that February afternoon of 1941, and least of all the station's directors. Maybe they were out to lunch.

When the Festival was over, emboldened by the favorable press and academic reception, I decided to do a series on contemporary avant-garde music; we called it "Composers of Today and Tomorrow". Most of the musicians on the programs were European refugees; though we couldn't pay them, they were glad to resume musical careers now in limbo because of the war. My husband warned me conservative listeners might object to such experimental music and urged me to form a support committee. I knew he was right but couldn't spare the time. When the attack came, it was not from irate listeners but from Mayor La Guardia himself. One night he called, just as a broadcast was winding down. The program had consisted of works by such distinguished composers as Stefan Wolpe and Arnold Schoenberg, the most dissonant music of the time, and performed by violinist Rudolph Kolisch and pianist Eduard Steuerman. "You call this music?" shouted the Mayor. "Who wants to listen to such noise? Tell Novik I want to see him in my office tomorrow morning at 9 o'clock!" And he hung up. It was the evening's last program; only my announcer and engineers heard the Mayor's call. "Oh, you're going to catch it now," they taunted me. "You've got your nerve, putting such junk on the air."

The next morning I arrived early, a little apprehensive but with my head held high; I settled down in my office to await Novik's return from the Mayor's office. Soon Brimberg appeared, all smiles, and reassured me: "Don't worry, nothing's going to happen." Novik had told the Mayor: "I don't like that music either, but if you want New York to be the musical center of the world, then you can't tell musicians what to play. Besides, it doesn't matter whether we like it or not." The Mayor calmed down and said, "Okay, you made your point." In retrospect, I have to admire both men -- Novik, for confronting the Mayor up front, and LaGuardia, for his wisdom and enlightened vision of the city.

But the episode didn't end there. Two days later, the radio column of the *World Telegram*, the afternoon daily, carried a story that the Mayor was canceling "Composers of Today and Tomorrow." That same day, Brimberg walked into my office. Twirling his moustache, he casually asked, "Do you know the radio columnist at the Telegram?" "No," I said, "what about him?" He showed me the article. I was aghast! "You don't think I had anything to do with this?" I yelled. "Of course not," he said. "I just wanted to check it out." He beamed at me and patted me on the shoulder, much relieved by my answer. I never found out who leaked the story, but it could have been anyone at the station. I did learn how easily I could make enemies.

As World War II loomed more menacing with each passing month, European musicians, intellectuals and artists found refuge in New York; many came to WNYC Unforgettable was Bela Bartok, the great Hungarian composer. In 1940, shortly after his arrival in the States, I met him at his hotel to arrange a broadcast in his honor. Theodor Adorno, the Viennese psychologist, also a refugee, went along with me, since he was to interview Bartok on the air. Bartok, a slender man with chiseled

33

features and a gentle demeanor greeted us courteously. Adorno, a Schoenberg disciple, immediately antagonized him: "Mr. Bartok," he said, "I have just read through your Fourth String Quartet. You have written an atonal work, have you not?" (atonality was the cornerstone of Schoenberg's theories of composition). Bartok looked him square in the face; his icy blue eyes seemed to burn as he coldly said in perfect English: "Mr. Adorno, you may believe anything you like." It was certainly one of the great put-downs in musical history.

Several weeks later we broadcast the concert, Adorno carefully avoiding any controversial subject. Rudolph Kolisch (of the Kolisch Quartet) and Eduard Steuerman performed Bartok's Second Violin and Piano Sonata admirably; the studio audience, however, was impressed more by Kolisch's violin technique than the music. His right arm disabled in World War I, he had shifted his fingering to the right hand and bowed with the left. I heard comments about it for weeks afterward.

Of all the refugees none was more distinguished than the great conductor and charismatic personality Otto Klemperer, with whom I had several curious encounters. One day I received a frantic call from our receptionist. "Chenk, can you come out to the lobby? There's a man here and he's threatening me." I rushed out to find Mr. Klemperer pacing up and down. Now, Klemperer was a most terrifying figure in those days: more than six feet tall, he had just been operated on for a non-malignant brain tumor, and had made newspaper headlines for some weird behavior. With a black patch over one eye, his mouth a bit twisted to one side, and brandishing a cane, he was a menacing figure. "What's the trouble, Mr. Klemperer?" I asked in silken tones. Brandishing his cane at me, he growled: "The taxi is waiting downstairs. I will not conduct the rehearsal unless you pay the fare!" I rushed to the director's office, got the money, and sent someone to pay the taxi driver waiting on the street twenty-five floors below. Klemperer smiled graciously at me and disappeared into the rehearsal studio. I returned to my office.

Twenty minutes later the telephone rang again. This time the call came from the engineers in the control room: "Chenk, please come. We're fifteen minutes from broadcast time and we haven't had a mike test." "Well, why not?" I asked. "Because we're afraid of him, that's why!" they replied. Quietly I entered the studio where a rehearsal of a Bach harpsichord concerto was in full swing, Klemperer conducting the orchestra and Edith Weiss-Mann at the harpsichord. "Mr. Klemperer," I said, my voice rising as I competed with the sound of 25 instruments going at full blast, "the engineers must have a mike test." He glared at me for an instant, put the baton down, and smiled at me. "Of course," he said, graciously, "why didn't they ask me?" From then on he was as gentle as a lamb, and the broadcast went off without a hitch.

Shortly afterward I saw Klemperer at a party at Rudy Kolisch's house. All the Schoenbergites were there: Adorno, Steuerman, Weiss-Mann, and Oscar Levant, the pianist of Gershwin fame, also a Schoenberg disciple. Everyone carefully avoided looking directly at Klemperer, their old friend and admired colleague, still with visible marks of his operation. Finally, KIemperer faced his friends, "Look at me!" he demanded with obvious annoyance, yanking off the patch from his eye. " What's the matter, can't you bear the truth?" Everyone was embarrassed, but as liquor and food were passed around the tension evaporated.

The last time I saw KIemperer was in Mexico City, shortly after my arrival there in 1941. The U.S. embassy had rung me up: Mr. Klemperer was in town as a visiting conductor and needed some help. Would I oblige? The next day he came to see me with his request: "As you know, I can conduct an orchestra but I can't write. Would you please write a letter for me?" I was delighted to help out. Although he tried, there was no way to disguise the fact that the letter was addressed to his lady love in New York, the same Hungarian singer he had accompanied on the broadcast the year before.

Poor Klemperer, he had such a tough time in Mexico. Contracted by a private management agency to conduct several orchestral concerts at the Palace of Fine Arts, the principal concert hall of the city, he had offended Carlos Chavez, the acknowledged musical czar of Mexico; no musician was tolerated unless invited by him. Chavez had his methods of displaying displeasure -- penalizing his own musicians for joining another orchestra, or luring away key players from rehearsals. Klemperer, however, pitted his wits against Chavez' power: When his musicians found the stage door barred at the last rehearsal for the last concert, he ordered them to begin playing outdoors behind the Palace. Within minutes the doors opened, and the rehearsal continued on stage.

But let me return to "Adventures in Music", the kingpin of my work at WNYC, and how my interest in music of other cultures began. In New Haven at age 16 I attended a lecture given by Yale anthropology professor George Herzog, illustrated by a few of his own field recordings of African music. Herzog, also a musician, was a disciple of Bela Bartok, one of the pioneers of folk music research. I was so excited by the music I heard; it was new, strange, different from all that I had ever heard before. It sparked an interest, nay, a passion I have retained the rest of my life.

In 1940, however great my interest to broadcast such music on "Adventures in Music", there were virtually no recordings commercially available. I decided to scour the city for live performers. Even in 1940, New York was home to numerous ethnic groups, all of them with talented musicians and dancers performing in civic centers, restaurants, at street fairs and holiday celebrations. Between 1940 and 41 I found a sitar player from India in a restaurant, someone brought a Spanish gypsy flamenco guitarist to the station, a Chinese scholar came to play the almond-shaped "pipa". One day, George Herzog himself came to the studio with his wife to play a primitive African marimba, a bundle of tuned wooden slats arranged on the floor according to pitch. They took turns playing them, faster and faster until someone missed the beat and was eliminated from the game. The elegant Brazilian soprano Elsie Houston sang her country's folk songs; the Calypsonian "The Duke of Iron" had his own weekly series.

Soon American folk music became my chief interest. With Franklin Roosevelt's election in 1932, Americanism was in the air, and one of its consequences was the birth of city interest in traditional country music. Towards the end of the 1930s, a colony of folk musicians from various regions settled in New York, primarily to raise money for political causes. I met the principal figures. -- Huddie Ledbetter (Leadbelly) from the black south, Woody Guthrie from the Oklahoma Dust Bowl, and Aunt Molly Jackson, her sister Sarah Ogan, and brother Jim Garland from the Kentucky mine fields, all trouble spots, all keepers of old-time rural musical traditions. Unlike the popular songs I knew, mostly about romantic love, their songs tracked every aspect of life from the history of their struggles to the intimate details of their private lives.

Sarah, Jim, and Woody appeared on one of the "Adventures in Music" first broadcasts. It was about the 20 year-old strike in the Kentucky mine fields to form a union of their own choice. Although a national issue it was seldom, if ever, discussed on the air except as a news item. I decided to bring their story to our listeners. Both Sarah and Jim were union organizers as well as singers. To help out on the broadcast they brought their friend Woody Guthrie, even though he was from another part of the South. Gentle Sarah sang her heartbreaking "I Am a Girl of Constant Sorrow", Jim his defiant "I Don't Want Your Millions, Mister".

> I don't want your millions, mister
> I don't want your diamond rings
> All I want's just live and let live
> Give me back my job again.
>
> I don't want your Rolls Royce, mister
> I don't want your pleasure yacht
> All I want is food for my babies
> Now give to me my old job back.

We heard first-hand about the dismal life in company-owned towns, their fight against company-hired Chicago gangsters, and government compliance. It was all tied together by a memorable script written by Paul Kresh, a fine writer and dear friend until his death in 1997.

Woody brought the program to a close with the ballad "Tom Joad", based on the hero of John Steinbeck's novel *The Grapes of Wrath* which he had just seen in its movie version. He stood at the microphone, swung his guitar (to which a sign was attached saying: This machine kills fascists) to playing position, strummed a moment or two, and began his song. When it was over, there was hardly a dry eye in the studio; everyone patted him on the back. The telephones kept on ringing; listeners telling us it was a great show. For the first time I rubbed shoulders with these courageous country people -- miners, migrants, union organizers, people I had only heard about but never met in the flesh.

Pete Seeger, whom I was to meet shortly, reported that Woody wrote "Tom Joad" in an apartment they shared on the sixth floor of an East 4th Street tenement. Woody typed away, stopping every now and then to try a verse on the guitar, then typed again. About one in the morning, Pete fell asleep. When he awoke the next morning he found Woody asleep on the floor, huddled in his overcoat, a half-empty jug of wine at his side, and the finished ballad in the typewriter.

Woody Guthrie was undoubtedly the key person in the then budding urban folk song movement. Even today, his "This Land Is Your Land" is the unofficial national anthem known to every school child in the nation. His songs, as well as his lifestyle inspired generations of folk musicians, notably Bob Dylan and scores of others. But in 1940 he was just another musician out of work. Recently arrived from California, he was the only one on that broadcast with previous radio experience. His politics, his opinions about life were his own; no one told him what or how to sing. He never proselytized but wrote from the heart, from experience, from life itself -- and did it with humor and a writer's skill. The irony was that he didn't trust us. We were too intellectual, too eastern, too big-city; we weren't part of his family. Being with Woody was like walking on glass; we always had to watch out for splinters. Although we admired his songs and integrity, it was difficult to be an intimate friend. Yes, Leadbelly and the Kentuckians talked his language, but we New Yorkers were suspect.

Marjorie Mazia, a member of Martha Graham's dance group, who later became Woody's second wife, once choreographed a dance to Woody's songs, called "Folksay". Years later Marjorie told me she made a chart indicating his entrances, what and how much to sing. But Woody, a freewheeling musician who loved making up verses on the spur of the moment, resented the endless repetition and split-second discipline. In the end the dance went off without a hitch, but Marjorie had a bad case of the jitters during the performance.

Woody originally came to New York in 1940 to help raise money for the Dust Bowl refugees, poverty-stricken migrants working in West Coast fruit orchards. Even after years in New York he never abandoned his small-town view of life, or his optimism and vision of a just and bountiful America. His idealism was expressed in his songs, but even more so in his writings. He loved the act of writing; he loved his typewriter. He would rewrite a song over and over again. In the years I knew him he would send me long letters rather than phone me. After his death, when I was writing his biography, I pored over essays, reprints of his West Coast newspaper column, "Woody Sez"; scribbles in book margins; lists of all kinds; stories about his youth as a hungry, homeless and jobless wanderer. During World War II he wrote literally hundreds of letters to Marjorie while he was in the Merchant Marine. Some of his musings were so poignant, so perceptive, so outrageously funny that I still enjoy quoting them to this day.

Here are a few of my favorites.

In describing himself he says: "I am five feet and some inches in my brother's socks feet. My hair is wavy when I'm two haircuts behind, and plumb curly when I'm four. I ain't got any

40

bad habits except my own and never take a drink unless I am by myself or with somebody."

Here is a short excerpt from a letter to a newborn niece, written in Woody's early youth in Texas: "May your days be toward a glittering harvest when your seasons blend at noontide and your morning stoops to kiss your midday. May your gladness ripen as a yellow sweet fruit and the radiance of your thinking invigorate the world. May you see the reality of affliction and realize the all-ness of God. For God is truth, love."

This poetic language and faith in God may come as a complete surprise to his admirers, but Woody was a complex man, not a country "yokel." To him Jesus was a champion of the poor, a workingman like himself, exhorting the rich to mend their ways. He sang about this belief in "Jesus Christ":

> Jesus Christ was a man who traveled through the land,
> A hard-working man, true and brave.
> He said to the rich, "Give your goods to the poor,"
> But they laid Jesus Christ in his grave.

Another favorite is Woody's incomparable comment on censorship on the broadcast media: "The radio agent gave us friendly talks about not singing any song that took sides with anyone, anywhere, on any fight, argument, idea, or belief from a religious, scientific, political, legal or illegal point of view, nor from any point of thought that would cause anybody, anywhere to think, act, move or perform any motion in any direction, to agree or disagree with any one single word of any one single song or conversation." (Note: The series was short-lived; he was fired.)

41

Woody was a southerner with no racial or religious prejudice, and his open-mindedness amazed us. He married a Jewish girl and had a lively relationship with his mother-in-law, a Yiddish poet. And he fought for black rights all his life, refusing to sing for segregated audiences.

The last time I saw Woody was shortly before his death. One day Pete Seeger called me: "Chenk, the Weavers are having a party at Tom and Jerry's restaurant for a new member. Please come, Woody will be there." I hadn't seen him for many years, but knew about his long battle with Huntington's Disease. My husband and I arrived at the restaurant on the appointed hour, spoke to a few friends, but did not see Woody. Just then, Pete entered the room. "Have you talked to him yet?" he asked anxiously, "There he is, over there." He pointed to a man strapped into a wheelchair, his cheeks sunken, surrounded by people. For a moment I didn't recognize him: his hair was almost gone, that mop of frizzy hair I remembered from his youth. I saw no sign of recognition when I approached. I greeted Marjorie and watched with consternation as someone lit his cigarette, and fed him.

We stayed another 10 minutes, said our goodbyes, and headed west. A few doors down the street, Marjorie and Woody were waiting for their car in the open door of a parking garage. I stopped to talk with them. "Woody," said Marjorie, "do you remember Henrietta from WNYC days? Just blink if you do." I waited anxiously for a sign of recognition, would he remember me? A moment later, Woody, no longer able to talk, blinked his eyes. I kissed Marjorie, touched Woody's hand, and walked away. As we got to Seventh Avenue, I burst into tears, sobbing so uncontrollably I thought my heart would break. Woody died the following year. My City College ensemble gave a memorial

42

concert, with songs and quotes from his writings, a truly moving tribute.

My relation to the Guthrie family continued into the next generation, especially with Arlo, Woody's eldest son by Marjorie. I arranged one of his first concerts at City College when he was still a teenager, but it was an uneventful affair. A few years later with the release of "Alice's Restaurant" he jumped to the top of the pop charts. Not everybody could turn a tale about illegal dumping of garbage on Thanksgiving Day into a protest against the Vietnam war but Arlo did. Like his father, he never preached or sloganized -- his sly humor made the military look ridiculous and the war a total waste.

Some time later, I was invited to Arlo's wedding in Stockbridge, Massachusetts the site of "Alice's Restaurant." Folk singers, theatrical folk, artists' agents and friends filled the bus Marjorie provided for the trip from New York. Arlo and his beautiful bride, both dressed in white satin wedding attire, greeted us on arrival. It was a lovely day; the green lawns and distant hills provided a picture-perfect setting. We all gathered in a semi-circle around the couple as the minister read the ceremony. Just then, Arlo's little dog began yapping at his heels. Looking bewildered, Arlo picked up the dog; the minister paused, and we all looked on helplessly. Finally someone took the dog away and the ceremony went on. To close, Majorie read the poem (quoted above) Woody had written to his niece so many years before. We all felt Woody's absence, but felt his presence at the same time.

The last thing I remember about that day was Alice's huge, multilayered wedding cake decorated with streaks of blue, purple, pink and white icing. There were no bride and groom dolls on top, no rosettes, nothing like a traditional wedding cake. But after all, what would you expect at a Guthrie wedding?

Oh yes, let me go back to 1940 and tell you about Pete Seeger. A voice on the telephone said: "My name is Pete Seeger. Woody told me about your folk song program. I sing folk songs. Could I audition for you?" We made an appointment, and I soon forgot it until I was called to the station lobby. Waiting for me was a long, lanky young man carrying a banjo. As we walked down the corridor to the studio I asked, "What did you say your name is?" "Pete Seeger," he replied. I looked at him closely: "Are you related to Charles Seeger, (the eminent musicologist)?" "Yes, I guess so," he said hesitantly. "He's my father." "Say," I said, "I met your father when I was sixteen; he was my idol. And tell me how did you to get into folk music?" Pete spoke an educated English. "It's like this," he said," I went to Harvard for a while, and the college and I decided, by mutual agreement, to part company. Then I spent some time in Appalachia, learning to play the banjo and swapping songs with the musicians there. I love the music. Maybe I was tired of singing madrigals at Harvard."

The engineer set up the microphone in the studio; Pete tuned his banjo and began to sing, his Adam's apple bobbing up and down. Within minutes we were all attention. The engineer reached for his telephone to alert the entire station, the control room filled with announcers, the program director and our publicity writers. We knew we had a star in our midst. "Pete," I said, "you're wonderful. Please, come here whenever you like." And we've remained friends since then.

Shortly afterwards, Pete invited me to meet his friends, the Almanac Singers, with whom he shared a huge loft on West 10th Street. As I climbed the stairs, the smell of baking bread assailed my senses. The baker was Lee Hays, a member of the group, an ex-lay preacher from Arkansas. Lee, a corpulent man with a relaxed air and an "all-welcome" smile, greeted me with a flour-dusted handshake, and invited me to try the bread just out of the oven. "Folk songs," he mused as he kneaded another batch of dough, "Well, I'll make one up right now, if you like!" That remark exploded another old myth; a song doesn't have to be old, doesn't have to have a long beard, before it can be called a "folk song".

The Almanacs soon became a center of folk song activity. City kids flocked to the loft to learn first hand America's country music, try their hand at guitar and banjo styles, learn the old songs and invent new ones along the way. Always hovering in the background was Alan Lomax, the son of John Lomax, a pioneer folklorist and ex-head of folk archives of the Library of Congress. Alan, a visionary, was also a practical man. Through his efforts the Almanacs, Guthrie and Leadbelly obtained their first recording contracts from Decca and RCA Victor. Those first recordings are still treasured items in my collection which now numbers thousands. The other members of the group were: Pete Hawes, a charming New Englander, the writer Mill Lampell, and Bess Lomax, Alan's sister.

Later on, in the 50s, Pete Seeger and Lee Hays achieved international fame as the nucleus of the Weavers. As Almanacs, they wore plaid shirt and jeans, as Weavers they appeared more formally in tuxedos. Nevertheless, it was the same audience as the pre-World War II left-wing crowd -- only grown older and more affluent. Bess Lomax became the director of the folk music program of the National Endowment for the Arts. Mill Lampell wrote scripts for Hollywood; blacklisted during the McCarthy era, he returned to shame fellow writers who had abandoned him. Pete Hawes lived in Puerto Rico until his death from a horseback riding accident, in the 1970s.

I became completely involved with Pete, his friends, Burl Ives, and stray folk singers who came to the station. They would perform on my programs and come back to my apartment to swap songs and tell stories. ("Kisses Sweeter than Wine", a favorite Weaver's song, was composed in my large bathroom on St. Marks Place.) One day we all went on a picnic at Bear Mountain Park, about an hour from the city. We sang, ate sandwiches and roasted hot dogs. At one point, Aunt Molly Jackson sauntered over to talk to me, Leadbelly eavesdropping nearby. Now Molly's reputation for frontal attack was well-known. She plunged in, "You know, Chenk, I've been hearing stories about you." "Really?" I asked, my voice rising with irritation. "What kind?" Molly smiled at me: "They say that you're uppity, but I tell them it's not true." I bridled. At that point, Leadbelly whispered in my ear, "She's the one who spreads the rumors!" I had neglected to invite Molly to appear on my first Kentucky program and now, I realized, she was taking revenge. I put my arms around her and said with all the nonchalance I could muster, "Molly, how would you like to sing on WNYC?" Suddenly she was all smiles: "Honey, I would love it anytime you say." Aunt Molly and I were reasonably good friends from then on, but I kept my distance -- always wary of those somewhat lethal claws!

That picnic at Bear Mountain was my first insight into "backwoods" literary skills. Everyone improvised, inventing new verses on the spot. However, Molly shone above the others; she was a natural-born poet, rhyming came as easily to her as breathing, and her rhythm was impeccable, even her ordinary speech was poetic. Hearing her at Bear Mountain I recalled my first sight of her at a demonstration, pleading for funds for the miners' union. Dressed in a shapeless dress, her hair pinned back, she cut a heroic figure as she sang, "I Am a Union Woman."

> I am a union woman as brave as I can be.
> I do not like the bosses and the bosses don't like me.
> Join the CIO, Join the CIO.

> The bosses ride the fine white horse, while we walk
>   in the mud
> Their flag's the old red, white and blue, while ours in
>   dipped in blood.
> Join the CIO, Join the CIO.

Leadbelly was the best musician of the group -- and everyone's teacher. He was a walking encyclopedia of Southern music, equally expert in both Afro-American and Anglo-American music. This should come as no surprise, since blacks and whites, though socially segregated, swapped songs and musical styles from each other. As Jim Garland once told me: "Negroes and whites worked together in the mines, alongside each other -- and we picked up their songs. Sure, we didn't sing the blues like them, but to us they were the blues."

Leadbelly's apartment on the East Side of Manhattan was another Mecca to city folk singers. He taught them the proper accompaniment for each kind of music; how to play work songs, the slow, sad blues and up-tempo happy blues, as well as British ballads, play-party songs, and Baptist and Methodist church hymn-singing. Leadbelly claimed all these were his own inventions, even though many had come not from his Southern back yard but from Europe. I can still hear his unforgettable version of a British ballad called "Hangman, Hangman" transformed into a story about black oppression in the United

47

States. Although everyone tried to sound like him, nobody could imitate his powerful voice or the clarity and pounding sonorities of his twelve-string guitar.

One day in 1940, I received a letter from Woody Guthrie, urging me to put Leadbelly on the air. Woody wrote: "Life hasn't been so smooth with Huddie, and what makes him good is that he simply wants to sing and tell how it has treated him, and what he has learned from it, and he wants to be honest about it, without any pretty put on. I honestly believe that of all the living folk singers I've ever seen that Leadbelly is ahead of them all. I am lucky enough to study under Huddie which is to me one of New York's greatest pleasures. I argue that it is a mistake for the people in the radio world to leave Leadbelly out of the picture, its [sic] like leaving the alcohol out of the wine or leaving the spring out of the clock. Huddie plays a little old $4 accordion and you can actually hear the sad note of his people ringing in the swamps and jungles and echoing in the Louisiana moss."

We gave Leadbelly his own 15-minute weekly spot called "Folk Songs of America". He always arrived on time. I could set my clock by his arrival, neatly dressed in a double-breasted grey suit, white shirt and dark bow tie. We would sit in my office and plot out a skeleton script. Once on the air, Leadbelly would ad lib commentaries about his life, his youth on Fanning Street, a red-light district, his experiences with cocaine, backbreaking field work, his sexual exploits and disappointments, and his years on prison farms. He would recall the time spent as the "eyes" of the great bluesman Blind Lemon Jefferson, leading him through southern streets to play for nickels and dimes. After each broadcast Leadbelly would ask me, "Did you understand everything I said? Folks up north don't understand southern talk, and I want them to know what I'm talking about." But he really had no cause to worry; the meaning of his songs was never in question. Each program had its own theme. I would listen, enthralled, to rough ballads like "John Henry", "Frankie and Albert", and "Railroad Bill." But Leadbelly also loved to sing "sukey jump" play-party songs and dances for children. Even today, I entertain my grandchildren with his "Grey Goose", a song about a bird so powerful that even cut up, boiled, and killed he came back to life. There was no doubt he was talking about the regenerative strength of his own people. And, of course, his blues had the ring of truth about small-town black life. We mailed copies of the lyrics to our listeners on request. Each week Leadbelly or his wife, Martha, would write them out on his stationery by hand.

When Leadbelly was released from prison in the 1930s, he was placed in the custody of John Lomax and his son, Alan. He traveled North, performing at the Modern Language Association and universities. He came to live in New York just as the Harlem Renaissance, a brilliant period of sophisticated jazz, Blues, and fine literature, was winding down. Leadbelly, a country bluesman from the southern backwoods with a prison record, represented everything Harlem intellectuals wanted to forget. To further denigrate him, ugly rumors were circulated that Leadbelly was exploited by the Left for political purposes. During the Depression the Left had a clear policy on race; they fought for black rights long before the 1960s Civil Rights struggle. While Leadbelly might have had his difficulties in adjusting to white society, nobody in our circle "chunked" him a nickel for his singing or made him come in the back door. We liked him the way he was, let him be himself, and were grateful that he was part of our lives.

Leadbelly did not compose political tracts; however, "Bourgeois Blues," a song on racism in the nation's capital, was a rare and memorable example.

49

I'm gonna tell all the colored people,
I want 'em to understand.
Washington ain't no place
For no colored man.

'Cause it's a bourgeois town,
Ooh, it's a bourgeois town.
I got the Bourgeois Blues,
I'm sure gonna spread the news.

The white folks in Washington,
They know how.
They chunk you a nickel
Just to see a nigger bow.

Once, at a party at my house, his eyes a little bloodshot from drinking wine, Leadbelly cornered Rufino Tamayo, the great Mexican painter. "Sing us a Mexican blues," he demanded. "We don't have blues in Mexico," said Rufino, a little frightened. (Leadbelly had recently served a sentence at Riker's Island for assault.) He handed Rufino a guitar. After a moment's hesitation, he sang "La Llorona," a lament about love's frustration, a tender song from Mexico's Isthmus of Tehuantepec. Leadbelly listened attentively and, obviously moved by the pathos of its melody, slapped Rufino on the back: "See, Mr. Tamayo, didn't I tell you? Everybody got the blues." Leadbelly was perceptive, he heard the blues even in a language and music not his own.

Although my work at WNYC was completely engrossing and took up most of my time, Chenk and I managed to meet other people besides musicians. Often, I would come home from the station to find the evening's guest waiting with a pork chop in a bag, a contribution to the evening meal. Chenk had done wonders with our floor-through brownstone apartment. What we couldn't afford to buy in expensive furniture stores we picked up in junk shops around town, or he made himself. On one wall of the living room was an enormous blow-up photograph of Sabu, the young hero of the film "Elephant Boy." Except for our bedroom, the rest of the apartment was Chenk's studio, crowded with paint and half-finished canvases.

Most of the people who came to our apartment shared our ideas about art and politics. But sometimes things went awry. One evening Margaret Mead and her husband, Gregory Bateson, came to dinner. Chenk had assisted her in designing an American Indian exhibit at the Museum of Modern Art, and was quite impressed with her lectures at the Museum of Natural History. But the evening was marred, not by my unremarkable cooking, but by a heated exchange of opinions. Chenk and I defended the people's right to protest and change unjust laws. Margaret insisted that rebellions upset the social equilibrium, and created neurotics. Despite differences I continued to see her over many years and came to appreciate her considerable talents; a thorough academic, she never used professional jargon but spoke ordinary garden variety English. Last but not least, she was charismatic and influenced not only heads of government but students in droves.

One night we were invited to Margaret's home to see several films about Bali. Among the guests were the Mexican painter Miguel Covarrubias and his wife, Rosa, Colin McPhee, the Canadian composer who had revived the Balinese gamelan orchestra, and his anthropologist wife, Jane Belo. All of them had spent time in beautiful Bali, like Tahiti in Gauguin's time, the intellectuals' paradise of the moment. Of the three films, the Covarrubias' color film was the most esthetically pleasing.

51

Margaret's own black and white film, later edited as "Trance and Dance", was the more profound, showing the importance of ritual in Balinese life. As the evening wore on, Margaret, now in her ninth month of pregnancy, began to look a little piqued. Jane Belo whispered to each of us, "Let's go, Margaret looks exhausted." The next morning her daughter was born, with Margaret herself directing the filming of her birth! Only a super-woman could do that!

We resumed our argument, the one about rebellion and society, started in the 1930s, in the 1960s when we accidentally met at a national meeting of anthropologists. She had just emerged from a heated exchange with students, many passionately involved in the Civil Rights struggle and protest against the Vietnam war. We stopped to talk, "I keep on telling them," she exploded, "that anthropology is a fact-finding discipline, not a springboard for social action, but they don't listen." She advocated change on some issues and kept silent about others, like the Vietnam war, which she opposed only when it was about to end. However, she made many good decisions on social issues concerning women and children.

Let me end my recollections of the pre-World War II years in New York with a few words about an extraordinary man I met at WNYC. One weekly series I produced was "South American Way" featuring recorded Latin American popular music. When its host Evans Clark, the director of the foundation "Twentieth Century Fund", departed for Latin America on a fact-finding mission, he turned the program over to a Spanish refugee, Gustavo Durán, a handsome, charismatic man who spoke impeccable English. Gustavo was no ordinary refugee; he had been Madrid's supreme military commander during the Spanish Civil War. Over lunches and parties at my house, we gradually learned about the other side of his life: long before the war he had been a composer. Ernest Hemingway described him as *"el niño bonito"*, the esthete, friend and colleague of Europe's leading artists and intellectuals. Later on he was eulogized as the war's hero in Andre Malraux's novel on the Spanish War *L'Espoir* (Man's Fate). Rescued at the war's end Gustavo, now in England, married Bonte Crompton, an American heiress, and arrived in America in 1940, shortly before I met him.

I did not see him again until my return from Mexico in 1946. After much searching I finally located him -- of all places -- in the State Department; during the war he had been a principal political advisor to Spruille Braden, our ambassador to Cuba and later Argentina during the Peron dictatorship. The next time I saw him was in 1953 as director of an United Nations agency in New York. "Give me some advice," I asked him, "I'm leaving for Spain next week." "I guess they'll understand your Spanish," he said with a pat on the shoulder. I laughed, it was a good-natured remark, for I spoke the language fluently, perhaps marred somewhat by a Mexican accent. The last time I saw him was at a party at Alan Lomax' house. There he was, older, but still the same dynamic man. He grabbed my arm and drew me into a corner. "Ah, Henrietta, I know what it is to die," he said in an agonized whisper. " I had a heart attack, yes, I think I died for a second, and came back." I was terribly shaken, but we chatted about our families, his wife Bonte, now in a wheelchair, and my work in Spain and Morocco. A few years later he died in Greece while on UN business. Ignored for generations in his native Spain, he has lately been eulogized in a biography entitled *El soldado de porcelana* (The Porcelain Soldier) by Horacio Vazquez-Rial. Yes, better late than never. He was an unforgettable man, a man with a mission, a man of superior gifts, and above all, a human being. It may seem strange to conclude my New York memories about a hero of the Spanish war. But his story reminds me of my first year, 1936, in the city.   Each night during that war Chenk and I would walk to Times Square to watch the latest bulletins flashed around the New York Times Building.   We were devastated when the final defeat came. To us it was the beginning of the end. The handwriting was on the wall, in our hearts we knew that a global war was in the making, this time a big one that would engulf us all.

***

New York 2
1946-69

Return to Washington in 1946 left me with no plans for the future. My first concern was my family. The war over, my brother, safe and sound, soon married beautiful Rebecca; my sister Ruth and her husband, Dave, had their first child, the lively copper-headed Annie. My mother, however, had had a painful a hip infection, soon afterward her first heart attack. A tower of strength she survived my beloved father by five years. Even today, they are sorely missed.

Although I decided to live with Chenk again, not even the birth of our only child, Peter, healed the breach between us. When Peter was six months old we moved from Washington to Troy, New York, where Chenk taught architecture at Rensselaer Polytechnic Institute. The two years in this ugly provincial town were the worst years of my life; I once attended a meeting of faculty wives where the chief activity was planning a bridge tournament. I felt suffocated, brain dead. Only Peter kept me from perishing of sheer boredom. Finally Chenk received a

54

commission to design a health center in Harlem, and we returned to New York.

Never did life seem so bright. I renewed old friendships, my family was nearby, and concerts, museums and libraries were only a subway ride away. Every day I wheeled Peter in his stroller to the park. The nip of fall was in the air, the leaves gently falling to the ground; it was glorious, invigorating, and I felt alive again. I would take Peter shopping downtown. Poor little fellow, he would fall asleep on the subway as we headed home. Yet, even half asleep he managed to walk, stumbling a little but valiantly keeping up with me. He was a beautiful child with a calm unruffled air. One day, as we entered the elevator of our apartment building, a neighbor said to him, "My, what a big boy you are!" Peter, then two years old, replied, "No, I'm not, I'm a little boy stuck!" He was never in a hurry to grow up, and I, for one, loved his babyhood, wanted him close to my side, his little hand always in mine. One day, I picked him up at nursery school. "Promise me, Mommy," he pleaded, "that you'll always come for me after school." "Even when you go to college and you're grown up?" I asked. "Yes, Mommy, even when I'm grown up, promise." I promised. Even now that he's married to a wonderful wife, Ingrid, and has two beautiful and talented children, Nicholas and Helen, I see him every week -- though my after-school services are no longer needed.

Happy though I was in New York, by the time Peter was four I had grown restless. My dream of a home of my own, of settling down was not to be; I was permanently scarred. My wanderings began again, to last the rest of my life. Tricked into a divorce settlement by a wily lawyer I agreed that Peter live with his father, a decision I regret to this very day. For a while I earned a precarious living, first at an ad agency, from which I was promptly fired and then as cultural director of an old people's home. It kept the wolf from the door, but no more than that.

Finally, in the late '50s, I was back in my own world again; folk music was enjoying popularity for the first time since the Depression. I became folk music editor for the prestigious *American Record Guide* and *Musical America*, wrote record notes, published three books, numerous articles, received grants from several foundations for research in Spain and North Africa, and attended meetings all over the world. Best of all, I returned to broadcasting, first for a chain of FM stations, then a year at WBAI, and once more at WNYC.

All these activities kept me on the run, but brought little money. Teaching came to my rescue; first I took over Henry Cowell's pioneer classes in world folk music at the New School, then I gave courses at New York University and Brooklyn College. When, in 1964, I received a full time appointment at the City College of New York, my financial woes came to an end -- and there I remained for 25 happy years.

Teaching folk music in the music department was not, however, like teaching counterpoint or 20th century serialism; it had to be taught as music, to be sure, but, to me, it was fraught with other meanings. My tenure at the university coincided with a tumultuous era -- the Vietnam war, Civil Rights movement, African independence, Black Power, feminism, gay and lesbian liberation. Our campus, like others, was the scene of protest, take-overs, teach-ins, demonstrations, etc. All the issues were expressed in song. Except for the Depression never were music and politics so closely intertwined.

Musically, the country was in an intense creative mood. Every week I would take stock of new recordings in our college bookstore; each week there were new bands, new singers, and new record companies. One could take one's pick from the folk music revival's Joan Baez, Judy Collins or its old-time star, Pete Seeger. Then there was Soul, particularly the great Aretha Franklin, Nashville's Dolly Parton and Johnny Cash, or modern blues -- Muddy Waters' Blues Band from Chicago. Then came Rock, the newest musical craze, and like a tree, it grew many branches. Its stars -- Jimi Hendrix, Janis Joplin, Grateful Dead and, most of all, the Beatles and Bob Dylan -- soon became international idols worshiped not only for their innovative music but for messages of freedom and justice.

At first the campus seemed to pull together on social issues. But presently separatism began to float in the air: "You stay with yours and we'll stay with ours" was the message from black colleagues, and it applied not only to politics but to music as well. At meetings I heard remarks condemning whites for playing blues or jazz. From my own black students I heard complaints like, "Hey, why don't they (whites) leave our stuff alone?" White musicians had not only initiated the 1960s blues revival, but had learned to play the music as well. I reminded them that imitation was the sincerest form of flattery. "And," I added, "maybe you should stop singing 'Silent Night', 'Happy Birthday', and 'We Shall Overcome' (the Civil Rights anthem), because that's a white hymn. "Anyway", I added, "people have been 'stealing' music from each other since the Dead Sea was sick, and you haven't got a case." My words must have hit the bull's eye, for black students flocked to my blues class for years afterward.

I did what I could to focus the college on black culture; little did I know then what tragedy was about to happen. In 1968, I asked Mura Dehn, the Russian-born dancer, an authority on black dance, to organize a concert to highlight its history. She

57

knew all the tap dancers and blues singers in the city, gifted performers who had disappeared into the woodwork after the demise of the Harlem Renaissance of the 1920s. From this talent pool she selected the best for the college concert.

The university went all out, built a special stage in the ballroom (we had no concert hall), and raised money to pay musicians and dancers. Everything was ready to go. It was minutes to curtain time, a packed audience was already seated, the musicians on stage -- when tragedy struck. I was in Dean Ed Sarfaty's office when a student rushed in: "We've just heard it on the news," he said, "Martin Luther King has just been shot!" Ten minutes later, he reappeared to announce he was dead. The president of City College, Buell Gallagher, came on stage and told the audience, mostly from Harlem, the sad news. First there was dead silence, then cries and moans arose from the crowd. One man walked up and down the aisle moaning, "They killed my son, they killed my son," in the most anguished tones. The performers, stunned, tried to sing something – anything -- but were choked with tears. Silently, everyone walked out of the auditorium to the street; the police had been mobilized to guide them safely to subways and buses. I was told later that then Mayor Lindsay rushed to 125th Street, Harlem's center, to calm the situation; fires were already raging and threatened to engulf the area.

We rescheduled the concert three weeks later as a memorial to Dr. King. I am sure he would have been proud to have seen it. That performance at City College was the beginning of a second career for Mura Dehn's group. Subsequently they performed in the Mexican Olympics of 1968 and in several African countries, on a State Department sponsored tour.

Except for opposition to the Vietnam war, I considered student political activities basically romantic, although their sympathy for the poor was genuine. I used to tell my (non-black) students, "You can wear torn jeans and march for black rights, even spend a night in jail, but your parents will bail you out; you can go home, and drive the family car to a Grateful Dead concert. In the 1930s, when I was growing up, poor was poor."

With time, the student movement spun out of control, awash in drugs; sex became so casual that all previous sexual revolutions seemed puritanical by comparison. Once CCNY students took over Finley Hall, the student center, and barricaded themselves in for the night. The sit-in began with speeches against the Vietnam war and ended with students behind locked classroom doors for a night of sex. For a while the main corridor of the music department was invaded by Harlem drug sellers, the faculty so terrified it took months before we threw them out. The worst debacle was the destruction by fire of our only concert hall, a 19th-century architectural gem, a city landmark, a needless act of arson unexplained to this very day.

At long last, the Vietnam war ended in 1974 and the "rebellion" died down to a whimper. The campus, once a battlefield, was strewn with old leaflets, memories of high-flown rhetoric, the faint echo of "Freedom Now" -- and not much else. The students, tired of the controversy and uncertainty, called the "revolution" off; it could wait another day, as one of my students explained.

With peace on campus, I offered workshops in African, Balkan, Caribbean and Hindu music, where students learned to perform music they had known only through recordings. I organized concerts of the best talent of the time, though we paid them a pittance. Besides Arlo Guthrie, mentioned earlier, Judy

59

Collins, guitarist Danny Kalb's Blues Project, and Tom Paxton, all sang on campus. So did many old-time southern bluesmen -- Skip James, Mississippi Joe Williams, Sonny Terry and Brownie McGhee. The blind street singer, Reverend Gary Davis, led by a student, his "eyes" of the moment, came to class. "Reverend Davis," someone asked, "what is the blues?" "The truth," he said, "yes, the truth about life. The blues tells it like it is."

Then there was young Julius Lester, who wrote a wonderful book about the blacks of John's Island, South Carolina, and inspired me to make several recording trips there. Julius later became a convert to Judaism, thereby angering other Black intellectuals. Finally, I formed a student ensemble which performed every semester for years. After all, I always believed the best way to learn about music was to do it.

There was room for all kinds of music in the 1960s. Sometimes we glanced backward to listen to music of the past. One day, Victoria Spivey gave a concert with Louis Metcalf's jazz band in our concert lounge. Victoria had been a blues star, like her mentor Bessie Smith, during the Prohibition era when she sang in luxurious theaters and elegant night-clubs, dressed in sumptuous gowns, before an elite audience, both black and white. To my students, blues was country blues, the remarkable poignant music of poor blacks. However, for my black students, country blues was a reminder of slavery and poverty, and better forgotten.

Then there was the marvelous Mabel Hillery who brought black life of the Old South right into my home and classroom. A member of the excellent Georgia Sea Island Singers, she had barnstormed with the group for several years and now wanted a chance to live in the big city. With Alan Lomax' help and mine, she settled in New York and became a close friend. Every

Sunday over breakfast she would talk about her life, the poverty, her abusive husband, her six children and her hard-drinking mother. "My mother would disappear for long periods and come back now and then all dressed in fine clothes. She'd hang around for a while; all we had to do to keep her happy was give her a bottle of gin and cigarettes. And when she got real bored she'd leave."

Mabel, a courageous fighter by nature, teamed up with several gifted white and black musicians, the talented Hazel Dickens, from a Kentucky mining community, Mike Seeger, Pete's half-brother, and the blues singer Johnny Hodges. They barnstormed around the south, performing at soldiers' cafes near military training camps to spread an anti-Vietnam message. In those days, such a mixed racial group was an act of daring in the segregated South. Mabel said, "I would go over to the drinking fountain where the sign read, 'For Whites Only,' put my hand over it, and drink, and nobody dared stop me!" Mabel was even-handed about race. Chided for her friendships with whites by Harlem friends, she would fire back, "Well, they help me and you don't do me no good." Once her eldest son called from Georgia: "I'm in jail, please come and bail me out." When she learned he had been arrested for speeding in the center of town, she said, "If it was a civil rights issue I'd be down in a minute, but you broke the law and endangered people's lives. You stay in jail until they let you out."

Mabel appeared on my radio program, taught school children, and sang in churches and folk music clubs. A natural musician, a born leader; she would start a song, let the audience warm up, and at the climax, stand motionless hands at her sides. Yet, the audience, swinging with the rhythm, was never aware she had stopped, her presence was so powerful.

61

One day as I sat in my college office, the telephone rang. It was Alan Lomax. "Mabel died this morning." Brownie (McGhee) had taken her to the hospital thinking she had a stomach disorder. An hour later the doctor came out. "She's gone," he said. A memorial, planned at my house, was later held at the splendid Cathedral of St. John the Divine, almost across the street from her last home. All her friends were there -- Alan Lomax, Pete Seeger, Hedy West, Mike Seeger, a children's chorus she had directed, and everyone sang. But Brownie, who had been her special friend, sang only one song, and grief-stricken, left the stage overwhelmed by tears.

Of all the musicians I interviewed on WNYC, no one has played a more brilliant role in American popular music than Bob Dylan. I reviewed his first recording for the American Record Guide. Almost immediately, I received a call from his agent, Albert Grossman. Would I be interested in having him on my radio program? Sure, I said, and arranged to meet Dylan at his office for a preliminary interview. When I arrived at Grossman's luxurious office, Bob was waiting for me, dressed in his signature railroad worker's cap and jeans. Looking me straight in the eye, his first words were: "I read your review." (It hadn't been too flattering.) I was about to say something conciliatory when he stopped me. "You were right, I was drunk at the time, and thanks, you were the only one to tell the truth."

The following week Bob appeared at WNYC right on time. He was terribly excited. "Guess what," he said, "I just got my first telephone bill. Would you believe it, $300 -- I've been calling my friends in London, just everyone I know." The taping began, with the producer in the control room, and Bob and me seated on either side of the microphone. "How did you happen to come to New York?" I asked, to begin the interview. He was non-committal. "I can't tell you," he said, "because it would involve other people." "Which people?" I pressed on. "I can't tell you. I came with them from Minneapolis." "What did you do those first few days in the city?" I persisted. "Well," he said, scratching his head, "I better not say 'cause my friends wouldn't like it."

For the next half hour, Bob evaded every question. The conversation bogged down hopelessly. Finally, in utter frustration, I signed off. To this day, I don't know if the program was aired; I left the decision up to my producer, who probably patched it together with snatches of talk and songs from his album. The engineer and production personnel said goodbye, gathered up the microphone and left the two of us in the studio. I confronted Dylan. "We haven't got a program," I said angrily. "Why bother to come and then say nothing?" And then, gentle as a lamb, he said, "What do you want to know?" "Everything," I said. "Why you came to New York, what you did, and why you stayed here." "OK," he said, "I'll tell you." For the next half hour I listened to his story. Although I couldn't tape it, I remembered all the important things. Bob had come by car from Minnesota with a few friends for a short visit, mainly to see Woody Guthrie, by then in the hospital, seriously ill with Huntington's disease. The first night was spent in a Greenwich Village cafe, swapping songs for food.

At four in the morning when the cafe closed down, Bob wandered the streets and was picked by a homosexual from whom he fled. On the street again, a middle-aged man approached him, offering him somewhere to stay in exchange for cleaning up the place. For the next four days he slept on a tabletop in a union headquarters off Union Square. Then Bob made an important decision: not to return to Minnesota, and to try his luck in New York. "One day," he said, "I watched the children playing in Washington Square Park; they were so happy, I decided that I could be happy here, too."

Dylan spent those first months in the city frequenting the many Village folk music clubs. "I wrote wherever I happened to be," he told me. "Sometimes I'd spend a whole day sitting at a corner table in a coffee house just writing whatever came into my head. I'd look at people for hours, and I'd make up things about them, or I'd think, what kind of song would they like to hear, and I'd make one up."

Then Robert Shelton, the *New York Times* critic, heard him, and the rest, as they say, is history. I reviewed his concerts, even the famous one with Joan Baez; wrote several articles about him, but had no more personal contact with him. When I was writing my biography of Woody Guthrie, however, I asked permission to use his "Song for Woody" featured on his first album. It took six months before I received an answer. He granted permission, but only after reading my manuscript. I may assume he liked what I wrote.

Dylan was not only a songwriter but a philosopher as well, as concerned with social problems as with personal conflicts. At first he was the darling of the Left, writing protest songs on numerous issues: His first hit, "Blowin' in the Wind", almost supplanted Guthrie's "This Land Is Your Land" in popularity. But he ran afoul of a rigid folk music establishment at the 1965 Newport Folk Festival where the audience booed him because he was backed by a rock band. Later Tom Paxton in the folk music journal "Sing Out!" foolishly called his brand of "folk-rock" "folk rot". By this time Dylan was a hero to a young, hip audience and cared not a fig for the Old Guard.

The 1960s produced an encyclopedia of American vernacular music. Yet, the New York appetite for music went beyond its own borders. Music and dance groups from all over the world flocked to the city. I reviewed those events and brought many of the musicians to WNYC. Y.G. Srimati, the talented painter and musician from South India, gave workshops at the University and became a life-long friend. Then, there was Jean Redpath, the great Scottish singer. What a glorious voice, what heavenly songs! Our apartment was her second home in New York. Evenings she would perch on the edge of my bed, and sing, verily like a thrush on the wing. One day, about to review an LP just released, I played one of the songs, "The Gathering of the Clan", a graphic description of the amorous proceedings of a Scottish clan meeting. She listened in stony silence, her face deadpan. When it finished, she said, "Well, if it's dirrrty songs you're wanting," her voice ringing with a true Scottish burr, "I'll sing you some more!" And she did, another 10 verses or so, until we collapsed with laughter.

"One day," she said, "I was singing around the house when my mother appeared. 'How dare you sing such indecent songs?' she exploded. 'Mother,' I said, 'I learned them from you.' " Then she added; "We 'dour' Scots long ago sang songs about illicit love, without condemning it, that is. Trouble was that in the 18th century well-meaning but puritanical preachers collected them from country folk; shocked at what they heard they 'cleaned' up the offending verses. Fortunately people like Bobbie Burns and later collectors found the originals and published them. Those are the ones I sing now." I met Mrs. Redpath on a visit to Scotland one year. "Bluebell" was a formidable lady of 5 feet 10 inches, or so. I only recall one incident; when my husband and I mentioned (not complained) that the tea was strong, she retorted, "When I want water, I drink water; when I want tea I drink tea!" We said no more after that, we dared not.

"The Gathering of the Clan" appeared on the flip side of a recording of Mark Twain's "601", an essay read by Dyer-Bennett. This sophisticated tenor, a popular singer of folk songs before World War II, later became a record producer. The longish essay was Twain's imaginary re-creation of a gathering in Queen Elizabeth I's private chambers of her favorite literary figures. Francis Bacon, Shakespeare, and Walter Drake hold forth, not on weighty literary matters but on sex and bodily functions, Twain imitating the style of each writer to perfection. I invited Dyer-Bennett to a broadcast even though we couldn't play the work (the FCC would have closed the station down). Dyer-Bennett merely described it and played some songs from the flip side, except "The Gathering of the Clan", which also was taboo on the air.

Afterwards we walked across City Hall Park to a lovely 19th century coffee house on West Broadway, he to regale me with stories and me to listen. He said the Reverend Twitchell, Twain's close friend and neighbor in Hartford, Connecticut, had the work published in a limited edition at the Sing Sing prison press; it had been refused publication elsewhere. Franklin Roosevelt owned a copy, and rumor had it that he enjoyed reading parts at informal cabinet get-togethers. Only Jesse Jones, the Reconstruction Finance Minister, a Puritan at heart, demurred. "But Jesse," said the President, "you gave it to me."

Of all the stories told me that afternoon, the most memorable was about a squire in the time of Elizabeth, a tale Dyer-Bennett found in an ancient document. It seemed that, having performed many services for the crown, this worthy man was summoned to the palace to receive a knighthood. As he walked down the aisle and faced the Queen, about to make his reverential bow, he passed wind. The unfortunate man backed out of the room and disappeared. It is said he sold his property and moved to the Netherlands. Years later, having again served the crown, he was recalled to London. As he stood before the Queen, again about to bow, she said, "You know, we would have forgotten you had it not been for the fart." Richard said, "In Elizabeth's time, they talked quite frankly about bodily functions. Today, it's considered dirty." Not by me, or my friends; we laughed for weeks afterwards.

I loved broadcasting, and when I could get away with it, presented many controversial programs. Although the McCarthy era was about over, television and radio were particularly squeamish, careful to avoid hiring anyone with the least taint of Leftism. However, I decided to make a bold move. One February, when WNYC's annual American Music Festival rolled around, I planned a broadcast to honor Leadbelly. Alan Lomax, who had known him better than anyone, kindly consented to record the introductory remarks, a beautiful 20-minute eulogy. I notified our news department of his appearance. When a week passed and nothing appeared in the press I complained. "Sorry," they said with some embarrassment, "we can't send it; Siegel (Seymour Siegal, the station's director) said no." I confronted Siegel. "You know why," he said by way of explanation, and walked away. Yes, I did know why: Lomax was still persona non grata. He had spent the McCarthy years in Europe recording folk music for Columbia Records; his "crime" was not making himself available to McCarthy's committee. Nevertheless, I didn't bow to Siegal's decision; I broadcasted two programs instead of one over several weeks, making sure Alan's remarks appeared on both programs.

Recently, both Lomax and Seeger received the coveted national awards at the Kennedy Center in Washington. I noticed during the televised program that President Clinton and Vice

President Gore, their families, and some members of Congress sang along with the performers on stage; they were students in the 1960s and knew the songs, like everyone else.

***

John's Island, South Carolina, 1970 and 1971

In 1970, during the Easter break, I took my blues class to John's Island, South Carolina, just off the coast from Charleston on Mabel Hillery's suggestion. Everyone was terribly excited, their first exposure to the rural South. I set down some rules. Yes, I told them, you've got to dress decently because everyone will be wearing their best on Easter Sunday. "Cut your hair, trim your beards," I warned the boys, "and wear decent jeans with no holes, a tie and a clean shirt." Pandemonium broke out in the classroom. "Hey, whadayou trying to do to us?" they shouted. I was accused of robbing them of their manhood. The girls, however, offered no objections when advised to wear a dress and a hat for the Easter service. Although they didn't own such things (who wore a hat in those days?) they found them tucked away in old trunks, dusted them off, and packed them in their suitcases. After a sleepless train ride, we were met in Charleston by Esau Jenkins, head of the island's credit union, and driven to the island along a causeway built in the 1930s. "Yes," said Jenkins as we left the mainland, "in the old days you would've been ferried across in little flat-bottomed boats, so we've made some progress. And by the way, this flat, marshy land was once haven for runaway slaves." Huge oak trees covered in Spanish moss came into view and soon clapboard houses scattered in the grassy terrain. Only the new brick Methodist church, a few schools and private houses reminded us that it was 1970 and not 1900. First, we dropped our belongings off at the Progressive Club, our "hotel" for the week's stay. Years before it had been the island headquarters for voters' registration. Now it was a community center with a gym, a small grocery store, several rooms with two-layered bunks, and one lone bathroom.

Then we headed to a welcome party at Janey Hunter's house. Janey, a mother of 13 children and numerous grandchildren, was the center of John's Island's musical life. Our car turned off the main road onto a path obscured by the grass grown tall and dense. The last few yards, too muddy for the car, we managed on foot. Two short steps brought us to the porch supported by rotting timbers. Janey, at the door, drew us inside with words of welcome. Despite the rickety outside, the living room was nicely furnished, neatly arranged with old but comfortable upholstered sofas. In no time we were surrounded by children of all sizes, everyone talking at once, everyone with plans for our stay. They led us into the dining room where a lovely buffet was spread out. After we ate, we watched them dance to music by Aretha Franklin and James Brown. When Mabel started singing and clapping the rhythms of gospel, we joined in. As my student John Helak later wrote, "We were northern white college students in a poor black section of the South, and we were so self-conscious that we were very deliberate in our actions and speech and didn't know how to act." When the party ended with the singing of "May the Circle Be Unbroken" the ice had been broken.

Easter morning dawned gray and overcast. As we entered the church for the service we heard sounds of prayers and laments, but soon the entire congregation burst into song, clapping and foot stamping reverberated on all sides. Quietly we set up our recording equipment. Soon Reverend Goodwin, the minister, entered. More than six feet tall he towered above the congregation. "Beautiful, beautiful, church, you sound beautiful this Easter morning," he said, his long arms outspread like an eagle in flight. As he began his sermon, we heard the rain pelting down on the roof outside. His thundering voice, rising above the storm, and the message of rebirth left a deep impression on all of us. This was my students' first time in a black church. It was also the first time they had ever heard a preacher as eloquent or intelligent as Reverend Goodwin. That sermon, directed more at my students than his parishioners, clarified the civil rights issues better than demonstrations and strikes back in New York. The rest of the week was filled with activities at the church, at Janie's house, fishing with Janie's grandchildren for guppies in nearby ponds, or exploring the outer reaches of the island. The boys hung on the periphery, unable to join. "We're a bunch of rednecks," they'd say despondently, feeling guilty and out of place. With Mabel as organizer, the children taught us singing games about animals, counting-out rhymes, clapping games, and silly songs which only children can sing with a straight face. Afterwards back in New York, I taught them to my classes, year after year. Here is one we learned:

> Old lady come from Booster
> She had two hens and a rooster
> The rooster died, the old lady cried
> She couldn't get eggs like she use-ta

The Sea Islands on the Atlantic coast stretch for hundreds of miles, some so close together only a footbridge separates them. Sometimes we stumbled on abandoned, dilapidated plantations, the damp earth overgrown with exotic plants, tall grasses, moss-covered trees, and flowers blooming in the early April spring. We held round table discussions with members of other Protestant churches, argued about culture and politics. In Charleston we visited the old slave market now a historical monument, but the sight of the huge, elegant homes of its ex-slave owners spoke even more eloquently about pre-Civil War era; those wealthy merchants lived like royalty from the profits of slavery. In the 1970s I saw the descendants of those slaves coming up from the muck of centuries, still discriminated against, still second-class citizens, but now fighting for their rights.

When we returned to New York we raised money, collected clothes for the poor of the Island, and entertained Reverend Goodwin when he came to town. Oh, yes, I must remember to report that the boys recovered from their alienation, and became fierce, almost belligerent partisans of the Islanders. We did several radio programs on WNYC and I edited an album for Folkways Records. In 1971 I took another class back to John's Island. Again we saw the old dilapidated plantations and the mossy trees. "Couldn't we have a field center here?" they asked. It was a lovely but unrealizable dream. At least my students have the wonderful songs learned on John's Island, and wonderful memories. I often recall those wonderful weeks on the island, the children so eager to share with us, but then I remember one disturbing recollection: one day as we gathered at Janie's house to dance and sing, Alice Wine, the manager of the Progressive Club, sent her son to invite us to a singing session in progress at the nearby "Moving Star Hall", a pre-Civil War slave church. In this ancient clapboard hall a small chorus rehearsed the oldest form of gospel singing preserved on the island, a style dating back to pre-Civil Wartime. I missed the cue, and missed the opportunity to hear it in person. Fortunately, someone else, Guy Carawan, recorded it, and it can be heard on a Folkways album.

***

71

1-Mother and father, Rebecca and
Edward Weiss, New Haven,
Connecticut. At the monument on
East Rock, 1941.

2-Sister and brother, Ruth and
Nathan Weiss, December 1941.

3-Sister Ruth Lester with husband
David Lester, New Jersey, 1985.

4-Basil Yurchenco. Graduate of Yale University, New Haven, Connecticut, 1936.

5-Basil Yurchenco. Taxco, Mexico, 1941.

6-Black and white painting of Henrietta Yurchenco by Basil Yurchenco. 3' X 2 1/2'. Background was never completed. Influenced by the artist Rufino Tamayo. Painted in the Yurchencos' apartment on St. Marks Place in Manhattan, New York. *Photo: Emilio Espinosa, 1941.*

7-Son Peter Yurchenco and 1-year old grandson, Nicholas. New Jersey. *Photo: Ingrid Yurchenco, 1990.*

8- Ingrid Yurchenco and 2-year old Helen. *Photo: Peter Yurchenco, July 1989.*

9- Grandchildren, Helen and Nicholas Yurchenco, Christmas. *Photo: Ingrid Yurchenco, 2001.*

10-At my apartment with Pete Seeger. New York @ 1995.

11-With a leading citizen of the Island and member of the Methodist Church that served as a focus of my research among the African American Gullah-speakers of John's Island, South Carolina. *Photo: David Lewiston, American Folklife Center, 1971.*

Chapter Three – Mexico

I probably never would have gone to Mexico had it not been for our friendship with Rufino Tamayo, the great Mexican painter. Tamayo and his beautiful wife, Olga, came to live in New York during the 1930s, long before he became world famous. Chenk and I used to visit them in their tiny, rather dark but cheerful apartment in midtown Manhattan. With no room to spare everything was neat and orderly; his easel in a corner of the living room near the window to catch the daylight, his tubes of paints, brushes, turpentine and paint rags placed on stools around him. Finished paintings were neatly stacked against the wall.

For years our visits had been filled with talk about Mexico. To Chenk it was the promised land. Like many other American painters he was inspired by the great Mexicans -- Siquieros, Rivera and Orozco -- whose works portrayed the life of the poor and Mexico's revolutionary ideals. However, no one influenced him more than Tamayo; he was the painters' painter, the great stylist, the magician that transformed the lowliest subject into high art.

The Tamayos gave us our introduction not only to Mexican arts but to the country itself. I listened avidly to their stories about ancient tribes in remote mountain regions, of strange music and masked dances, and descriptions of the magnificent Aztec, Toltec and Mayan ruins. The most visible symbol of that ancient past was Rufino's own remarkable face, similar to ancient sculpture we were to see later on.

One day, in the spring of 1941, Rufino telephoned to say he and Olga had just bought a car. Would we like to go to Mexico with them? Since my job at WNYC and Chenk's on the WPA Art Project were winding down, we eagerly accepted the invitation.

Besides, the excitement of the previous decade, with its lively arts scene and intellectual debate, had slowed to a crawl. An atmosphere of suspicion and distrust prevailed, and we were glad to leave the country. We meant to stay away as long as our money held out.

In June of 1941 we headed south along the Eastern seaboard, southwestward to Texas, and crossed the Mexico-United States border at Laredo. It was a frightening time: The day before, the Germans had marched into Poland, Soviet territory; the shaky pact between the Nazis and the Soviets was over, and the war, already in progress since 1939, had assumed menacing proportions. Even then we felt in our bones that America would soon be involved. Nevertheless, although anxious about the future, we continued our journey, traveling south on the world's straightest highway from the U.S. border to the city of Monterrey. Then the road climbed through mountains; one moment in chilly high-altitude country and the next in steaming hot lowlands. Finally, the Valley of Mexico stretched out before us, and soon we were in Mexico City.

My first sight of the city filled me with wonder. I was unaccustomed to such clear, bright sunlight where every building was etched sharply against the azure blue sky. The long, slender palm trees that lined the streets swayed in the gentle breeze. It was the beginning of the rainy season, and Mexico was in full bloom. Flower markets abounded with sprigs of purple orchids, long-stemmed white lilies and red carnations, pink, white and yellow roses and delicate violets.

Like other tourists we saw the sights -- the Toltec pyramids at Teotihuacan, the ancient floating-gardens at Xochimilco, the shrine to the Virgin of Guadalupe, Mexico's gentle patron saint,

Porfirio Diaz' 19th-century marble Palace of Fine Arts, now irrevocably sinking into the city's mud bottom. I marveled at the vast proportions of the *zocalo*, the principal square, with Cortes' elegant palace on one side and, at right angles to it, the ornate Churruguesque cathedral -- the twin seats of power -- government and the Church. On the far side of the *zocalo* was the *Monte de Piedad,* the national pawn shop where precious jewelry could be bought for a song. How I longed for the amethysts, rubies and diamond earrings sparkling in the glass-covered showcases. But alas, I never had the money to buy those things and was grateful for the few treasures I came to possess over the years.

On our walks in Alameda Park near the Palace of Fine Arts, I imagined myself in 18th-century Mexico on a Sunday afternoon stroll: Elegant *galanes* (gentlemen) mounted on stalwart black horses rode along its paths, flirting with well-chaperoned young ladies; to shield myself from the afternoon heat, I held aloft a silk parasol and fanned myself with a lacy Spanish fan. "Stop dreaming!" my husband would murmur in my ear. "You're in the 20th century." How right he was; there were no aristocrats to be seen, just poor people selling trinkets to weary tourists.

We had to adjust ourselves to new conditions, such as the high altitude which left us exhausted after the least effort -- and the food. Unlike many foreigners I was apparently immune to 'Montezuma's' revenge', which wreaks havoc with one's digestive system. Not mine, however, I must have an iron-clad stomach, for no microbe has dared attack me during all the years in Mexico. My palate adjusted easily to the new diet. *Huevos rancheros,* tortillas, black frijoles and dainty sweetbreads tasted just as good as the bagels and lox I had left behind in New York. Special treats were *gusanos de magey* (maguey worms, which taste like soft-shelled crab), iguana and *cuitlacoche* soup (corn fungus) and tamales (especially the meat-filled ones from Oaxaca steamed in banana leaves).

Besides these exotic dishes there was a staggering array of fruit: Instead of our northern apples, peaches, plums and pears we had ripe bananas, some as tiny as your finger (appropriately called *dedos*) and other enormous red ones for cooking. The pineapples dripped with golden juice, and we feasted on fruits like mango, *zapote negro*, papaya, *tuna and pithaya* (cactus fruits). Today, most of these tropical fruits can be bought in New York markets. Like vanilla, chocolate, tomatoes and hot chiles, all these had been part of the Mexican diet long before the European conquest.

Everything was new and exciting -- pre-hispanic ruins, colonial churches and shrines. But it was the people who thronged the city that most aroused my curiosity. I was used to rubbing shoulders with races from every corner of the globe and hearing numerous languages in the subway, the grocery store, in movie houses and parks. In Mexico, however, there was a more homogenous population: remnants of old pale-skinned Spanish families, a mestizo majority (the mixture of Spanish and Indian), and Indians, the lowest rung of the social ladder, all speaking Spanish.

In our first year in Mexico we met mostly middle class families. Our first lodgings was a room in the home of a "respectable" middle-class family fallen on hard times. The matriarch of the family would awake at ten every morning, have her breakfast served in bed, read her mail, confer with the cook and gardener until two in the afternoon, when she would rise to preside at the dinner table. Immediately afterward she'd retire for the daily siesta, awake for afternoon tea and hold audiences with relatives until bedtime. This was her daily routine, which rarely changed from one day to the next.

Some educated middle-class women, however, worked for a

living as secretaries or teachers. It was not yet common for them to work outside the home. Besides, intelligence and talent in a woman were often considered liabilities; a smart woman hid her capabilities and deferred to men, especially her husband. I met many brilliant women whose lives were severely curtailed by this ancient social code.

For example, among my friends was a gifted American-educated dancer, from a wealthy, socially prominent family. When she decided to marry a young and brilliant lawyer, her family objected furiously. "He's a liberal," they said, "and not our kind." But Amalia, educated in the United States, fought back, and they were duly married. For the first six months her life was an exciting round of concerts and art exhibits; they compiled a fine library and bought paintings. Then, almost imperceptibly, her life changed -- there were no more concerts; the husband quietly removed the books to read them in the privacy of his office. The young wife began to despair as her husband laid down the law: He would not tolerate any activity that deprived him of her total attention. When she pleaded for a divorce, her parents sided with the husband. Only when physicians warned the parents that her life was in danger did they finally agree to the divorce. Later on she became one of Mexico's most illustrious women, although she married and divorced several times She was, however, an exception to the rule.

While talented women were admired within artistic circles, they were seldom rewarded with jobs. For example, all the famous murals on government buildings during the enlightened regime of Lazaro Cardenas had been painted by men. Even gifted painters like Frida Kahlo and Olga Costa, the wives of Diego Rivera and Jose Chavez Morado, respectively, deferred to their illustrious husbands. Decades would pass before these gifted women received the recognition they richly deserved. Today, Frida Kahlo has become an icon, but in those days she was Diego's wife who also painted.

The opera, theater, literature and dance were open to women, but with conditions. The symphony orchestra, for example, allowed women to join, but the few who did were members in name only. When Mexico's film industry flowered in the 1940s, dance became essential. Since most dancers were women, their male relatives were up in arms: They didn't want the spotlight on the girls' legs, or close-ups of their faces. After all, what decent man would marry a girl who "exhibited" herself for the whole world to see and ogle?!! And so, the best dancers were often shunted to the last row of the lineup, where they were hardly seen.

Much has changed since the '40s. Women are educated (more than half the students at the National University are women), have their own careers, and many prefer a single life to marriage; many men, on the other hand, are having a tough time reconciling themselves to the change in their long-held privileged status.

My favorite observation point of middle-class socializing was Sanborn's, the famous American-owned store and restaurant located in one of Mexico City's most beautiful buildings, its facade entirely of blue tiles. Respectable ladies dressed to the nines would meet their friends and relatives for American delicacies like pancakes and waffles. It was the equivalent of having tea at New York's Plaza Hotel. But Latin American women outstripped American women by their elegance. Never had I seen such sparkling earrings, such brilliant makeup, such tight little sexy dresses and spike heels -- for early morning family get-togethers! They even wore fox furs, complete with head and tail, in the warm summer months.

I learned a new way to cement a relationship. At Sanborn's I watched people greet each other with kisses and embraces. At first I thought they were all close friends or family members. But I learned that many were total strangers, meeting for the first time. In the 1940s Americans did not hug mere acquaintances; a handshake was sufficient. However, I acquired the habit: to this day, it takes only a moment before the initial handshake leads to an embrace, and a bond is formed. The embrace is merely an acknowledgment of one's presence, a gesture of good will (even if the relationship turns sour along the way).

But, I was especially intrigued by certain women dressed in black from head to toe. Despite the funereal clothes they were brilliantly made-up and lavishly bejeweled." Who are they?" I asked my friends. "They are widows", they laughed, "just announcing they're in the market for a new man." Although legal in Mexico, divorce was considered a social disgrace by the middle class; accordingly, a divorced woman was expected to live like a nun, shunning contact with men. But I took this information with a grain of salt for, as one wise woman told me, "*Las leyes son una cosa, y la vida otra*" (Rules are one thing, life is another). Part of my education was learning how Mexican women cleverly circumvented the rules. Men would carry on their love affairs openly, without serious condemnation from the community. Women, however, had to be smart and disguise every move. Their elaborate plans to deceive husbands, mothers, fathers and brothers are rivaled only by Muslim women, who are most skilled in the art of deception according to recently published folk tales collected from women in Middle Eastern countries.

Coming from Depression America, I was all too familiar with the sight of homeless, unemployed men picking over garbage in search of an edible morsel or two. But as I wandered through Mexico City on my own, away from friends to guide me, I was once again surrounded by the sights of poverty. Indian women sat on the sidewalks amid their possessions, babies cradled in *rebozos*, eating cold tortillas. Although virtually destitute, their colorful clothes, gay woven belts and jewelry of silver, seeds and shells indicated that poverty did not necessarily negate artistic sensibility. These encounters with Indians on the streets of Mexico City were brief and superficial but stirred my curiosity: Who were they? Where did they come from? How did they live?

My first real encounter with Indian life was in the city of Oaxaca in December 1941. Chenk and I had spent the summer in San Miguel de Allende, in the state of Guanajuato, and the fall in Taxco, the famous silver-manufacturing town in the state of Guerrero. Although we met many Mexicans, they were, like ourselves, people in the arts. In Taxco we listened to the famous Bill Spratling, the gifted American founder of the modern silver industry, tell risqué tales of Mexican upper-class life; we marveled at the imaginative ways Mexicans celebrated their saints' days, the costumes, masks, and fireworks in the form of castles and bulls. But there were too many American tourists in San Miguel and Taxco for my taste, and I wanted to lose sight of them. After all, I hadn't traveled thousands of miles just to hang out with the same guys I saw every day on the streets of New York.

***

Oaxaca - 1941

Friendship with the Tamayos had aroused our curiosity about Oaxaca, Rufino's birthplace. One day we booked passage on the train. By this time we had become accustomed to the second-class buses that lurched laboriously along back roads with market-bound Indians loaded down with live chickens, strings of onions and baskets of huge papayas. But the train was a new experience. Every year, during the rainy season, the railroad bridges between Mexico City and Oaxaca, loosened by flooded rivers, would collapse into deep ravines. And every year, temporary structures were assembled hopefully to last until the next rainy season. I can still recall how our train shook as it slowly, painstakingly, passed over each bridge. Would we get to Oaxaca alive? I feared the worst. But we finally arrived, 24 hours later. (These days I make the same trip by air, a 45-minute plane ride!)

What a city! With its pale green stone buildings and wide, gracious plazas, Oaxaca was a colonial gem! The cathedral of Santo Domingo, with its magnificently carved ceiling and maze of interior patios, reminded me yet again of the awesome power of the Catholic church and its hold on mestizos and Indians alike.

Luck was with us. Everywhere posters announced the upcoming Indian fair. Indians from Oaxaca's seven regions were to convene for a week of festivities! The special feature was a re-enactment of the *guelaguetza,* a pre-hispanic ceremony honoring tribal chieftains, forgotten for hundreds of years. Performed on a mountain high above the city, near the awe-inspiring ruins of Monte Alban, the center of pre-hispanic Mixtec-Zapotec civilization, the ritual was pure theater, solemn and regal.

We were not the only outsiders at the Oaxaca fair. It was there I met many of Mexico's leading musicians, painters and anthropologists. Many became life-long friends and colleagues. I remember Blas Galindo, the gifted composer just back from studies in the United States, Luis Sandi, the head of music in the Department of Education, and Frances Toor, the one expatriot and tireless folklorist from the States. We traipsed around the city searching out Indian musicians. We heard simple tunes and dance rhythms on primitive drums and reed flutes. "Tell me," I asked my new friends, "how old is this music?" "What you heard," they said, "is their way of playing music brought by the Spaniards." I persisted, "Is anything left of the past, the pre-hispanic past?" "Oh

81

yes," they said, "but not here. You'd have to travel far from here to hear it." My curiosity was aroused. "Has anything been recorded?" I asked. "No," they said, "only written down in notation." Although I did not know it at the time, I would soon be the one to do the job.

Although unimpressed by the tunes played by the Oaxacan Indians, I was truly excited by a band from the Isthmus of Tehuantepec featuring guitars, wind instruments, and marimba. They were marvelous; the trumpeter as good as the best jazzman back home and the marimba player a gifted improviser and virtuoso. Though in Mexico City I had heard the best mariachi bands and small ensembles from Vera Cruz coast, the Isthmus bands were to leave a lasting impression on me.

Oaxaca also introduced me to Indian theater, part of every festival, religious or secular. Although called 'dances,' they are really theatrical presentations, replete with story, music, dance, dialogue and costumes. As described by 16th and 17th century Spanish chroniclers, the ancient Mayas and Aztecs dramatized every aspect of life; even their bloody sacrifices were theatrical events. The theater was so important that tribal kings and chieftains maintained at their palaces huge companies of actors, singers, musicians, dancers and mimes. Once the Conquest was accomplished, festivals honoring Christian saints supplanted many of the old pagan celebrations.

In Oaxaca I saw for the first time the most popular post-conquest drama: *El Baile de los Moros y Cristianos* (Dance of the Moors and Christians). This 'dance', originally a lavish 13th century court pageant, is a re-enactment of the Spanish victory over the Moors in the wars of the Reconquest. It was taught by Catholic priests to the Indians all over Latin America to demonstrate Christian power. I often have wondered why the Indians identified with their conquerors when they, like the Moors, were a defeated people. Sometimes, however, even the best plans go awry. I was once told that somewhere in southern Mexico a note, scribbled in the margins of a church record book, reported the killing of the priest who had taught them the drama. Could it be that they had identified with the defeated Moors, and killed the priest in revenge?

At this early date, my Spanish was shaky, but Chenk, born in Argentina, led me where I could not have gone alone. To see a special *huipil* (pre-hispanic blouse) from Yalalag, a mountain village in northern Oaxaca, we wandered into the patio of a house where the Indian women were staying during the fair. "Can we take your pictures?" Chenk asked. They immediately invited us in. "Wouldn't you like to try on our clothes? ", the women asked me. The next moment a white cotton *huipil* with a purple tassel was slipped over my head, then they wrapped me in a hand-loomed blue skirt. The crowning glory was an enormous black headdress of twisted woolen strands. Chenk took pictures. I felt like a queen. I loved those flowing garments, so comfortable, and so dramatic. I'm sure that dressing me in their clothes was an act of hospitality. However, on second thought they might have thought my clothes were ugly. (I was once told my dress was *sucio* [dirty], meaning just plain awful.) I have treasured those photographs all my life.

Finally the festival ended, we waved our friends from Mexico City goodbye as they boarded the train. We watched as the last Indians packed masks, costumes and musical instruments on their burros and headed down the road for home. Without a moment for relaxation Chenk and I were plunged into Oaxaca City's own holiday entertainment. It was now almost Christmas and, like the rest of the country, the round of parties known as the *posadas* was in full swing. But Oaxaca's celebration was unique: a few nights before Christmas Eve we sauntered out to the main plaza to find push-carts everywhere selling little dolls made of large radishes, which the women had dressed in local costumes. The next night, we followed huge masked figures on stilts (like the kind I was to see in Spain later on) as they lumbered through the streets. The following night the plaza was ringed with pushcarts selling *buñuelos*, hot crisp waffles, drenched in sweet syrup and served on crude earthenware plates. These we tossed on the ground when finished. By two in the morning the square was littered with broken crockery. When we came out for our morning coffee the next day, the streets were clean as a whistle: overnight; the entire prison population was let out to clean up the mess!

By now it was Christmas Eve, and Chenk and I were feeling homesick. What could possibly take the place of our shimmering Christmas tree, carol singing, my father's spicy pumpkin pies and the warmth and intimacy of family and friends? I missed the frost of winter, the nip in the air, the glitter of lights on Fifth Avenue. And here we northerners were in balmy, sunny, Oaxaca with tall palm trees and cactus instead of snow and ice.

We were not without anxiety. It was December of 1941; the Japanese attack on our naval fleet at Pearl Harbor had taken place, and our country was at war. Soon the Mexicans joined the Allied cause, sending an air squadron as their contribution to the war effort. Would Chenk have to go back and join the army, what about my brother Nate, and so many friends? The last week in Oaxaca was perhaps our last time together. We agreed to enjoy ourselves as much as possible and face reality upon return to Mexico City.

Christmas Eve was the culmination of the holiday season: like everywhere in Spanish America, the birth of Christ is celebrated by a Midnight Mass. However, Oaxacans have a unique custom: each *barrio* (district) forms a procession of lights, called *calendas*, and marches to the central cathedral for the Mass. To light the way through the dark night they make candle-lit lanterns shaped like airplanes, cars, trains, or whatever, and attach them to tall poles. A brass band precedes each procession, playing marches and popular songs.

We watched the flickering lights of the *calendas* from a hillside high above the city. From our vantage point they seemed dream-like, mysterious and illusive! Then we rushed down the hill to see the conclusion of the event; hundreds of Indians had crowded into the cathedral for the mass -- the air filled with the aroma of incense, flowers, and the cries of babies wrapped tightly in the folds of their mothers' rebozos. Although we were spending Christmas away from home, we were not alone. By this time we had made friends who shared the evening with us drinking mezcal and gorging on those heavenly Oaxacan tamales.

After all the festivities, Christmas Day was quiet. Was everybody asleep, or working off the hangover of the night before? When would the children receive their presents? In those days presents were distributed on January 6th, *Dia de los Reyes* (Three Kings Day), when Jesus received the gifts of gold, myrrh and frankincense. Today, many Mexicans, seduced by the glitter of our Christmas trees, buy plastic imitations and decorate them with fake snow and brightly colored baubles. The lucky kids get presents on Christmas Day and *El Dia de los Reyes*.

When the celebrations ended, we said our goodbyes, ate our last tamales and headed back to Mexico City by train. The war still seemed far away and surreal. Stopping at Puebla en route we bought the newspaper for the latest war news. Chenk struck up a conversation with two Indian teenagers on their way to Mexico City in search of jobs. He tried to explain the war to them. "The U.S. and Mexico are at war with Japan," Chenk told them, "which is far away from Mexico on the other side of the Pacific Ocean."

They looked pleased. *"Que bonita, la revolución!"* they responded. "No, no," protested my husband, "it's not a revolution, it's a war." But they didn't understand. Revolution was the only kind of fighting they knew: You fight people you know and who have done you wrong; a war against people you've never seen and haven't harmed you was simply barbaric to their way of thinking.

***

Mexico City - 1942

Back in Mexico City we felt unsure of our next move. Our summer holiday had extended into the winter, yet we had no plans to return home. Were we to remain tourists or were we to settle in? In the midst of our confusion we met Waldeen, an American dancer living in Mexico, who helped shape the next crucial years of my life. From the moment we met until her death in 1995 we remained the closest, most loving friends. A few years my senior, she was like a sister to me. A few years earlier, Waldeen had taken Mexico by storm as prima ballerina of a famous ballet company directed by the Japanese dancer, Micho Ito. Waldeen's delicate beauty and charismatic personality had so charmed Mexico's arts' patrons they invited her back to form a company of her own. However, by that time Waldeen had done an about-face, abandoning the ballet technique for the modern dance. Under the auspices of the Union of Electrical Workers, she founded the modern dance movement in Mexico and was active as choreographer and teacher until the end of her life.

The year before my arrival she had made dance history with her ballet, *La Coronela* (The Woman Colonel), about women fighters in the 1910 Mexican Revolution. The great Silvestre Revueltas wrote the musical score, and the painter Gabriel Ledesma designed a

86

stunning set based on popular Mexican folklore. An early feminist, her *Coronela* was the first of many works based on women's history in Latin America, their trials as well as their triumphs.

Waldeen was a powerful figure, both on stage and off. Sometimes her regal manner and strong opinions antagonized even her closest friends, who often called her the "Duchess." Nevertheless, her dancers respected her absolutely. One of my great pleasures was watching her when, with a few friends, she would improvise to music; she understood Bach like a musician, aware of the interplay of different musical voices. Her appearance on stage, beautiful arms lifted, head poised like a bird in flight, would bring the audience to its feet in wild applause. Her mother, a southern "lady," and her father, of a minor German aristocratic family, had nurtured and protected the budding artist; she lived purely for her art in a privileged atmosphere. But with time Waldeen became a rebel -- in her art, her politics, and her person. Only the fine manners acquired in her youth betrayed her genteel past.

Waldeen had just ended a relationship of several years with Seki Sano, a Japanese film and stage director, her collaborator at the Union. Seki was probably the most gifted man I ever knew. I remember him as a charming friend, a wonderful cook, and a great storyteller. He spoke 14 languages, and years before had played the oboe in the Tokyo symphony orchestra. Born to a wealthy Samurai family, he had founded the western-style Little Theater movement in Japan. Like many other Japanese intellectuals, he was attracted to Marxism and subsequently was imprisoned and tortured for those ideas. He escaped to the Soviet Union some time in the early '30s, worked in film, came to the United States and finally to Mexico. Until his death in the 1960s, he was the respected theater director, and teacher of such notables as Ricardo Montalban, later a Hollywood star. Unfortunately, he was also violent at times, and that destroyed his relationship with Waldeen.

Waldeen, Chenk and I, all of us homeless, decided to pool our resources. We had been living quite comfortably at the home of a Russian friend, but it was time to strike out on our own. We rented an apartment near the Diana statue at the entrance to Chapultepec Park. Even though our combined income was meager, we managed to eat three meals a day, pay the rent, the electricity and even the services of a maid. Faced with no money, we prowled through flea markets and small shops for bargains; we bought for pennies the bounty of Mexico's handicrafts -- hand-loomed fabrics, baskets, and serapes for the floor, pottery, masks and other decorative items. Every Sunday we walked to the neighborhood flower market and for a dollar bought enough long-stemmed white lilies, sprays of purple orchids, red carnations, and bunches of delicate violets to fill every bowl in the apartment. They were so colorful, and the aroma so beguiling, nobody noticed the lack of furniture. The blessings of our modern apartment were floor-to-ceiling windows and a working fireplace! (Mexico is a tropical country, but at 7,800 feet above sea level, mornings and evenings are downright chilly.) Despite the war, Mexicans suffered few inconveniences. When the tanks of gas ran out, for instance, Petra, our housekeeper, used charcoal to heat bath water and cook, just as her ancestors had done for centuries. Mexico had two telephone companies -- Telefonos Mexicanos, American owned, and Telefonos Eriksson, Swedish owned, but few of our friends had both, so messages were often hand-delivered.

Mexico City during the war resembled New York -- it was fast becoming a lively international city. The process had begun at the end of the Spanish Civil War when the Mexican government rescued many Spanish intellectuals interned in French refugee camps. To give them employment they founded a new university, *el Colegio de Mexico*, and a publishing house, el *Fondo de Cultura*

Economica, which even today are considered quality institutions. Fighters in the International Brigades and the American Abraham Lincoln Brigade also found a friendly home; I remember meeting Isabel Palencia, a patrician freedom fighter during the short-lived Spanish Republic, the German writer Bodo Uhse, the Spanish anthropologist Juan Comas, Bill Miller, an American film man, and the Polish Ambassador in Exile for Latin America and his wife, and others whose names I have now forgotten.

The news from home was disturbing; my brother in the navy, friends in the army, my father a night watchman in a factory, and my mother in a munitions plant. Even so, the war seemed far away and remote, even though we read the papers and partied at benefits for the Allied cause. But mostly life was pleasant with outings to the countryside, trips to Indian village fiestas, and dancing the *danzon* at the elegant Reforma Hotel. When the racetrack opened, we welcomed it as a diversion and possibly a source of money. (Our funds were fast disappearing.) But I proved to be nothing but bad luck; I'd bet other people's money and lose every cent.

As foreigners we were always aware of Mexican hostility towards us Americans. The artistic colony considered our culture definitely second-class, not to be emulated by any intellectual with a head on his shoulders. Upper class Mexicans sent their children to English, or preferably French schools. Since independence from Spain in the early 19th century, Mexico City's architecture turned towards France: Chapultepec Castle, Emperor Maximilian and Carlota's residence (now the Historical Museum), Porfirio Diaz' grandiose marble Palacio de Bellas Artes, and the lovely Paseo de la Reforma, the city's main thoroughfare, a replica of Paris' Champs Élysées. I had a taste of French adulation early in my stay: When planning my first recording trip, I approached the poet Carlos Pellicer, then director of the Palace of Fine Arts for support. He put me off with

89

his very first question: "You speak French, of course?" "No, I don't," I said, surprised at the question. "Well, why not?" he asked. Why I needed French to record Indian Mexico I'll never understand, but it was probably his way of gauging my cultural savvy. No doubt, I failed miserably, but it really didn't matter; shortly thereafter he was replaced by Benito Coquet, who was most cordial and helpful in every way.

Anyway, at the time of my arrival, Spain, the traditional *bete noir*, and France, the 19th century invader, were both confined to the past. The real enemy was the United States. Cordial as Mexicans were to American dancers, anthropologists, and musicians like myself who worked with them, they viewed us with suspicion. After all, we came from *El Coloso del Norte* (the Colossus of the North), the great Goliath, always a threat. "Just send us your girls," they'd say with a wink and a smile, and I would smile back with a shrug of my shoulders. When the U.S. established a branch of the Economic War Board in Mexico City at the Hotel Imperial, it was immediately dubbed "*Hotel Imperialista*". To further poison Mexican-U.S. relations, there were the so-called "zoot-suit riots" in Los Angeles, where Mexicans were badly beaten by the police. For a long time afterwards, some of our Mexican friends stopped talking to us -- wouldn't look us in the eye, as if holding us responsible for the violence.

When the U.S. government established the Good Neighbor policy under Nelson Rockefeller, we Americans hailed it, hoping for a change in attitude towards Latin America. But the program started off on the wrong foot. Hoping to enlist cooperation with Mexican intellectuals and artists, the State Department sent a cultural attaché to Mexico City. Within days he was exposed as a '*franquista*', a supporter of the Spanish *caudillo*, Francisco Franco. Given the leftist sentiments of the art colony, he was the worst choice the U.S. could have made. His first blunder was to deny a visa to Luis Sandi, an official of the Department of Education, invited to an educational conference in the United States. When I asked him for an explanation, he declared Sandi was obviously a Red because of his membership in the artists and professional union. "But," I said, "nobody can get a government wall to paint, or a grant unless you're a member." If I remember correctly, the State Department ultimately overruled him and granted Sandi the visa.

His next blunder was to invite Mexico's leading artists to a dull party, a sad affair without entertainment, little food or liquor. The speeches about cooperation between neighbors in a time of crisis, etc., etc., did not sweeten the sour atmosphere. Some time later the State Department replaced him with a career diplomat who, although he accomplished little, at least didn't offend people. Somebody in Washington must have gotten the message

At the same time, the Russian Embassy was winning over the Mexicans in droves: their parties were the talk of the town. Being new to the scene, I myself was never invited, but Waldeen, much in the news at that time, was on their guest list, and reported all the details of the parties to me. The Russians loaded their tables with legendary delicacies like sturgeon, caviar, blini and rich pastries. In a haze of champagne and vodka, guests were regaled with poetry readings, balalaika music, and films on the progress of the latest Five-Year Plan.

Yes, the Russians were riding high in those war years. Their battle against the Nazis (the Soviet-Nazi Pact was never mentioned), industrial progress, claims of eliminating poverty, etc., generated admiration and even envy. Yet one claim proved groundless when tested out on Mexican soil: that a new man had been created under Socialism, one that regarded women as equals, not as sexual objects. As it turned out, within a short time the

91

young men of the Embassy were chasing Mexican women in the old-fashioned, capitalist manner. When one of them came to our door looking for Waldeen (she had given him her address at one of those parties), our maid Petra sent him on his way. Opening the door a crack, she said (lying through her teeth), " The señorita is not at home." Waldeen had been hiding behind the door! "A man is a man for all that," she said after he had gone, acknowledging her great disappointment in the New Soviet Man.

But nobody was regarded with more respect and honest affection than the Chilean poet Pablo Neruda. As Chile's Consul General to Mexico, I'm sure he took care of the usual duties -- commerce, politics, etc. -- but we knew him as a delightful and charming friend. Pablo made no secret about his Communist sympathies, yet he had been Chilean Consul in more than a dozen countries before Mexico. (Later on, I learned that Latin American governments regularly rid themselves of their radical intellectuals by shipping them off to obscure embassy posts overseas.) Pablo was a frequent visitor at our apartment, mainly because he admired Waldeen as a dancer, but also because she translated his poetry into English. One day I delivered a note from her to Pablo at the consulate. Enrique Davalos, another Chilean writer and Pablo's right-hand man, greeted me: "I'll see if he's awake; there was a party last night..." Soon I was led into his study, where he greeted me in a bathrobe, his eyes bleary. Always the genial host, he squired me around the room. "Come, Henrietta," he said, "let me show you those glass cases over there. The shells you see I found myself." His government had sent him to various islands and little coastal countries, as far away from Chile as possible. But he enjoyed passing the time by looking for shells on the beach. It was the loveliest array of shells I had ever seen outside a museum -- pink, pale yellow and orange, fragile little gems from the sea. "Do you know that it's been called the best collection in the world?" he informed me proudly.

I saw Pablo again when he left Mexico, having been recalled to Chile by his government. All his friends trouped out to the airport to bid a final farewell; two mariachi bands played "Las Mañanitas", Mexico's handy, all-purpose, celebratory song, people wept when he boarded the plane, and waved goodbye until the aircraft disappeared from view. He visited New York several times after the war, to read his poetry at the 92nd Steet Y's Poetry Center (after which, I was told, his admirers carried him through the streets on their shoulders). I was in Chile during the campaign of 1970 when the ill-fated Allende was elected president. I tried to see Pablo but missed him. Cancer was given as the cause of death, but was that the whole truth?

What I found upon arrival in Mexico from Oaxaca in January of 1942 was an intense dedication to everything Indian, a movement initiated during the regime of Lazaro Cardenas, Mexico's great president in the 1930s. In art circles Indian handiworks, like jewelry, pottery, and paintings, were avidly sought. But, by the early 1940s, most antique Indian jewelry had been bought up by savvy collectors; to find a genuine embossed silver cross, or seed pearl, coral or turquoise earrings, was like discovering a treasure in Tutankhamen's tomb.

The churches, however, were deposits of real treasures, not the elaborate silver altarpieces but popular art, walls lined with paintings on wood or tin by local artisans. These *milagros* (miracles), as they were called, were offerings to the saints, thanks for their help in curing illness, intervention in accidents, natural disasters, trouble of all kinds. For years the *milagros* were looted by quick-fingered collectors but eventually became available for a price. When I encountered them at Bazaar Sabado, Mexico's huge art market in San Angel (Mexico City's elegant residential area), they were too expensive for my slender purse.

93

***

One day, I received a letter from John H. Green, a recording engineer I had known in New York. Planning to come to Mexico with his recording equipment, an enormous Fairchild machine, he hoped I could arrange a field trip somewhere. Well, my heart jumped with excitement: but how was I to arrange this? After all, I had no money of my own, no reputation as a folklorist, and was totally unknown.

Waldeen came to the rescue. She introduced me to Dr. Enrique Arreguín, former rector of the University of San Nicolás in the state of Michoacán. Within a few days he had written to Dr. Anguiano, then rector of the university, and obtained his approval of my project. Next, I appealed to Benito Coquet, director of the Palace of Fine Arts, for additional help. Lo and behold, to my complete surprise, he promised to provide me with a closed van and a chauffeur.

I was so happy about my success in convincing the Mexican officials that I didn't stop to wonder, until much later on, why they trusted a mere slip of a girl, an American at that, with no field experience, knowledge of the country, and only basic Spanish. Perhaps they were testing me. But, after all, what did they have to lose? Mexico had few recording machines appropriate for fieldwork. For some years the Department of Education had sent musicians to several Indian areas to notate the music, although they surely knew that a written score was a flawed document, and at best, a mere skeleton without flesh or bones.

John arrived from New York on the appointed day, impatient to leave. In desperation, I pleaded with Benito Coquet. "When do you want to go?", he asked me. "Tomorrow," I said. "The truck will be ready for you at 9 a.m. I'm sending Roberto Tellez Girón, from the Department of Education, with you." Although my Spanish had improved since my arrival in the country, I nevertheless welcomed Roberto's help.

***

Michoacán - 1942

The next morning, April 1st, we took off for Morelia, the Capital city of the state of Michoacán. I still had no final word from Dr. Anguiano, but I decided to take a chance. It was a bold move on my part. After all, what could happen to us? We had the equipment, an experienced sound engineer, two musicians, and a car and driver to take us where we wanted to go. Upon arrival in Michoacán, we immediately went to the university. I introduced myself, bold as brass. Lic Anguiano welcomed me warmly, as if he had been expecting me all along. Within a half hour he had signed official vouchers to pay for gasoline and hotel, and given us letters of recommendation and plenty of advice.

The next day we headed towards Patzcuaro, our first destination. We turned off from the main highway and cut through the Indian towns of Santa Fe de la Laguna and Tzintzunzan, a famous pottery center. Finally, as the road curved and twisted through the red-clay earth, I had my first glimpse of Lake Patzcuaro. How serene, how majestic it was, nestled among the hazy blue hills and dotted with little islands! Now I understood why it was sacred ground to the Purepecha Indians, and why it had been the center of their ancient empire.

The town of Patzcuaro was a colonial city. Its great cathedral, houses and narrow streets were built around flowered patios noisy with the chirping of brilliantly-hued tropical birds. But the Indian presence was alive and palpable in the town's two open marketplaces. I still remember my first impressions of the women vendors in long, full, dark skirts and white blouses, their straight black hair braided with colored ribbons. How decorative they were! Rows of silver fish dangled from their red seed necklaces, black-and-blue-striped rebozos held babies in their folds, and their waists were wrapped in woven multi-colored sashes.

In front of the vendors, arranged neatly on the ground, was the produce of the lake and surrounding mountains: long, green-stemmed white onions; freshly-caught whitefish and glimmering trout; bright red tomatoes; chile peppers and beans of all colors and shapes. In the surrounding plazas, jacaranda trees were already shedding their blossoms, covering the walks with a layer of lavender petals.

Soon we presented our letter of introduction to the director of an experimental fishing station in Patzcuaro, a gracious and cultured man with detailed knowledge of the area. He immediately notified villagers around the lake to come to Patzcuaro to record their songs. Within a few days we were besieged by Indians ready to sing. Best of all were the youngsters from a government-run Indian boarding school at the nearby town of Paracho, a center of guitar manufacture. Those boys and girls, who sang in duos or trios to guitar accompaniment, knew an endless number of songs from their native villages. In three weeks in Michoacán we recorded more than 125 songs, most of them in the Indian language (Purepecha). What I learned on this trip confirmed the ideas I had acquired in New York: that music doesn't have to be hallowed by age, created by anonymous composers, or passed on from generation to generation to be called a "folk song." Folk songs are created every day, and often forgotten as new songs take their place! The "Purepecha Hit Parade" consisted of the latest tunes, most of which -- like our own popular music back home -- were love songs, serenades to woo the girls.

By the time I returned to Mexico City, I was hooked. Somehow or other, I would find a way to continue the research in Indian music. By this time I had met people active in Indian affairs. My field trip had stirred a lot of interest, and everybody wanted to hear the recordings. In order to preserve the delicate acetate disks, which, at best, would deteriorate after a dozen playings, I decided to present them at a public lecture.

Roberto Weitlaner, an anthropologist working at the museum, referred me to Dr. Daniel Rubín de la Borbolla, director of the School of Anthropology, for help. My Spanish was still shaky, so Weitlaner and Chenk came along to translate. Little did I know that Borbolla had been trained in England and spoke English perfectly, without a trace of an accent. But at our first meeting, he pretended not to understand a word I said!

Dr. Borbolla became my lifelong friend and benefactor until his death in 1991. One of Mexico's great men, he was a leading authority in the folk arts, not only of Mexico, but all Latin America. I shall always remember him as a spell-binding story teller, one who could elaborate on any theme, weaving together threads as diverse as politics, technology, myth, and history into a single integrated whole. He was also a kind and generous man, as concerned with the craftsmen as with their products. Today, I am on intimate terms with his wife, the gifted writer Sol Arguedas, his children (especially Sol Rubin de la Borbolla, director of the Museum of Popular Culture), and grandchildren, Inti, Roberto and Rosalpina.

Under the auspices of the Society of Anthropology, I gave my first public appearance in Mexico at the Benjamin Franklin Library, an agency of the American Embassy. I wrote the talk in English (I still have the original in my files); it was translated into Spanish by Salvador Ordoñez, director of the Conservatory of Music, and presented by Roberto Tellez Girón, who had accompanied me on the expedition.

My role in the event was minimal: I sat on the stage and dropped the needle down in the appropriate places on the disks. However, I was dressed for the occasion, in a handsome lime-green suit with my head wrapped in a high turban of sulfarino pink, a favorite Mexican color. (The effect was startling, according to my friends in the audience.)

Now things began to really happen. Dr. Manuel Gamio, the director of the newly-formed Interamerican Indian Institute, asked me to prepare a series of radio programs. Somebody had told him about my radio experience in the United States and my first collecting trip to Michoacán. Jointly sponsored by the Institute and the Music Division of the Pan American Union under Charles Seeger, I commissioned some of the leading Latin American composers to write orchestral pieces based on Indian themes, to be woven into the hour-long broadcasts. For the next year I worked closely with Dr. Gamio, whose encyclopedic knowledge about Latin American Indians gave me my first academic introduction to the field. Dr. Gamio remained my friend and mentor until I left Mexico in 1946, and the Institute became my headquarters. There I met many leading anthropologists and policy makers of the time: genial but troubled Franz Blum, author of *Tribes and Temples*, a pioneer work on Maya archeology, lately come from the States. With him was Gertrude (Trudy) Duby, a Swiss journalist and photographer, later his wife and co-founder of an important center of Indian Studies in San Cristobal de las Casas, and young, over-confident Oscar Lewis, the American anthropologist, later to win fame and fortune for his books on Mexico, and many others. At the Institute I also met Juan Comas, the Spanish refugee anthropologist, Dr. Gamio's right hand man, who was to play an unexpected and turbulent role in my life, first as advisor, and then, after my husband's departure, my lover.

Dr. Gamio was Mexico's first professional anthropologist. An early student of Franz Boaz at Columbia University, he had become renowned for his work at Teotihuacan, the Toltec ruins in the valley of Mexico. By the time I met him he was in his 60s. He was a gentleman of the old school, tall and thin, a dignified and elegant but lovable man. Always formally attired, he would sit at his desk smoking a cigarette through a long holder, the ashes falling on his vest. Not given to small talk, in a moment of candor he once said to me: "My dear, long ago I decided to forgo love affairs for the joys of a *gallinero* (chicken coop), a reference to his many children and grandchildren.

***

Chiapas –
The Isthmus of Tehuantepec – 1942

Shortly after my return from Michoacán, I was invited by the Governor of the state of Chiapas, Dr. Pascasio Gamboa, to record music there. Dr. Gamboa, who had just sponsored a conference on anthropology, was anxious to expand his state's cultural activities. Chiapas had long been famous for the excavations at Mayan centers, Palenque and Yashi Lan, but anthropological research was only in its infancy. The cities of the old Mayan empire in Chiapas had been abandoned by its ruling classes in the 9th century for reasons still shrouded in mystery, but the poor Indians of the region's many tribes (Tzotzil, Tzeltal, Lacandon and Tojolobal) never left their ancestral villages.

One day I had a visit from Bernardo Reyes, a photographer and the governor's right-hand man. "We've heard about you and your work in Michoacán," he said. "How would you like to come to Chiapas?" Well, of course I was delighted and accepted immediately, even though I didn't know where I would find recording equipment, now that John Green's machine was no longer available. "First," he said, "I must write to the governor for his final approval." And we left it at that.

We went for a walk together, and Bernardo took photos of me in my black tailored suit and wide-brimmed straw hat. What I didn't know was that he sent them to the governor. I've never been quite sure whether he was impressed by my professional qualifications or my good looks, but shortly thereafter I received a letter approving the project. Alfonso Caso, the distinguished director of the Institute of Anthropology and History, loaned me his recording equipment and disks. I also acquired an assistant, Raul Guerrero, an anthropologist interested in music.

We made the long, tedious journey to Chiapas by train: first, overnight to Vera Cruz, the principal port city on the Gulf of Mexico; then, a whole day south and across the Isthmus of Tehuantepec to Ixtepec, our first destination. On our first night in the Isthmus we were greeted by a real tropical storm. The rain came down in torrents and made a sea of the unpaved streets. Since Guerrero was engaged to Rosita, a girl from the Isthmus, we visited her family. The next day we explored the marketplace. To my utter surprise, all the stands selling produce, pottery and clothes were run by women. But they weren't like the Indian women I had observed elsewhere carrying huge packs on their backs, trudging on foot along the road while their men rode donkeys. These women of the Isthmus had stature, strength of character and a sense of purpose. Later, walking along the banks of the Tehuantepec River, I saw the gently swaying palm trees, and in the distance, soft blue and gray hills that had inspired Miguel Covarrubias to compare Tehuantepec to Bali, which he had visited in the 1930s.

My diary from that trip has the following entry: "August 17th. Up at 7:00. All of us -- Rosita, her two sisters, Raul and I bathe at 8 in the river. The girls wear sarongs, naked to the waist; their skin so smooth, brown and shiny, their long pitch-black hair streaming down their backs. It is so funny to see women, at any time of day, clothes parked on the bank, tranquilly bathing or washing their clothes, while men lead oxen across the river. They don't even look at each other."

We had our first recording session that same afternoon. We recorded Zenobio, the legendary Indian reed piper now old and blind, accompanied by his young drummer. Then a band appeared, and I recognized the trumpeter as the one I had heard in Oaxaca at the Indian fair in December of 1941. We had a lively session, the first of many I was to record over the next 5 years!

But things did not go smoothly. The machine had temperamental fits; worse yet, while I hand-held the microphone and Raul did the actual recording, a swarm of sand flies attacked my legs. Since I had to stand motionless they made a meal of me, and blood dripped from every pore. I began to understand why a long skirt is preferable to a short, knee-length modern dress: the bugs can't get at you!

The next day, August 18th, we traveled to Tuxtla Gutierrez, the capital of Chiapas. Our visit had been anticipated in the papers; there was even a dispatch from the Associated Press. The governor offered us everything we might need -- disks, even a guide to smooth our encounters with the Indians. Several days later we continued the journey to San Cristobal de las Casas, the center of the Indian world. Rain pursued us during the entire trip, pouring as it does only in the tropics, in torrents. The road was nothing but slippery mud all the way.

My diary notes our first recording session in the village of Tenejapa: "September 5th. Our first sight of the town is out of this world. From above we saw the plaza filled with people. We announced our arrival by blowing our horn. Impossible for our *camioneta*, we start through the mud into town on foot. The recording session was a howl; we were surrounded by hundreds of people, the kids up high in the trees, leaves and flowers falling all over us as we record."

When it was over, we climbed up to the road and drove back to San Cristobal in the pouring rain. All this time I was learning about Mexican men and their ways with women. My diary notes that I attended weddings, parties and dances, and that at times I was frightened. Everyone is polite, they say all the proper things, bow and kiss my hand, but.........!

From my diary comes the following: "September 13. I go to the casino and get in heaps of trouble. Ye gods, this place is giving me the creeps. The guys all carry guns, too many are stinking drunk, and there was a fight over me. It is utterly impossible for me to conform to their way of thinking and living. For one thing, I'm a foreigner and stick out like a sore thumb. Second, I'm a woman alone!"

At this point in my life I decided that I would never flirt, never wear revealing clothes, never party without an official escort while I was on location. I learned to be neuter, just smile a lot, and act like a nun, untouchable, and remote. That way I stayed out of trouble -- most of the time.

The day I arrived at Chiapa de Corso, a tropical town in the lowlands, two events occurred: first, a ten-second earthquake in Chiapa de Corso that scared me to death, and second, a call from the governor: "a group of workers are going to Comitán," he said, "to extend the telephone lines there, do you want to go with them? You'll be traveling most of the journey by motor launch up the Grijalva River, close to the Guatemalan border." I jumped at the chance. Early the next morning, the sun shining, the earthquake forgotten, I boarded the boat and settled back in my seat to enjoy the journey. On both sides were deep forests, huge trees spanned the river shading us from the murderous sun; alligators floated peacefully by, and brilliantly-hued bluebirds streaked by overhead. A perfect day.

There was more to come; towards midday we stopped at a clearing in the forest. Up the sandy embankment we climbed. There, a fabulous cook served us and a small battalion of wood-cutters an array of dishes -- chicken mole, chicken with special herbs, chicken and rice -- all cooked to such perfection that to this day my mouth waters thinking of it. And in the midst of the Chiapas wilderness -- incredible!

After lunch and a short siesta under the trees we continued our journey to a small ranch where horses were waiting for us to take us to San Bartolome, a large Indian town. My diary says:

"September 22nd. Changed my clothes and off we started. By this time it was twilight, then came darkness, and with it a full moon. On the road we sang and I learned a new song, at the next ranch we were greeted by a *marimba*, ate marvelous cheese, and finally retired for the night on a *petate*, the thin woven mat that is

103

the mattress for most rural peoples."

At San Bartolome the musicians, as well as the delightful local *cura* (priest), came out to meet us and we prepared to record. There were harps, violins, guitars, drums and trumpets, most of them of local manufacture. But disaster struck! We plugged our AC machine into the town's DC current and burned out the wiring. Not everything was lost. "Don't worry," said the priest, "you'll find a master electrician, a German, in Comitán, your destination. He can fix anything." He also suggested the musicians go along with us to Comitán to record there. The Indians agreed, anxious to please the priest.

The next morning we left for what was to be a 12-hour journey, I on horseback, the Indians on foot. For hours we plodded through the forest, in mud up to the horses' ankles; I passed the time counting the numerous orchid plants (the source of Governor Gamboa's orchid collection) sprouting from the trees.

Finally I could hear the roar of rushing water as we approached the river, now swollen from the torrential rain. I had been trailing behind my companions for a while. When I came to the banks I saw no one; they had simply disappeared. Which way had they gone -- to the right or the left? Remembering an old folk saying that a horse, given rein, would follow the other horses, I let the horse have his way, and he turned left. For the next fifteen minutes we meandered down a narrow path along the river's edge. But not a soul was in sight; I was lost. Just then an Indian passed by. "You're going the wrong way," he said. "Your friends went the other way." A moment later my companions galloped up to meet me, and I was rescued. I had remembered the saying wrong: When you give the horse rein, it will return to his own stable!

The next problem was crossing the raging river. The sight of cascades of water pouring over huge boulders terrified me. How was I to cross the river on this poor horse? But waiting for us on the other side were local mestizos ranchers accustomed to the yearly rising waters. I exchanged my nag for a huge white horse. Clutching the hub as tightly as I could, my feet raised high, I plunged the horse into the water. What a marvelous beast! After a few stumbles on the boulders, he landed me safely on solid ground. However, the Indians refused to budge; the sight of the wild river filled them with alarm. "Why are you afraid?", asked a rancher. Didn't you see the señora go across?" "Oh," they replied, *Ella es un diablo, quiere morir, y nosotros no*" (She's a devil. She wants to die, but we don't). With that they disappeared down the road towards San Bartolome, and that was the last we saw of them.

Part of our cargo received a soaking, some floated down the river, but our recording equipment was safe. I was happy to be alive and not a casualty of nature's tantrums. We spent the night at the home of a local rancher. It was there, amidst drunken hilarity and good-natured jokes about my bravery, that my mettle was tested once more. Luis Mendoza, my host, offered me a chile. "I can't eat hot food," I said, eyeing the little green pepper with alarm. "Tsk, tsk," he cajoled. "Don't worry, it's sweet." Cautiously, I bit off a piece and gasped with agony: my mouth was on fire! I almost jumped to the ceiling. It took at least ten minutes before I was back among the living. Some joke, I thought; but my feelings were assuaged by Luis' apologies and genuine concern.

By this time the endless drinking of the local firewater, called *comiteco*, the wild gestures and general excess began to tire me, and I longed to go to sleep. However, the night was not over yet. I had noticed that Luis' wife, a shy, diminutive woman, never sat at the table herself, even after all the men had been served dinner. Being a brash American, I insisted that I would not eat unless she sat next to me. She shook her head in embarrassment and continued

105

to serve her guests until everyone had left the table. Then, and only then, did she express her feelings by holding my hand tightly in hers; no words passed between us. She was literally a servant in her husband's house.

I learned a lesson that night: Not everyone, certainly not women, enjoyed the freedom I took as my right. Nevertheless, my views on their Mexicans' social customs were tolerated because I had good manners and delivered my opinions with womanly charm. Besides, as a foreigner -- and especially a woman -- I was allowed transgressions denied their own people. However, tolerance did not mean agreement; they listened and kept their opinions to themselves. In later years, I was to shout and argue with those who disagreed with me, but I was gentler in my youth.

That night I slept like the dead. I needed the rest, for the next day's trip would be another long and tedious horseback ride to Comitán. My diary reads:

"October 1st. Our friends accompany us part of the way, and then we go on alone. What a journey, mud and stones all the way. Our first sight of Comitán is magnificent: You can see for miles layers and layers of mountains, blues and grays. The tropical vegetation, and date palms seem to reach into the sky, all pink by this time." The 12-hour trip left me stiff as a board and I had to be bodily lifted from the horse and placed on my feet. Even in my weakened state I was aware of the hubbub around me -- the bishop, marimba bands, and the crowds of people welcoming us. For the first time in a week, I slept that night in a hotel with a mattress, spring, and clean sheets!

What we had been told in San Bartolome was absolutely true: The electrical engineer repaired our machine, and it was as good as new in no time. Because the roads were almost impassable, Indian musicians from nearby villages walked to Comitán for the recordings. Strangely enough we didn't record a single song during this trip to Chiapas. Later I was to learn: when you ask an Indian to play 'musica,' that only means instrumental music; if you want 'songs,' you use the word *cancion*. On a later trip in 1945 I recorded many songs.

The first expedition to these Mayan-speaking people had come to an end, but the prospect of another ten days through mud and slime was more than I could bear. The governor must have heard my thoughts, for he sent a plane to take me back to Tuxtla. Suddenly, we were told we would be leaving immediately. According to my diary:

October 7th. Rush back to the hotel, grab our stuff and arrive at the airstrip. Raul and I and squeeze into the tiny plane, me up front with the pilot. We leave at 12:10. Up in the clouds, how really pleasant it is -- no mud, no donkeys, just sky, beautiful blue sky! We landed in Tuxtla at 1 p.m., a 50-minute trip that had taken ten days by horse. That trip on a little puddle-jumper was my first ever by plane, and I marveled then at the wonders of civilization.

A message from the governor was waiting for me, an invitation to join him on an inspection of the Pan American Highway then under construction between Tuxtla and San Cristobal. When money ran out, constructions sites, particularly in jungle areas, were sometimes left unfinished; vegetation grew back, and when funds were again available, construction started from scratch. Such was the case, I was told, in Chiapas. But under Gamboa, the highways were finally being paved.

The next morning, Bernardo Reyes (Gamboa's right-hand man) met me at the hotel. I was surprised not to find Raul;

apparently not invited. We headed out to the construction site, Bernardo, the governor and me in one car, and several state officials in other cars. At the site, lunch was served under the trees on tables spread with lovely hand-loomed cloths, and servants offered one delicious dish after another.

After inspection we started back to Tuxtla. Soon the governor was holding my hand while Bernardo pretended to see nothing. "You need a baby," the governor whispered in English in my ear. Like a hole in my head, I thought. So, now I knew the purpose of this little excursion. Then he offered me one of his two prize black orchids and a plot of land on which he would build a little house for me. I thought to myself, how do I get out of this? Here I am with the highest authority of the state, his henchman in the front seat. If I scream, who will hear me? As I reviewed my options, none, to be sure, except personal persuasion, we arrived at the town of Chamula. A murder had just been committed and the governor was obliged to stay. I returned to Tuxtla with my virtue intact. Before returning to Mexico City, I said a fond farewell to Bernardo, not without giving him a sly smile. You lost, didn't you? It didn't go according to plan, I thought to myself. Too bad!

The next day Raul and I arrived in the Isthmus and took a cab to the city of Tehuantepec. It was time for his wedding, and I was ready for a good time. In borrowed clothes as a Tehuana, I danced the seductive *sandunga* with both men and women partners, as a brass band blared forth the sensuous melody. I ate enormous amounts of my favorite tamales, fresh juicy pineapple, papaya and pastries.

We had arrived just in time to catch the last day of a fiesta honoring the women, the organizers of the holiday. I wandered the streets with Charlie Frey, an American amateur archeologist I had met previously at the beginning of my trip. Suddenly we were swept up in a parade. Preceded by a brass band, a procession of women holding aloft the banners of their cooperative society marched down the road. Gaily attired in sumptuous silk and satin holiday dress, they balanced on their heads huge painted gourd-baskets filled with fruit, sweets and toys tossed to the children lining the streets. Ox-carts creaked along the sandy road, trailing banana branches in the dust. From within the carts came the sound of flutes and drums, joyously announcing the festivities.

Near a small plaza a group of women were dancing and drinking. We joined the men watching nearby, obviously proud of their lively women. As soon as they saw us, the only foreigners, they generously offered us a drink from the bottle, or, as was my undoing, from a little cup. I am not a drinker, and have a reputation as the cheapest drunk this side of the Atlantic. I get drunk smelling the cork. But now I was trapped; there was no way to refuse a drink without offending the women. I drank until I was reeling. Suddenly, Charlie and I were pushed towards the patio of the majordomo's house (the festival sponsor). A feast was in progress, and as guests of honor, we were plied with stewed iguana (the gourmet dish of the Isthmus), pineapple and, of course, more liquor. In a haze we were led out onto the dance floor to dance with the women. Every now and then shrieks would rend the air as a hefty Tehuana collapsed to the floor, felled by quantities of mezcal. Five minutes later, revived by who knows what alchemy, she was back on the floor, swaying to the music.

By this time, my head was pounding and I was dead tired. I managed, with Charlie's help, to return to my *pension*. My only wish was to lie down in the patio hammock, and sleep, sleep, sleep. No luck; there was a young girl with a baby in her arms lying in the coveted hammock. I glared at her, hoping she'd get up and go away, but she ignored me. As I sat there, miserable with an aching head, I gradually realized she was singing, and singing one beautiful song after another. I caught snatches of the words:

Ay, Sandunga	Oh, Sandunga
Sandunga, mama por dios	Sandunga, mother of god
Sandunga, no seas ingrata,	Sandunga, don't be ungrateful
Mama de mi corazón	Mother of my heart

Then I heard the song Tamayo had sung at my party in New York, *La Llorona*, the legendary weeping woman, Mexico's folk heroine who appears to people in the mist, in the forest, forever a tragic figure:

Ay, de mi Llorona	Oh, my Llorona
Llorona de azul celeste	Llorona, so heavenly blue
aunque me cuesta la vida, Llorona Llorona	Though it costs me my life,
no dejaré de quererte	I'll never stop loving you

But there I was helpless, no way of recording those lovely songs. Our work done in Chiapas, we had sent the recording equipment back to Mexico City! But I resolved that I would come back, and I did, many times, over the next 50 years. I still think those songs from the Isthmus are among the most sensual, the most intoxicating songs in the entire world of music.

***

Library of Congress Project - 1942

One day early in 1942, as I walked into the Interamerican Indian Institute to work on my radio programs, I was met by Dr.

Gamio. "I have just received a letter from the Library of Congress," he said. "They want to know if we wish to co-sponsor a project to record folk music in Mexico. They offer us equipment, disks and a small sum to cover field expenses. We in Mexico would pay salary and travel. Are you interested?" My heart leaped forward; my dream was about to come true. Quickly, my answer tumbled out: "Of course," I almost shouted. "Of course, I want to do it!" After returning from Chiapas I had drawn up a similar project and submitted it to the cultural attaché at the American Embassy, but nothing had come of it. Now, help was coming from an unsuspected source.

I never doubted that any future research I might do would focus on Indian music rather than mestizo, particularly the possible survivals of pre-hispanic culture. Though I knew Spaniards had explored every nook and cranny of the country and left their mark everywhere, anthropologists and musicians assured me that if I went far enough into the mountains I would find primitive tribes living like their ancestors. "If you record it you will be doing us a service," said my Mexican colleagues.

On a more personal note Gamio warned me of the dangers of fieldwork in remote areas. "For a delicate woman like yourself, the road will be long and hard, and you can expect deadly insects, poisonous snakes, bad water, and no comforts at all." But his dire warnings fell on deaf ears. Who cared? With the arrogance of youth, I was sure I could overcome any difficulty. Hadn't I already been baptized in Chiapas, and hadn't I survived interminable horseback trips, sleeping on the ground, and insect attacks? Wasn't that proof enough of my stamina?

Shortly thereafter, Gamio presented the project to the then Minister of Education, the poet Torres Bodet (later director of UNESCO), who gave his immediate approval. No one in Mexico could possibly say no to Gamio, this distinguished man whose archeological discoveries had been heralded around the world. He also pleaded on my behalf for a traveling companion. Torres Bodet agreed; a Department photographer, Agustin Maya, would go with me. However, the amount of my salary was not on the bargaining table; it was little more than glorified tip, but I never complained about it, I just wanted to work.

Soon a letter arrived from Washington. Benjamin Botkin, chief of the Archive of American Folksong at the Library of Congress, notified us that all the equipment had been mailed to us and would arrive shortly in Mexico City. Unbeknownst to us, it was held up at the border for six months, for reasons never made clear. But time was not wasted; I learned to wait, to cool my heels, control my temper when things didn't go my way immediately. It was invaluable training, for the next few years would sorely test my patience to the breaking point.

Meanwhile, life went on in Mexico City. Our apartment on Avenida Vera Cruz was warm and friendly. We had no money, and when dead broke we sometimes borrowed from Petra, our housekeeper, who hoarded parts of her salary for such eventualities. A Protestant from the state of Guerrero, she was a lively woman who brought nothing but joy in our lives.

Then the inevitable happened: Chenk received orders to return home for induction in the army. We knew it was coming but it was a shock nonetheless. For his last evening in Mexico, Petra made an enormous cake which she called *pastel de tristeza* (a sadness cake). The 18-egg cake was heavy indeed, and nobody at the party could down more than a thin slice. Petra, however, believed that proof of generosity was in direct proportion to the number of eggs used. Only *los codos* (literally "elbows," but signifying stingy folk) would make a cake with a few eggs. As she said this, disdain visible on her face, she would tap the elbow of her left hand with the fingers of her right, a gesture indicating stinginess. Then she cut a huge wedge, wrapped it in paper, and gave it to Chenk for the long train ride back to the States. Poor Chenk, he had no intention of taking it with him and pleaded an upset stomach. But Petra was as stubborn as a mule. "When you return," she said, "I shall make you a *pastel de alegria* (a happiness cake)." She never carried out the "threat," for when he returned many years later, Petra was working for someone else.

Saying goodbye at the railroad station was sad indeed, but I also felt a certain sense of relief. Our marriage, despite many common interests and his total support for my efforts, was beginning to be burdensome. With his departure I felt liberated, on my own; I didn't have to check in with him. Besides, a new career had blossomed for me, and I was blind to everything else. We both agreed that it would be foolish for me to return to the States while he joined the army, and so I remained in Mexico. As it turned out, Chenk was rejected by the army because of a childhood knee injury. Instead, he went to Harvard where he studied architecture with Walter Gropius and Marcel Breuer, refugees from Nazi Germany, and directors of the famous Bauhaus, the citadel of modern architecture and design.

Life went on, the war was far away, and only the newspaper headlines and parties in support of the Allied cause reminded us of the human tragedy taking place elsewhere. Waiting for the Library of Congress project to begin, I formed many friendships. Among our friends were Susana Gamboa and her husband, Fernando, soon to be director of the National Historical Museum. Susana was the director of a newly-formed gallery of modern art. Originally from Brooklyn, New York, she was a handsome woman to whom men were attracted like flies to honey. "Listen, gals," she'd say, bursting into laughter, "wait until you hear the latest." A prospective client once invited her to lunch at the most elegant French restaurant in the city. Obviously taken with her beauty, he showered her with compliments. "Just then," said Susana, "a young woman entered the restaurant, and he followed her with his eyes until she sat down at one of the tables. So I said to him 'Do you realize as you were praising me, you didn't take your eyes off that girl?' 'Oh,' he said, 'is there anything wrong in that?' Can you beat that for nerve?"

American women had questionable reputations, admired for our free ways, and condemned for them as well. One day, I came out of my room to find two complete strangers having tea with Waldeen. I detested them from the moment I saw them, perhaps because they seemed to be sneering at us. The conversation got off to a bad start. "You women from the States are ruining our women" was their opening sally. "We don't want them to be like you. We rule the house, we are the boss, and you set a bad example." To make things worse we were called "las Americanitas," comparing us to "las Mexicanitas," a well-known whorehouse in our neighborhood. Waldeen was ready to do battle with them, but I shooed them out the door, and we never saw them again.

Besides Waldeen, Dasha, a New York painter whom I had met in Taxco, became a close friend, a friendship that has lasted to this very day. At that time she was living with Paul Kirchhoff, the famous German anthropologist. When the Library of Congress' equipment arrived, after months of delay, I decided to do a test run in Tepoztlan, where Paul had a house. Tepoztlan is a beautiful town near Cuernavaca in the shadow of a dark, craggy mountain called el Tepozteco, home of witches, according to local belief. In actuality, these women were *curanderas*, medical practitioners skilled in herbal medicine and pre-hispanic practices.

One of Paul's neighbors was an Indian craftsman known for

114

his interest in pre-hispanic instruments. Several years before he had made an exquisite copy of a pre-Conquest drum, *teponastli*, a two-toned, hollowed-out tree trunk, one of several revered by ancient Aztecs and Mayas. The original instrument had lain in the cornfields for hundreds of years, partially eaten away by earthworms. Finally, removed for safe keeping behind the church altar, it could be seen for a small fee. Dasha and I went to visit the craftsman. When he claimed his copy was the original, we looked skeptical, and he backed off. But, more intriguing than the drum was the clutter of instruments strewn around the cabin - painted drums made of old oil cans, wind instruments of rubber tubing attached to tin whistles. Obviously, most of them could never sound. While Dasha did drawings of the instruments I talked to this remarkable man. "These are all copies of pre-hispanic instruments. How did you know what they looked like?" I asked him. "Señora," he said proudly, "every week for a whole year I walked to the National Library in Mexico City and made drawings of the instruments in the codices. And then I came home and made the copies with whatever material I could find. We take them out every year for the celebration of our patron saint." "They are very beautiful," I said, "but what music do you play? You know as I do that your forefathers left no record of it." There was a long silence in the room. Then he said, "Next week we are having a town meeting; we will decide then."

I, too, had questions about the past. I tried playing the flutes in museums (when allowed), but I knew nothing about the technique they used. Did the players half-stop the holes, did they overblow, or perhaps growl into their instruments? I was totally in the dark.

For information about the performing arts I turned to 16th and 17th century chronicles written by educated Spanish clerics. These writings described dances, music, and lavish theatrical

115

performances with lavish detail (even as the participants watched their own companions sacrificed to Aztec and Maya gods). Thousands of young and talented dancers and singers of the ruling classes performed at huge religious ceremonies; every family and civic event was celebrated with pageants and music composed especially for the occasion, just like Europe in the time of Haydn and Mozart.

What a glorious past, but dead and gone, buried in the rubble of destroyed temples and monuments. The world I was about to enter was a different one, inhabited by primitive tribesmen. These people had had little or no contact with the great Indian empires in their heyday before the European invasion. I was to find them, still living in the same isolated mountain and desert communities as their ancestors, unchanged for centuries, if not millennia.

***

Cora – Huichol – 1944

After several weeks of hectic consultation and miles of red tape, everything was ready. The train pulled out for Cora country one warm May day, carrying myself, two hundred pounds of recording equipment, sleeping bags, and anti-scorpion serum provided by the Department of Indian Affairs. My only companion was Agustin Maya, photographer from the Ministry of Education. Agustin accompanied me for the next few years on several trips. He was the perfect companion; he lightened the burden of those long and arduous journeys through Mexico's difficult terrain, a true and unforgettable friend. His photographs are among the great photographic documents of his country and people, intimate, loving, perceptive.

Arriving in Tepic, a city on the northwest coast, we went straight to the governor's office to ask for assistance for our trip across the Sierra Madre, Mexico's wild and craggy western mountain range. We were in luck! An army captain and colonel were just about to make the same perilous trip to Jesus Maria, a small town in the Mesa Del Nayar, our destination. Since their purpose was to distribute money to the community for a land sale, accompanying them would help our own mission, put the Indians in a good mood, or so we thought.

Before heading into the mountains by horse we had a grueling four-hour train ride from Tepic to a town situated at the foothills of the Sierra Madre. Somehow or other we piled our cumbersome equipment onto the train, and left it in charge of the captain. It was nighttime by then, the heat was suffocating and the train was packed. I finally found a seat next to a young man, pulled out a book to read, and found myself the object of his curiosity. After a long time, he asked, "Why do you read? Isn't it hard work?" I assured him it was easy once you knew how. But I'm sure he remained unconvinced.

Finally, the onerous trip was over and we found a small *pension* to spend the night. It was here that I had my first encounter with a deadly scorpion. In the environs of Mexico City scorpions sometimes emerge from bathroom pipes or lurk on the ceiling. Even if they bite you, they cause no more than a rash, or leave you feeling sick for a day. However, we were now in an area home to deadly scorpions that kill in an hour or so. The pension had no electricity, so Agustin examined every inch from floor to ceiling with a flashlight. Finding nothing, we said good night, he went into his own room and I prepared for bed. I washed my face at the water stand, used the potty and stored it under my cot. As I stretched out, exhausted from the day's activities, I suddenly remembered I hadn't brushed my teeth. Flashlight in hand, I

117

pointed it down on my shoes where I had left them a moment before. There, on my sock, was a green scorpion. I immediately killed it with the other shoe. I shudder to think what would have happened had I not looked first.

Certainly, I was not prepared for the rigors of the trip across the mountains. Unlike the snow-covered Andes, the Sierra Madre is low and craggy. Rather than wind around the mountains in easy stages, the Indians here are accustomed to climbing straight up the steep mountain sides and down again, now in cool pine forest and a half hour later in steamy hot tropics. Agustin headed the procession of burros and mules laden down with our gear and equipment, in the middle came the mule driver and owner of the animals, the colonel and the captain, and I brought up the rear. As we climbed the steep mountainside, I could see the mule carrying the recording machine stop after every two steps, its sides heaving with the effort. Climbing the mountain was easier than descending, the terrain was so stony and so precipitous that mules had to jump down from one rock to another; loose stones made them slip and slide and I hung on to the saddle hub for dear life.

One day, as we descended a sleep decline to the river, one of our mules lay down on top of the box containing the recordings. Frantically, we pulled the poor exhausted mule to its feet. But all was intact, nothing had been damaged, and we drew a sigh of relief. I had taken care of such eventualities: the disks were stored in a metal container stuffed with paper and then placed in a thick wooden box.

Each day's journey began at daybreak; we rolled up our sleeping bags, built a fire, prepared coffee, and ate tortillas and beans for breakfast. When breakfast was over, the animals were fed and the equipment securely packed, we started on our way, properly dressed for the weather. The early morning was the best time of all, cool

118

and fresh. But soon the sun rose; first I discarded my leather jacket, then a sweater, then my handkerchief, and finally my gloves. By 11 a.m., my hands and my nose were bright red from the sun's rays; the heat was insufferable, and we would stop until the late afternoon when evening breezes again cooled the earth. To avoid the heat we sometimes rode at night, especially when the moon was full. These were among the most beautiful hours of all. Plants, cactus and trees, motionless in the pale blue light, had a mysterious aura that enhanced my sense of adventure. Reality returned upon passing through sleepy, dark villages along the route. As we approached starving dogs snarled and snapped at our animals, causing them to rear, and giving me a panic attack.

Besides barking dogs, we had to contend with other dangers. Mexico is known for its polluted water supply. No one in his right mind should assume that clear, sparkling river water is safe to drink. Although we used chlorine pills to purify suspicious water supplies, we knew not to trust it. Maybe it was just luck, maybe I have an iron-clad stomach, but I never had so much as a stomach-ache all the years on the road!

Although we carried a few provisions, like canned goods and coffee, we depended on finding food along the way. But sometimes days went by without seeing a soul, just miles and miles of mountain ranges in the distance, dry dusty empty spaces; not even a snake or rabbit crossed our path. One day we arrived at a small mestizo settlement near a pine forest where woodcutters were at work. Agustin dashed off to ask the lady of the house for food for me.

"I'm so sorry," she said, "I have nothing to give you." Agustin pressed on: "Not even tortillas and frijoles?" he begged. "Sí, of course I have tortillas and frijoles." "An egg, perhaps?" he wheedled. "Yes," she said, "I can give the señora an egg, and some chicken, if she likes, but no meat, that's out of the question." To her thinking, a meal without meat was no meal at all. I had a marvelous dinner, and we continued on our way until nightfall, and made camp in an open field under the stars.

Out in the Mexican wilderness I became used to vast mountain ranges, maguey cactus, Indians with long hair, and smoke-filled huts, but there were some surprises: In one tiny hamlet in Cora country we found an American couple, the young wife pregnant and a day's journey away from the nearest health facility. They were Protestant missionaries from the "Summer School of Linguistics," an organization dedicated to committing Indian languages to writing -- for Bible translation.

In another remote village we found two American priests. As they were afraid to invite us to their parish house for fear tongues would wag, we spoke in front of the church. "What are you doing here?" I asked. "This village," they said, "hasn't had a resident priest since the Calles regime," referring to the 1926 campaign against the Catholic Church. The people are so grateful to have Mass said every day, they feed and take care of us." These priests, supported by the church in the United States, neither spoke Spanish nor performed social services. In a village as dirty and neglected as this one, it seemed to me the height of indifference to be so unconcerned. When I chided them, they said, "That is not our mission; we are here to say mass and hear confession." Without knowing the language?

Before we left Mexico City, anthropologists had warned me of possible trouble with the Coras, a tribe with a long history of antagonism towards outsiders. Nevertheless, in recent times they had received some benefits from the Federal government. A school established by the Department of Indian Affairs in Jesus Maria had trained Indians in much-needed skills and elementary literacy. For reasons never explained it had been shut down and moved elsewhere. The school building was still there when I arrived, but in ruins.

Upon our arrival the entire town assembled for the distribution of money sent by the governor. We foolishly thought the money would establish good relations between the people and us. It didn't happen that way. They fought among themselves about the division of the money, and ignored us completely. When they finally did notice us, they accused us of coming to "steal their music." I was disheartened but sought help from the authorities. Finally, the tribal governor came to our rescue and helped us in every way. My offer of remuneration, of course, changed the atmosphere; soon everyone wanted to sing or play for the machine.

Even so, we had troubles. In May, just before the rainy season, most Cora men work as hired hands on coastal haciendas or nearby mestizo farms Besides, many Coras live in distant ranches far from town and difficult to contact. Worse yet, their shamans who preserve pre-hispanic ceremonies live in isolated caves in the countryside.

Nevertheless, the news of our mission traveled: each night musicians came to record their songs. With no electricity we worked by candle and flashlight. Maybe it was the lure of money that brought them, maybe it was pride in their culture, but they came. The few pesos we offered put everyone in a cordial mood, and the music brought everyone together.

In the Cora-Huichol region I was to find, concentrated and in grand profusion, Mexico's history; its ancient indigenous roots, the European invasion and subsequent modernization. I have seen pagan curing rituals and the enactment of Christ's Passion, and heard pre-hispanic drums and European guitars and violins, shamans' ancient chants and songs in Western harmony.

But most exciting to me were the shamans' chants, the most ancient of all. A shaman is a native priest whose origins were mostly likely in Asia. Like his counterparts in Siberia, Korea and Japan, he is the healer, guardian of tribal myths, singer and chief officiate at the yearly cycle of festivals. I never saw a woman shaman (although they do exist) and was told that at least one-quarter of the male Huichol-Cora population receive the call.

Luck was with me, a Cora festival in progress. Now I could see with my own eyes a real Indian ceremony. In the center of the festival grounds, amidst the confusion of food preparation, noisy children and yelping dogs, an old man played an instrument I had never seen before -- a hunter's bow used as a percussion instrument, called a *mitote*. The bow, placed on top of a large gourd resonator resting on the ground, is held in place by the shaman's foot while he strikes the bowstring with two thin sticks. That afternoon he sang the ancient chants for the coming planting season, the rainy season. "Who taught you the chants?" I asked. "God gave them to me, I knew them when I was born." "And the *mitote*?" "God sent it." But a minute later he sadly admitted: "When I die," he said tapping the *mitote* with his stick, "all this will die with me. My son will have nothing to do with it." When I pressed him to tell me the words of his songs, he said, "They are in a language we no longer speak, and the meaning is unknown."

Is it possible that what I heard more than 50 years ago was an ancient musical style brought by the first Asians to come to America thousands of years ago? Well, just a few years ago, singers from the Sakalin Islands, then part of the Soviet Union, gave a concert of their music at New York's Asia Society. The songs I heard had an uncanny resemblance to the shaman's songs heard in Mexico in the 1940s!

122

The music preferred by the younger Coras was decidedly Mexican. Sure, they attended the old agricultural rituals, but without turning a hair, they celebrated the whole panoply of Christian saints' days, the Passion of Christ, and Christmas. Each year for Lent they made new bamboo flutes, burned them at Easter, and muffled the strident sounds of their drums as a sign of mourning for the dead Christ. Temples, palaces, and bones crumble to dust, but songs, stories, and myths, told and retold, live on as the true voices of the people.

A week later we were on our way out of Cora territory en route to the Huichols in the state of Jalisco. Riding in the intense heat through rugged terrain, I recalled a Huichol legend I had read in Mexico City: In the beginning, they say, the earth was flat and full of water, so the corn rotted. A wrinkled old bat came to the rescue. Darting violently through the air, he cut outlets for the water but made the valleys too deep and the mountains too steep. "What have you done to us?" cried the Huichol elders. Off flew the bat again, made the slopes an easier incline and thoughtfully left some level land. Thus the world remained! All very well, I thought irritably, as we laboriously climbed and descended almost perpendicular mountains, but couldn't he have done a better job?

Eight days later, sunburned, unkempt, exhausted and hating the sight of four-legged animals, we arrived in Bolaños, a hot little mestizo town on the banks of a wide river. Years before, American silver prospectors had built a bridge across it; successive political upheavals and revolution finally forced these entrepreneurs to abandon the mines. In 1944, the bridge was in terrible shape, rusty and covered with rotting floorboards; crossing it on foot was a hair-raising experience.

In Bolaños we were joined by members of a cultural mission from the Department of Education who were to be our guides into

123

Indian country. For the next few days we sweltered in the heat, for this dry, dusty town offered not a single civilized comfort. But one day, a man came across the mountains with a package: a chunk of ice wrapped in a leather pouch. Alas, having traveled hours in withering heat, the ice had shrunk to the size of a tennis ball. As the only woman in the group it was offered to me; I shall never forget those first few drops of icy water trickling down my parched throat. It was pure heaven! After a few days' rest we set off for the heart of Huichol country, a male nurse to vaccinate the Indians against smallpox, the gentle director of the mission, Sr. Bonilla, his aides, Agustin and myself. The first evening we camped in a dry riverbed between impossibly high mountains. As we sat around the fire, Sr. Bonilla, told me about his work in this isolated, god-forsaken part of the country:

"You have seen the river Bolaños at its lowest ebb. Everything is fine now. During the dry season the river supplies all the town's needs, however, when the rainy season begins it becomes a swirling, muddy mess, undrinkable unless every drop is filtered. When we established the mission a few years ago, we set up classes to teach the women to use a sewing machine, the men carpentry, etc. In addition, we proposed to build a dam; the government promised to supply the materials if the villagers would provide the manual labor. They agreed enthusiastically. But when I called a meeting a few days later, no one came, nor the next day either, and people avoided me. Finally, I spoke to one who had been my assistant. He said, 'We haven't come to see you because the priest threatened to excommunicate us if we had anything to do with you.' So, señora, that was the end of the plan. Every year since then the rising river continues to cause nothing but misery. And we cannot fight the priest; the people have to do that, not us." He shook his head in despair.

As he spoke, we noticed the moon disappear behind black,

rain-filled clouds. Everyone looked anxiously at the sky; the rainy season was about to begin. Bonilla continued: "In these mountains, new paths are made very year because the rains destroy the ones of the previous year, they simply slide down the mountain sides. If the rains catch you here it is almost impossible to get out, sometimes for months." My heart sank. I realized what a fool I had been to start my trip in May, almost the beginning of the rainy season. But here I was in the middle of nowhere and I would have to take my chances. Forever afterwards I was to fear the rain more than poisonous snakes or wild animals!

Sr. Bonilla went on: "Tomorrow we will arrive at Huilotita, a settlement of a few families, to see a curing ceremony which you will be able to record. It is typical of mountain Huichols. They live dispersed over a huge area, and only come together during fiesta time. They have no towns, only religious centers, and widely scattered ranches." "By the way," I interrupted, "I haven't seen any animals in these hills. How come? " "There weren't any, " he said, "until the Spaniards came -- no horses, no burros, no chickens or sheep, only deer, which are sacred. Now they have a few, as you will see later on. "

Bonilla continued. "You, señora, are in for surprises. The Huichols are polygamous, and each man in these mountain communities takes three wives, the first is the most important, next maybe a widowed relative, and the third, a younger child, never touched until puberty. On the surface the system seems to work, but then, who knows what really goes on. "

I interrupted Bonilla. "But these Indians are Christians, aren't they?" I asked. "Yes," he said, "but every six months or so, a Catholic priest wanders through the area, marries as many couples as he can, baptizes the children, and goes on his way. He knows his limitations and never bothers to preach Christian morality or the evil of their pagan ways. In the 17th century they were converted to Christianity but they never gave up their pagan gods, just added Christ and the saints to their roster of deities. We tried to make modern Mexicans of them, taught them our national songs and dances, but they just watch us and do nothing. In colonial times, some musical friars brought them the violin and guitar, but they invented their own way of playing them. The only change we've made in their lives is this: After the ceremony at Huilotita is over, we will travel to Tuxpan, a religious center. There are two wells there, a polluted one nearby, and a little further on, a clean one. It took two years to convince them to walk the extra steps to the clean well."

We arrived at Huilotita at noon and watched the preparations for the curing ceremony held because of malaria and death by scorpions. My stomach turned when, upon lifting a rock from the ground, half-dozen scorpions scurried out. I was given a hut on stilts to sleep in, and Agustin helped me surround my sleeping bag with mosquito netting. Scorpions are vicious little beasts, which, unlike mosquitoes, can't be heard. They don't buzz, they crawl under things, fall from the roof, and hide in your clothes. So every time I dressed each garment had to be turned inside-out, every seam examined.

Soon the shaman, called *maracami* in Huichol, arrived and visited each sick person. Although I did not witness it, I was told he said prayers and administered native herbs. A handsome and dignified man, the *maracami* was beautifully dressed in traditional garments -- a triangular shawl ringed with multi-colored bead pendants, a bright woven belt, a red hip girdle of small square pouches, and white cotton shirt and pants bordered in woven animals and birds. "Where do those fanciful designs come from? " I asked Bonilla. "They don't look like real animals to me." Bonilla laughed. "They visualize their peyote hallucinations." That was the first time I heard the word peyote; later I was to learn its importance for the Huichols, as well as for other groups in northern Mexico.

In the distance we could see a man carrying a heavy load in a cotton wrapper. When uncovered, it proved to be a huge wooden figure of Christ, the kind sold by mestizo traders. The man had carried it all the way from Tuxpan, an eight-hour walk. Bonilla admonished him: "Why did you come?" he asked, "It's planting time, not fiesta time." The man wiped his brow and let loose a string of invectives. "It's not my idea," he said, "it's just that this guy" -- pointing to the Christ figure -- "loves a party, and I have to take him where he wants to go." I shook my head in disbelief. To their way of thinking everything was alive -- not only people, animals and plants, but all of nature. Mountains, for instance, were not the dwelling places of gods but were the very gods themselves.

By evening we had set up our equipment in the festival area. One of the missionaries held the mike as close to the singers as he could get. As the moonless night deepened, only the fire in the center of the clearing illuminated the serious faces of the Indians gathered in a circle for the sacred rites. Seated in his ceremonial chair, flanked by two solemn assistants, the *maracami* soon began to chant in clear tones. The assistants responded in chorus, joined intermittently by women and children. On into the night the *maracami* intoned tribal legends, entreating the old nature gods of fire and earth -- as well as the Christian saints -- to heal the sick. Finally, he bestowed blessings on all, including our party. I recorded at every change in the melody, praying also to my own private god, the god of electricity, for a steady power supply to run the recording machine! Only once did the *maracami* interrupt the proceedings -- to hear the recording. Pleased with what he heard, he continued chanting until the first rays of light appeared in the

127

east.

Then the drowsy, yawning crowd came to life. Holding lighted candles, they moved close to the *maracami* as the ritual sacrifices began. They brought chickens, a bull, and we brought a sheep. I couldn't see who did the actual killing but when it was over the *maracami*, with sweeping gestures, threw blood offerings into the fire (the center of the earth), and then, in turn, to the four directions (where Huichol gods are said to live just under the horizon). Finally, he dabbed a little blood on the Christ figure and a painting of the Virgin of Guadalupe which had been standing by all night along. What a perfect mix of Christianity and paganism.

The sacrifices over, everybody -- including us -- set upon the food the women had prepared (tortillas, tamales, fruit and *tesguino*, their sacred corn beer). Urged by Bonilla, the Huichols danced for hours on end to the unrelenting beat of a pre-hispanic drum known to the Aztecs as *panhuehuetl*, a three-legged hollowed-out log with a deerskin drumhead. Agustin, who had been unable to photograph the all-night singing session, now took photographs, the best a spectacular shot of the *maracami* blessing the crowd at dawn.

A most intelligent man, the *maracami* engaged us in conversation. I am sure he wanted us to understand the ceremony we had just seen. After all, like a Catholic priest or a Jewish Rabbi, he is a man of knowledge, he knows the history and traditions of his people and guards their laws. "Long ago," he began, "we were nomads living on deer and peyote. Then the gods gave us maize, which is necessary for life. But we do not forget deer and peyote; we honor them, for that way we insure good crops. We eat peyote only at fiesta time, and we ask God not to make us insane." (Would that our modern mescaline, heroin and crack addicts had that much sense!)

I was very curious about peyote and asked Bonilla to tell me about it. "Every year Huichols -- men, women and children -- go on a pilgrimage to San Luis Potosi to gather peyote. It's a narcotic cactus with an awful taste that Huichols have worshiped as a symbol of their tribal beginnings for untold centuries. To commemorate their origins, they follow the same route, perform the same ceremonies, at the same places where their ancestors stopped so long ago."

"What kind of hallucinations do they have?" I asked Bonilla, "Once the cactus is eaten," he said, "they see visions connecting peyote, deer, and maize -- corn popping and deer jumping on the peyote." How neat a theory! I thought. It embodies their actual history; the Huichols, like many other people, were first gatherers (here represented by peyote), then hunters (the deer), then agriculturalists (maize). No doubt about it, hallucinations are culturally derived. No modern mescaline addict has visions of deer and popcorn!

My next question to Bonilla was about relations between men and women, not a burning issue in the 1940s but of interest to me. About sex Bonilla's response was fragmentary. Anthropologists in those days knew the laws relating to family relationships, kinship, marital and courtship customs but not actual practice. "I don't know much about it," he said, "but I know that on the six-week trip for peyote, wives left behind are expected to be faithful to their absent husbands. When they return there is a reckoning, women are expected to confess their infidelities, and the guilty ones are punished." "What about the men?" I asked, "are they punished for their sins?" "No," he laughed, "they go scot free."

True, I said to myself, nobody likes strangers snooping around their private life. I remembered that a renowned American

129

anthropologist was run out of a village for asking the Indians about sex. The curing ceremony I had recorded was a public affair, open to all, even outsiders like myself. Nobody objected to our recording the ceremony, they even seemed pleased. Surely, Huichols like people everywhere, have songs about their private lives. Surely, mothers sing to their babies, and lovers sing love songs. But, I realized, this is a private realm, and probably impenetrable. Then one day, the door opened. El Secre (short for "secretary"), Bonilla's helper, said to me: "My sister knows lots of songs, ask her to sing." The girl, a delicate beauty with great natural charm, agreed on condition that her mother not be told. With everybody slightly drunk from the festival *tesguino*, nobody noticed what we were doing. There, in her tiny house, dark except for a few candles, we recorded her songs. The short melodies were like the ritual music recorded the night before but the words were different. "What are the songs about?" I asked her. Shyly, hardly speaking above a whisper, she said one song was about her brother's impressions of a trip to Tepic; another about his drinking beer in a cantina, another described an airplane in the sky, and finally, a love song. Yes, I thought, the Huichols inhabit another world, but these songs are universal; and I would have missed them if not for El Secre who honored me with his confidence.

Saying farewell to the Huichols was not easy. We had been together for more than a week, made friends, played cards with them (I taught them Rummy), been shown a primitive god (minus arms and legs) buried in the ground, seen all the religious articles in their special "god house". The mission's male nurse had vaccinated everyone in sight against smallpox. Agustin had taken pictures of everyone, but on our last day, suddenly a horseman appeared at full gallop. He had come from a distant mestizo settlement, his sister had been bitten by a scorpion. "Do you have anti-scorpion serum?" he asked. We gave it to him and he sped away. Later we learned she had died even before his return.

130

The rainy season was upon us, a signal for the spring planting to begin. From now until harvest time the Huichols would be working their cornfields on nearby mountain slopes. I tried to call them back to help me with translations of the chants, but they refused to return. Nothing is more sacred than the planting season, for without corn, they would starve.

We packed our equipment and headed back to headquarters. A day's travel brought us to the riverbed where we had camped on our way into Huichol country. The dry stream was now a raging river. Upon arrival in Bolaños, we learned the missionaries who had left a day earlier had barely escaped drowning. "When we camped there that night," they said, "it was dry. In the middle of the night we were awakened by a terrible roar and a moment later the water poured down in torrents from the mountains. We escaped just in time."

We spent an uneventful night there and continued on the next day. The dark clouds hung over us, and we rode as fast as we could. Finally, finally, Bolaños River was in sight, the last obstacle before reaching the safety of the village. To our horror, the waters had risen precipitously, now a swirling muddy torrent, just as Bonilla had described earlier. We abandoned the idea of fording it. What saved our lives was the old, decrepit, rusty bridge, abandoned years before by Americans. We dismounted our horses and walked across it, carefully avoiding the huge gaps between the rotting slats that threatened to deposit us into a watery grave. It was a harrowing trip, but we were finally safely out of the mountains.

Bonilla urged us to leave as soon as possible; the next part of our trip along a dirt road would be dangerous with the threatening rain. How right he was! For two full days we plowed through mud up to the horses' ankles, spent a night in a rural *pension* where the "bathroom" was an open field inhabited by a vicious pig at the ready

131

to spring on helpless victims, and where yellow-green scorpions crawled over the walls. Finally, we arrived at a town with electricity, real pavements, restaurants, automobiles -- and a railroad depot. The long train ride to Mexico City was the pinnacle of luxury; there were no horses, no foul-mouthed mule drivers, no rain, no scorpions; and somebody else was doing the driving. Agustin and I watched the rain pelting down on the windows, unperturbed.

***

The Seris - 1944

Back home again, I was hardly recognizable, sunburned, my hands raw, my nose peeling, my hair matted, clothes beyond repair. I was a wreck, but happy. I spent the first day at the hairdresser, where my Russian friend Sasha put me back into civilized shape. Then I had a long lunch with Daniel de la Borbolla and gave him an account of all I had seen. Dr. Gamio, of course, was delighted. No one had ever recorded music in the Huichol-Cora region. I had performed a real service, and his confidence in me was unbounded.

Now, where was I to go next? By this time it was well into the rainy season, and travel to mountain tribes was out of the question. But, anxious to push on, we decided on the Seris, a non-Christian tribe of fisherman living somewhere in the vicinity of the Gulf of California. Although my reputation for good work was known to the Minister of Education, I still had to go through the usual red tape; I was put through the wringer. Here's how the system, known as *haciendo antesala* (literally doing the waiting room routine) works. Each item had to be approved by the minister separately; (1) travel (2) per diem expenses (3) my salary (4) supplies. Every day I would arrive at his office at 10 a.m., the waiting room already filled with delegations. Unseen by us, he would arrive through a private entrance at 11 a.m. I knew the exact moment because the shoe-shine boy, followed by a waiter with a coffee tray, were led into his office. Soon the petitioners filed in one by one, stayed a short time and left with much backslapping and embraces.

Each time somebody emerged from the sacred sanctuary I would bound over to Jose Luis' (his secretary) desk. No, I was told, have a little more patience; I'll speak to him in a minute. I sink back into my chair and wait. By this time, it is 2 p.m., closing time. I plead with him. "I'm so sorry," he says, "he just left. I'll try again tomorrow." A week later as I wearily return to the minister's office, Jose Luis rushes out, a sheaf of papers in his hand, crying, "Here are your travel vouchers, Henrietta!" "But what about the other things I need?" I ask. "Tomorrow," he promises.

Two weeks later, as Waldeen and I are having afternoon coffee, I hear my name called from the street. Jose Luis is in front of the house, shouting, "Henrietta, it's all signed, everything you wanted." I breathe a sigh of relief. Waldeen and I hug each other and dance around the room, and decide to have a victory party.

When Agustin and I left Mexico City on this our second trip together in the middle of August, 1944, we had only a vague idea where the Seris lived, somewhere in the northwestern state of Sonora. Before leaving I had read a 1930s report about them by the Mexican anthropologist Carlos Bausauri. He and his assistants had spent a day or so with the Seris on Tiburon Island, their traditional home in the Gulf of California, and were so frightened by the Seris' constant whispering all night long (not a word of which they understood) that they panicked and left the next morning. The Seris, it seems, had a frightening history, had fought the Mexicans, reputably killed and scalped their enemies. However, to the Jesuits of Sonora, eager to make converts, they

133

were a challenge. They raided the island, kidnapped as many as possible, housed and fed them at Villa de los Seris, a center near Hermosillo. But the Indians outwitted them: they never became Christians, gorged on the food and then ran away. Only the old and infirm remained behind. In our two-month stay in Desemboque I never saw a single cross, saint's image, or Christian celebration.

Upon arriving in Hermosillo, the state capitol, we paid a visit to the governor, Abelardo Rodriguez, a former president of Mexico. Before the advent of electricity, the Gulf of California had been a lucrative source of shark oil; in the 1940s it was a favorite fishing ground for American, European and Japanese boats.

My first question to the governor was, "Where do the Seris live? We read they lived on the island of Tiburón, just off the mainland." The governor smiled. "Your information is outdated," he said. They don't live there anymore. They have joined a fisherman's union and live in Desemboque, a village on the coast." He immediately called in the secretary of the union. Within minutes arrangements were made; the union truck would take us to Desemboque the following day.

What luck! Agustin and I thanked our lucky stars. Little did we know that we would be incommunicado for two months, and face innumerable problems. We had taken the recording machine with us but had sent the gasoline motor by rail. "Don't worry," said the union officials, "we'll bring it to you as soon as it arrives." And arrive it did, seven weeks later, while we cooled our heels in Desemboque, hungry and frazzled!

Since nobody knew where we were I wrote letters to Dr. Gamio and my husband in Cambridge, and left them at the hotel in Hermosillo with instructions to mail. Much later, I learned the letters were never sent. Meanwhile Chenk, upon reading a 1902 report by William McGee on the Seris at the Harvard Library, panicked. He wrote a scathing letter to Gamio, accusing him of sending this tender woman (me) into the lion's den. Gamio, alarmed, called the governor, who immediately assured him I was fine and living at Desemboque, and that the Indians, far from violent, had become peaceful, civilized people.

The next morning, bright and early, we bundled all our equipment into the truck and took off down the bumpy two-lane highway through the desert. A 10-hour ride through sweltering heat brought us to a ranch, where we obtained food but no lodging. I slept in the cab of the truck, so dead tired I didn't even notice the discomforts.

The next day we continued on our journey to the coast. Upon arrival we found Desemboque to be not a village, as described, but some shacks distributed haphazardly on the beach, the Seri camp. Nearby were a few run-down adobe huts where Mexicans lived. My "hotel" was the second floor of a stone building used as a refrigerator. During the fishing season, ice is brought in from God knows where; the day's catch is deposited there until trucks from the States haul it off. My room consisted of a cot and a tiny, rickety table, my bathroom the desert outside. Every day, a Seri girl would keep vigil while I attended to my necessities. Occasionally someone would walk by but never look my way, pretending I wasn't there. Agustin slept on somebody's floor in a sleeping bag. To make things worse, the day after our arrival the telegraph operator left to visit a sick relative in Nogales (read: his mistress), leaving us totally disconnected from the rest of the world for the next six weeks.

The beach was sandy, the sea calm and inviting, the days filled with sunlight, a perfect place for a holiday. The trouble was we were not on a holiday, and worse yet, there was little to eat. In 1944 the Indians didn't fish during the rainy season and grew no crops of their own; both Indians and mestizos depended on food brought in by the union. Years before, the Mexican government had tried an experiment; they had given each Seri family a plot of land and tools to encourage them to grow their own produce. But, after millennia as fishermen and hunters, they were not about to change their ways. They used to boast about their prowess: *"cuatro tiros, cuatro liebres"* (four bullets, four rabbits). They soon sold everything to neighboring mestizos. We visited one of those farms, a verdant green oasis in the Sonora desert, ate the sweetest watermelon I'd ever tasted, and marveled at lush fields of corn and squash.

With nothing to do I spent hours wandering along the sandy beach looking for shells. Antonio Burgos, a half-Yaqui, was always close behind me. "You like this beautiful shell?" he'd ask, or, "How about these baskets?" The baskets were beautiful and I bought all I could, and finally had to turn him down. "Antonio," I'd say, "I can't buy all the baskets you make, can I?" Being a reasonable man, he'd shake his head in disappointment and say, "I guess not," and he'd walk off. Antonio and I really cemented our friendship during the recording sessions; he was one of the best singers of the tribe.

Every day Agustin and I would wander into the Seri camp, he to take pictures and I to talk to the women. Seated on the ground amidst rags and hungry dogs, they would gather around me. I watched them etch pictures in the sand. One symbol really surprised me, a swastika, which is, after all, a universal symbol that the Nazis took over. But they also copied figures from comic books that occasionally fell into their hands. My first successful contact with them came through music: I learned to sing one of their songs. From then on, I was the talk of the settlement, proud of the recognition I had given them. I was to learn later that they seldom sang in front of the Mexicans, for fear of ridicule. The Seris are a very handsome people, and felt superior to their mestizo neighbors. Once they trusted me, they talked frankly about them. "Look at them," they'd say, "they're short, fat and ugly. You are like us, tall and slender with long, narrow feet." (At my full height I was only 5 feet 3 inches tall, but taller than the average rural Mexican.)

In 1944 the Seris numbered less than 200 in all -- men, women and children. A sneeze or a cough could send them into a tizzy of worry, for many had died of respiratory diseases. Their only modern remedy, as far as I could see, was Vicks Vapor-Rub, aside from, of course, the incantations and herbal cures of their shamans. A pregnant woman received royal treatment; the prospect of the birth of a baby brought unaccustomed luxuries for the mother-to-be. "Look at that poor woman," they would comment contemptuously of a pregnant Mexican woman. "She's working, working all the time. Seris only resting and eating all the time."

To while away the hot hours of the day, I'd go swimming (always accompanied by a group of women). While I wore a skimpy modern bathing suit, they went in the water fully dressed in a costume reminiscent of the Gibson Girl era --a long, wide skirt and high-necked, long-sleeved blouse. The women never commented about my near nakedness, and the men looked straight through me. I would swim out in the calm, warm sea, while they stood knee-deep in the water, lifting up and wringing out their skirts, now on one side, now on the other as a gesture of cleanliness.

Several women became my constant companions, but others caused me headaches. There was Sara Villalobos, a woman in her 50s with the carriage of a duchess, who stole my magenta lipstick. Then there were two sisters, Maria Luz and Manuela. Maria Luz did a little illegal trafficking in marijuana and flirted with the

Mexican soldiers stationed at the camp (to prevent Seris and mestizos from fighting each other), although she hated them. She stole my kerchief from under my eyes, had a terrible temper, always looked angry, and spread lies. Her sister was her exact opposite, kind, anxious to improve the lot of her people, but also hostile to Mexicans. I became used to the petty thievery and constant begging for money. But I was insistent on paying only for services and purchases I received from them, and finally they relented.

Agustin was also plagued with demands for money whenever he took pictures in the camp. He also had to cope with the strange notion that our modern equipment could change reality. One day, as I rested on my cot, I heard a disturbance outside. A very angry corpulent Seri woman was shouting at the top of her lungs. I came downstairs and was soon surrounded by others. "What's the matter?" I asked her. The entry in my diary reads: "She immediately calmed down and put her arms around me. I'm not angry, it's that Maria Luz, she put me up to it. She says my daughter (whom Agustin had photographed that morning) will come out naked (*va a salir biche*) in the photograph."

"You know that's a lie," I said. "She's just jealous because Agustin didn't take her photo." Soon she began to laugh and joke. "I only came to make a noise," she said as she walked back to her hut. The next day we invited Maria Luz to take some pictures. An hour later she appeared in full regalia, her face painted in a handsome design. She hugged and kissed me and happily posed for Agustin's camera.

Weeks had gone by and we were still completely cut off from the world. Night after night, Agustin and I would scan the desert for a light indicating the arrival of a car. And every night we were disappointed. Hunger pangs were beginning to slow us down; we were hungry. In desperation we asked the Seris to catch fish for us; just beyond the shore we could see schools of fish gliding by. We almost could have caught them with our bare hands. But fish to the Seris was a livelihood, not food. They sold it but they didn't eat it. What they really liked was coahuama, the huge sea turtles of the Gulf. From then on Agustin and I ate fish every day. It helped still the hunger pangs but left us unsatisfied. When I finally returned to Mexico City I had lost 12 pounds.

One day, someone brought a big pot of honey gathered from the nearby mountains. I witnessed a scene that will be engraved in my memory forever: As each person helped himself to handfuls of honey, thousands of flies buzzed around them, clinging to eyes, mouths, hands, hair and clothes. With each mouthful, they consumed innumerable flies as well. I was horrified by the spectacle, but realized that no harm was done. At least flies added protein to their diet!

Daily life in Desemboque was far from dull, maybe because it was so new to me and I was curious about every detail. The Indians loved showing us their skills -- how to build a fire by rubbing two sticks together, how to weave a basket with a design, and how to paint one's face. In the old days, face painting identified clan membership, but in the 1940s it was a form of adornment; each woman had her own favorite colors and design and these were applied like a painter with great skill. Often as the light faded and night darkened the camp, we sat in the sand in front of the Seris' huts and listened to their stories about ghost-inhabited caves, magical cures, and their warrior past. According to published reports, for centuries they periodically raided coastal ranches, killing their victims with poisoned arrows or by strangulation and biting. Yet here I was, listening to them sing and tell stories, and feeling no fear at all. In all the years of my work among Indians I never felt more at home than among these lively, intelligent and affectionate people. They opened their doors and let me in, and I am eternally grateful.

Two subjects occupied their conversations: the shortcomings of their mestizo neighbors and the miraculous qualities of their shamans. Like Huichols and Coras, Seri shamans are believed to have miraculous powers. Nacho Morales, the chief medicine man at the time of my visit, believed he was a son of god, knew how to fly, and talked to god. One day the Seris asked me for medicine for a baby ill with a cold. Taking my little medicine kit with me, I was led to the baby's shack. When I entered, Nacho was kneeling on the floor in front of the mother holding her child. I waited as he sang his songs and muttered, "shoo, shoo, shoo." Occasionally he spit on the red desert roots held in the palm of his hand. As soon as he saw me he stopped, moved over, and smiled at me. Manuela and I spoon-fed the baby with a little sulfa dissolved in a desert-root tea. When we finished, with a bow and smile he moved back to his original position and continued his chant. I had been recognized as a *curandera*, a member of the profession.

Nacho was not only a medicine man but also the composer of songs, which the Seris claim are of divine origin. "How do you know this?" I asked Manuela as we walked along the beach. "This is the story," she said. "One day Nacho went out to the *monte* to look for *pitaya* (a cactus fruit) and other things to eat. From a distance he saw a woman coming towards him. She had small feet and wore a full skirt and long-sleeved blouse. On her arm was a basket filled with fruit--grapes, oranges and pitaya. 'Don't you recognize me?' she asked him. 'I am your mother. I watch you from the heavens and know everything you do.' She gave him the fruit and told him to return to the tribe."

Manuela paused. I prodded her on. "Then what happened?" I asked. "They say that Nacho went back to his house and lay down on his bed for a whole year. Nobody saw him except the people who gave him his meals. During that year the people held fiestas every day, danced and drank *tepache* (a ritual alcoholic drink). The women braided their hair with flowers and ribbons. Everyone was happy because god had sent us a new prophet. When the year was over, Nacho called the whole tribe together. "Listen carefully," he said, "I'm going to sing the songs god taught me. Listen, so you may learn."

Manuela continued: "Soon everyone learned the songs. After that, people saw Nacho fly at night, with a knife stuck in his chest and a bullet hole in the back of his neck. And do you˚ know, Enriqueta, that when Nacho sings to the fish, they come right to the shore and our fishermen catch them with their hands? We all believe that Nacho has magical powers." Yes, music has magical powers, and long before Mozart and Bach, primitive peoples at the dawn of history had already discovered its magic.

Now seven weeks had passed and we were quite desperate over the long delay. Then, one day, a small boat filled with Seris from Tiburón Island arrived at our camp with a disturbing story. They told us our motor had been abandoned on the beach at Kino Bay, as well as their foodstuffs the union had promised to deliver. Kino Bay, 30 miles to the south, had once been a Seri settlement before Desemboque. That night the Seris, Agustin and I gathered in my room for a war council. "Rent a boat from the Yoris (Mexicans)," the Seris insisted, "and we'll row to Kino Bay and bring everything back." It sounded like a practical idea and I agreed; Agustin decided to go along with them. The next morning I waved them a worried goodbye and watched the boat, with five on board, disappear in the distance.

No sooner had they left when the long-absent telegraph operator returned from the States. Within a few hours we telegraphed union headquarters in Hermosillo. I heard a voice say,

"Your motor arrived a while back but we couldn't come because of the rains. Our truck got stuck in the mud. We will bring it the day after tomorrow. We'll also bring the provisions we promised." Sure enough, 24 hours later the truck pulled up, loaded down with food and equipment. The rest of the afternoon Seris, mestizos and I spent eating wheat tortillas, frijoles, and juicy watermelon (which gave everybody terrible stomach aches).

I installed the recording machine in my "office", and the motor down below out of earshot. The singers promised to sing on one condition: "no Mexicans when we sing!" I made appointments for each singer. Each singer waited patiently for his/her turn, announced the subject of each song and performed with a full heart. There were war songs (the trophies were enemy scalps), religious songs (sometimes the singers cried), cradle and love songs, songs for hunting and fishing, and special songs for matrons and young girls. Yes, the Seris told their story with music.

When the recording sessions were in full swing, the unexpected happened. I was told Sara Villalobos, my constant companion, was spreading rumors that singers would die if they sang for the machine. Quickly, I confronted her: "You know you're lying. You're just jealous because I didn't ask you to sing." Coyly, she smiled at me. "Come tomorrow morning," I said, "and I'll record your songs." Wreathed in smiles, she sauntered off to the camp, swaying her hips as she went. That was the end of rumors, and Sara sang admirably.

Within three days the work was done. All my disks were full, and there was no place to buy any more. Just as the last session ended, I heard the Seris shout. "Look," they said, "they've come back." I rushed outside; sure enough, in the distance I saw a small boat headed towards shore. As they approached I waded into the water, waving my arms frantically. "Agustin, Agustin," I shouted.

"I've finished! It's all done! We can go home now!"

Poor Agustin -- the trip had been not only a terrible ordeal but utterly useless. He and the Series camped on the shore the first night, attacked by thousands of sand flies. Arriving at Kino Bay the next day they found neither food nor motor. On the return trip they battled high winds, rain and dangerous waves. It was with mixed emotions we prepared to leave. The entire camp, including Nacho Morales himself, came to say goodbye. I was glad to have finished our work, but sorry to leave these imaginative, lovable people. There was Manuela, wiping the tears from her eyes; Maria Luz defiantly wearing the kerchief she had stolen from me; Sara with a smear of my magenta lipstick on her lips; and the mother who had complained her daughter would come out naked in our photographs. They showered blessings on us and asked when we would return.

The Mexicans were there, too. Maria, who had fed us in her ramshackle hut, a heavy-lidded, plump, unmarried woman with three children. I spent many hours with her; when household chores were done, she would sit outdoors in the shade, her hands folded across her ample belly and tell stories about the Seris as she watched her eight-month-old baby crawl in the sand. "*Mira, mira,*" she'd say admiringly, "*mira, los huevitos*" (Look, look, at his little balls).

One story I never forgot. "When we lived in Kino Bay," she said, "I was the baker and made fresh bread every day. One day, a Seri came into my shop and ordered 25 rolls. I put them in a bag and gave them to him. He sat down outside the door and ate them all. Then he ordered another 25 and ate them, too. I was horrified and a little frightened watching him devour the rolls one after the other." Yes, it is possible to eat enormous quantities, once you've been deprived. Upon my return to Mexico City I was constantly hungry. In no time at all, I regained the 12 pounds I had lost in Desemboque -- and then some.

***

Guatemala - 1945

In February of 1945 I boarded the train in Mexico City for the long trip to Guatemala. The U. S. State Department had given me money to cover my own expenses but not for a photographer. I felt bad about that; not having Agustin along was a definite loss, but hoped the Guatemalans would help once I arrived there. Today, the trip from Mexico City to Guatemala is a short one-hour air hop; in those days it was a laborious three-day journey by train. My diary records my discontent: "A holy terror," I wrote:

"Heat, dirt, bad food or no food at all. Anyone who does this trip by train ought to have his head examined! Most of all, mine."

The itinerary led westward to Veracruz, across the Isthmus of Tehuantepec from the Atlantic to the Pacific, and south to the Mexican-Guatemalan border at Suchiate.

Again from my diary: "All my troubles began there. The heat was unbearable, not a tree in sight, just the blazing sun beating down from a cloudless sky. A three-hour wait for the customs agent to inspect my luggage did not improve my temper one bit. He had overslept, and his assistants would be damned before they'd wake him up. Besides, unlike other passengers with goods to smuggle across the border, I was a legitimate traveler and not about to grease his palm with a bribe. When he did appear, disheveled and sleepy-eyed, he rumpled my baggage, and to add insult to injury, filched my favorite earrings. Was I mad! Then came the most punishing part of the trip-a long walk across the international bridge to Guatemala. A porter hauled my equipment in a handcart, with me trailing behind him panting in the suffocating heat. I will never understand why the train does not continue to the Guatemalan side and save thousands of weary passengers the tedious trek on foot. Once in Guatemala, a short walk brought me to Hotel Morelia, surely a place out of hell, here I spent the night. I slept with one eye open, for there was no secure lock on the door, and the clientele did not inspire confidence: The place was, I am sure, a smugglers' lair, inhabited by shifty-eyed characters and prostitutes, and the corridors smelt of cheap perfume and urine. Ayutla, the border town on the Guatemalan side, however, was a lot better than Suchiate. The Guatemalan customs control, quick and efficient, had advance notice of my arrival and I was whisked through in record time. Once again I boarded the train, this time bound for Guatemala City. The trip through the countryside was beautiful though miserably dusty. What made the trip fascinating was the sight of Indians along the way. The bright colors and ingenious designs were so stunning I could have torn them right off their backs had I half the chance. For miles and miles the train snaked through lush tropical growth. Palm trees and banana groves dotted the landscape as far as the eye could reach. No wonder the U.S. United Fruit Company held on so tenaciously to this territory. What a goldmine -- all those people working for practically nothing. "

Starved all the way, no food on the train. Finally at one stop I bought fruit and an avocado, for which I paid 25 cents while the other passengers paid 6 cents. The reason: The train pulled out before I got my change. My diary continues, "No one met me at the Guatemala City railroad station, so I found a room in the Hotel Continental and spent another bad night in an airless room. I felt completely abandoned."

The next day, however, my fortunes changed. Somehow I was discovered. James Webb, the cultural attaché of the American Embassy, had gone to the train station but missed me. As soon as he knew my whereabouts he took charge, and made sure I met everyone remotely connected with Indian affairs. I had a grand reunion with David Vela, the courageous newspaper editor who had fled the Ubico dictatorship, and whom I had already met as an exile in Mexico. Then there was the American-trained anthropologist Antonio Gouboud, from whom I learned so much. Later on, Antonio became his government's ambassador to Washington, but died a few years later.

My most lasting friendships were with Jorge Luis Arriola, then Minister of Education, and Salvador Ley, director of the Conservatory of Music, both life-time friends. Ley, of Jewish parents, had studied in Germany, was an excellent pianist and composer, and though thoroughly versed in European classics, devoted his life to promoting Latin American music.

I had planned a trip to Guatemala ever since my first field explorations in Mexico, but each time it was postponed because of the volatile political situation. Finally the long-time dictator, Jorge Ubico, was overthrown, and within a year his brutal henchman, General Ponce, as well. Shortly after my arrival in February of 1945, the new president, Jose Luis Arevalo, arrived from Argentina to take over the government. One of many intellectuals living in exile, he was Guatemala's first truly democratic ruler in more than 25 years and served his country, and the Allied cause, with distinction. With democratic forces in control, Guatemala went wild with joy. Not a night went by that I did not attend a reception, cocktail party, dinner or dancing at the local nightspots. Everyone offered me help and advice. In no time I had acquired a coterie of hangers-on, mostly eager young men, and was fast becoming a minor celebrity. In Mexico I had become used to an occasional newspaper or magazine article describing my exploits, but no more than that. My diary notes, "Jimmy Webb says I'm taking them by storm (my gift of gab)."

Within a few days of my arrival, Sr. Arriola had placed at my disposal a station wagon (more like a covered cargo truck); a chauffeur, Tadeo; and money for incidental expenses. After the usual delays in Mexico, the land of *mañana*, I was unprepared for such prompt attention, offers of expense money, and "Call us by phone if you need anything." Our first destination was Rabinal in the province of Baja Verapaz. Tadeo and I bumped along the unpaved highway, one of many built by Ubico to ensure swift arrival of his troops in case of Indian rebellions. Rabinal is a big Indian town in the middle of hot tropical country, where only a few *ladino* families live. *Ladino*, by the way, means people with Western ways. I found lodgings in an old colonial-style *pension* without electricity. In the five days I was there I dressed and undressed by candlelight. For privacy, both the windows to the street and the door to the patio had to be closed. Even when I took a shower I was in almost total darkness. Rigged up in the patio, the shower was a tiny, closet-sized, windowless room. I hung my clothes on a wall peg, showered, and retrieved them slightly damp from the water spray.

Upon return to Guatemala ten days later, dusty and dirty, my first thought was a shower in the *pension's* enormous bathroom lined with full-length mirrors. I almost fainted at the sight of myself! I was covered with red spots. I must have the measles, I thought. But no, I didn't have measles, or a mysterious tropical disease -- only flea bites. It is my nature not to feel their attack on my body! In a land of mean-spirited fleas, this is indeed a virtue, and one for which I have been envied.

In Rabinal we visited the homes of the musicians, examined

147

instruments and made appointments to record. Everybody was cooperative, in good humor and happy to play their music; it means a good time and a little money. One day, as I walked down the street, I heard cries of "*Señora, señora, espérese!*" I turned around, and there was the town priest in his long black cassock running across the plaza waving his arms at me. "I hear you have come to record the music of this village," he said breathlessly. "I am a music lover and I hope you will visit me at the parish house. I have a piano there and I would be honored if you would play for me. You play, don't you?" "Yes," I said. At this point in my life I was a very sloppy pianist; I hadn't played in years. But I did go to the parish house, and fortified by tea and cookies managed to play a little Mozart on his upright piano without disgracing myself. And after that the priest attended every recording session.

Then one day, when flutists and drummers were assembled in the patio ready to play, the priest whispered in my ear. "You know," he said, "I tried to wean these boys away from this old, pagan music. It's hard to do." I suppose he thought that since I played Mozart I would sympathize with his plight. "But," he continued, "I've taught some of the young boys to play guitar and violin and harp. Would you mind recording a few pieces the boys know?" I could hardly refuse him, but with only a limited number of aluminum discs and no way of getting any more, I recorded just a few short pieces. To my surprise they were *pasodobles*, the popular Spanish couple dance. "Tell me, Padre," I asked, "who is the author of these dances?" Alarm was in his voice. "No, no, no, " he exclaimed, "don't write anything, I can't tell you."

Later he confessed they were his own compositions. "If the bishop in Guatemala City finds out I write dance music, I'll be in trouble." My relationship with the priest of Rabinal ended when he told me he would be honored to receive me as a convert to the Catholic faith. I thanked him as gently as possible. It was the first of many requests for possession of my soul from Rosecrusians, Pentecostals, Catholics, Buddhists and believers of assorted cults that turned up in the course of my travels.

The first days of recording were routine, nothing exceptional or new. Then one day musicians carrying trumpets and a *teponastli* appeared at a recording session. This particular instrument sounded three tones instead of the usual two, making it in a sense, a melodic instrument. The trumpets played a wild soaring melody, interacting with the drum melody in unmistakable polyphony. It was the strangest music I had ever heard in Indian America. Later on, I was to find similar music in southern Mexico, but Guatemala was where I first heard it. This music was to be one of the great discoveries of my career; it was the music for the *Rabinal Achi*, a pre-hispanic theatrical masterpiece with an intriguing history worth telling:

In 1855, a brilliant Belgian cleric and ardent Indianist, Charles Etienne Brasseur de Bourbourg, was appointed ecclesiastical administrator of Rabinal. Soon after his arrival, one of his servants casually mentioned that his friend Bartolo Ziz could recite the lines of a long ancient story from beginning to end. His curiosity aroused, Brasseur summoned Ziz, who told him he had learned it from his father, and that it had been preserved by word of mouth for untold generations. The Abbe, a persuasive cleric, prevailed upon Ziz and his friends to assist him in writing it down. According to Brasseur's own account, he closeted himself with his Indian assistants for 12 days, wrote it down exactly as dictated in Quiche, and immediately translated it into Spanish and French, a remarkable feat.

The *Rabinal Achi* was a discovery of enormous importance, the only theatrical work of high Maya pre-hispanic civilization preserved to modern times. This 12th-century drama about the

149

rivalry of two Indian princes opens with the capture of the Quiche prince by the Rabinal prince after a bitter battle. They trade mutual recriminations, and the work finally ends with the sacrifice of the Quiche prince. As customary in pre-hispanic civilizations, while in detention (an entire year) the royal prisoner was showered with luxury and privileges. Only his request for the Rabinal's wife was turned down. The drama consists of long speeches (probably chanted) by the principle characters, enhanced by mime, song, dance and music. Years later I read the work in a Spanish translation by Luis Cardoza y Aragón, a Guatemalan writer. Barely hidden in the rhetoric was evidence of a hierarchal society, a war-like mentality, barbaric cruelty, intolerance towards neighboring tribes -- yet love of the arts. Like patriarchal societies worldwide, their women were instruments of male pleasure, and booty in war.

Not content with the *Rabinal Achi* as literature, Brasseur demanded an actual performance. And met with immediate opposition from the people. Was it right, they worried, to perform a work so un-Christian, hidden so long from authorities? Brasseur then devised a plan to bring his project to fruition: he quickly memorized part of the text, called the town elders together, and recited the lines to them. Completely astonished by this feat, the elders gave in. Brasseur paid all the expenses for the event, including costumes, music and masks.

But the Abbe had a Christian purpose in mind. The day before the performance, he called the people together to hear his benediction. According to his own recollections, as he made his entrance the war cry reverberated through the nave of the church; the sound of drums and trumpets filled the air, and the dancers with great dignity executed the initial dance. As the performers passed in front of him, bowing in the ancient manner, Brasseur made the sign of the cross over them. This was to remind them that they were Christians and that the old Maya past was over. Although the Rabinal Achi has nothing to do with Christianity, Brasseur did what Catholic priests have done since the Conquest in Indian America: use pre-hispanic ceremonies to honor Christian saints.

The next day the play was performed in its entirety. The Abbe presided high above the crowd, seated on a raised platform. There were 26 performers, men and women, and like our own theater, substitute actors, directors, and musicians. Brasseur had the foresight to commission his kapellmeister to notate the music during the performance. That was the last time it was given as a purely local affair, in what was believed to be "the ancient manner." When I later compared the notation of the music I recorded with Bourbourg's kappellmeister's, there was no resemblance, and no wonder, it was a devilishly difficult music to commit to our Western staff.

Tadeo and I returned to Guatemala City. I immediately reported to Dr. Arriola to make plans for a trip to the Western part of the country. To my surprise, he had just been appointed Ambassador to Portugal by the new president, Juan Arevalo. "I have a few days before leaving. Can I come along?" The next day, Salvador Ley called. "Henrietta, can I come too? I've never been on such an expedition." I was delighted. It was an unusual opportunity to work and also have a wonderful time.

I had also met an elderly American painter, Edith Hoyt. Edith, who was to lead me to another important discovery. One day, as we breakfasted together, she described a performance she had seen in Chajul, a remote Ixil village in the Quiche district. "It's called *El Baile de las Canastas* (Dance of the Baskets)," she said. "I know you will be interested because the music is so strange. Besides, nobody here knows anything about it." I was instantly intrigued and decided to head out to Chajul as soon as possible. Edith was right; no anthropologist or folklorist knew anything about it. But she had seen it with her own eyes, and I trusted her judgment. Now we had a specific goal in mind.

On the road again with Tadeo, Arriola, Salvador and Edith. A few hours of the usual dusty unpaved road led us to Chichicastenango, and I felt instantly at home; we were in Indian country again. It was now Holy Thursday, the streets jammed with people, and the main cathedral filled with worshipers. What a bizarre mixture! On one hand, high-arched European architecture, paintings and sculpture of Christian saints; on the other, dark-skinned people in ponchos, bright turbans, and colorful *huipiles*, kneeling on the cathedral floor surrounded by purple orchids and white lilies. The strong odor of copal incense was almost overwhelming. The babble of children's voices mingled with the murmur of prayers, but no one seemed to mind.

Chichicastenango is a big town and attracted tourists to its elegant Mayan Inn. The local kids knew some basic English, like "Wanna a superduper shine, lady?" But Indian life seemed undisturbed by the presence of foreigners. Catholicism long ago merged with worship of native gods. Franz Blum, the great archeologist, whom I knew in Mexico City, used to tell us stories about Father Rossbach, the Swiss priest resident in Chichicastenango for many years. An educated shrewd man, he knew the art of persuasion. Instead of excoriating the Quiches for not attending mass, he held services at a pre-hispanic shrine known as Pascal Abaj, high on a hill overlooking the valley and distant mountains. Indians had come for eons of time to petition their gods. But Father Rossbach placed both the Christian cross and the Maya cross, representing the four cardinal points, close together. Perhaps because they were so similar he hoped in time to eliminate one for the other. I'm not sure the strategy worked. Even though

Indians are Christians, they reluctantly give up the old gods for our new ones, perhaps in the belief that if your gods work for you, they can work for me too.

Father Rossbach was no longer in Chichicastenago in 1945, but I was curious to see Pascal Abaj with my own eyes. One day we climbed the steep hill that led to the shrine. Luck was with us: There, standing on the edge of the cliff, was an Indian. Raising his arms to heaven, he pleaded -- sometimes angry, sometimes in tears. I don't know what he said, but he seemed to be having a frank talk with the higher powers, who could be cajoled, coaxed or forced to act in his behalf.

For a few days we enjoyed the few creature comforts Chichicastenango offered, knowing full well they would be our last until our return to Guatemala City. At the Mayan Inn we swam, dined, drank good liquor, walked moon-lit nights in the gardens, danced the *danzon* and talked endlessly. While there, we added a few more people to our entourage: Maud Oakes, an American painter; and Ernestine, a Guatemalan photographer, along with her six-year-old boy and their dog. Each night we relaxed, going over the events of the day, the things we had seen, and the ideas we had formed about them. I don't think that a harsh word passed among us, we were so united, so affectionate with one another. Each one of the group was a person of accomplishments. Her first time in Guatemala, Maud had a Mellon Fellowship to study Indian Art, and eventually wrote several books on Todos Santos, a town famous because its local costume resembled our Uncle Sam's outfit --striped trousers and all. She became our official photographer; without her marvelous color slides we would have had no photographs of the momentous events that were yet to come. But once we left 'Chichi' and headed north to Ixil country, all resemblance to civilized comforts disappeared. On a short stop in the town of Quiche we found a bottle of genuine Scotch, tucked

153

away on a dusty shelf of a grocery store -- a real find in wartime. By doling it out in small doses it lasted a week. On route to Nebaj, the first Ixil village, we passed through vast mountain valleys dotted everywhere with grazing black, brown and white sheep. The land was so serene, so green with its patchwork of new growth, terraced gardens, and freshly-turned earth readied for the upcoming planting season, the rainy season. At Sacapulas, famous for enormous salt deposits in the dry riverbed just outside the village, we bought armfuls of local fruit, oranges, bananas for practically nothing. The papaya trees grew right in the village plaza. All told, we spent one American dollar for the fruit and received a papaya as a present from the fruit vender.

My diary reads: "What a road, the same dirt and bumps everywhere. I was lucky because I sat in front with Tadeo but all the others seated in the back were covered with red dust by the time we arrived in Nebaj. There in this Indian town we met Carlos Gordillo, a schoolteacher from Guatemala City born in Nebaj, but he was a god-send, a fountain of information. His family house, a charming colonial-type building, was our hotel for the next few days."

With plenty of booze on hand, and assorted *hambrientes*, appetizers, we spent the first evening listening to the marimba band that came to serenade us. Dr. Arriola, a little high and in a romantic mood, presented me with sprays of white roses from the bushes in the garden. Most of all, we listened to Carlos spin story after story about the Indians, whom he had known all his life. "What do you know about *El Baile de las Canastas*", I asked him at one point." To our complete surprise, he said, "Nothing, nothing at all."

The next day we took off for Chajul. Mobs of people came out to meet us. What extraordinary *huipils* the women wore! And the men in those black braided jackets. The musicians were already playing their instruments as we drove into town, guitars, strange square, leather-covered frame drums, reed flutes, metal trumpets and a teponaztli. We set up the equipment in a huge patio surrounded by at least half of the townspeople -- men, women carrying their babies, and swarms of children. And just as we were to begin, the electric motor balked, just wouldn't move. Patiently, the musicians waited while I fussed and fumed. Just as I was ready to give up, the motor sputtered and came to life. I leapt to my seat in front of the machine, put earphones on, and placed a shiny aluminum-based acetate disk on the turntable, ready to go. Well, I thought, I might just as well try. "Which of you musicians, " I said innocently, "play for *El Baile de las Canastas*?" A trumpeter and *teponastli* player stepped forward. "Tell me about it," I said, "nobody knows anything about it." They explained that it consisted of nine scenes, each one with its own music. For the next hour we recorded the music, so cheerful and rhythmically exciting, so unlike the doleful sound of the *Rabinal Achi*. Best of all, there was one short song.

That night we all gathered together over drinks (the Scotch we had bought in Quiche was fast dwindling). "What does the dance mean?" we asked. "What about the baskets," (which the townspeople had brought out for us to see), "what's the story behind the baskets?" Gordillo, who had spent the night before conferring with the local shamans (*balbastiches* in Ixil) told us the following story:

"The Dance of the Baskets," Carlos began, "celebrates the birth of corn. And as you know, such a myth indicates ancient history. Long ago, the Ixils, who lived by hunting, were starving because of scarcity of game. Desperately, their leaders looked about for a way to save the people. Finally, they discovered that the seed of the maize plant was concealed in the womb of a carefully guarded

155

young maiden named Mariquita, the ward of Matagtanic, an old sorcerer. Fortunately, a semi-god by the name of Tzunun, who lived amongst them, offered to steal Mariquita away and fertilize the seed. To distract Matagtanic, Tzunun, who could appear as man, a sparrow or quetzal bird, invited Matagtanic to join an expedition to hunt birds in the forest. While the party was off in the woods, Tzunun entered his house, won the girl's confidence and fertilized the seed. When Matagtanic discovered that his ward had been seduced, he flew into a rage and called upon the gods to kill Tzunun. However, as a semi-god with the power of regeneration, he revived. Despite the sorcerer's anger, Mariquita gave birth to the maize plant and saved the Ixils from starvation. Ever since, the Ixils have grown maize as their main crop."

"What about the baskets?" we asked. "What do they mean?" Carlos continued, "Don't you see, they were used as nets to catch the birds. That's why they are placed at the top of those very long poles, to reach the birds high in the trees." We had seen the baskets, recorded the music, and heard the legend which explained the meaning, but we had not seen the work with our own eyes. Dr. Arriola, who was returning to Guatemala City to prepare for his departure to Portugal, promised to send us a cameraman to film the work if we could convince the Indians to do it. Yes, yes, they said, we will do it, but we must have the proper costumes. Our next destination was Totonicapan to rent the costumes, and that's where we ran into trouble. My diary reads: "The man who rents costumes to the Indians is a horrid beast and Edith haggled with him for hours. First we argued, then we left in a huff, came back, argued again, and returned the next day for a final agreement. We paid the exorbitant price he asked, put the costumes in our truck, and sped down the highway, glad to be on our way again. It's really going to come off, we thought. All of us were happy again -- even Pixie, Ernestine's dog. (So funny, when I remind myself of Maud's struggle to train her not to pee every damn minute)."

Finally, we arrived at Chajul. By then we were eighteen passengers in all, including Miguel Angel, our cameraman just in from Guatemala City. The morning had been rainy, a steady drizzle, but as we pulled into the village it stopped. The entire town was on hand waiting for the fun to begin. Soon everything was ready, the baskets securely fastened to long poles tied to the dancers' backs, Edith helping them into their costumes, the Indians clamoring for more liquor, and demanding the money we'd promised them. But the clouds stubbornly refused to go away. We expected a downpour.

Suddenly, the sun burst out from behind the clouds. The trumpets and *teponaztli* started playing, the actor-dancers enacted the entire drama from start to finish. Edith madly painted the scene, Maud took photographs while the two cameramen filmed. Carlos and I noted down the musicians' description of each scene as it was played.

Finally it was over. The hundreds of people who had come to watch the spectacle left their perches on the hillside overlooking the plaza and headed for home. Even the marimba band stopped playing. We paid the musicians, collected the costumes and headed back to Nebaj for a much-needed rest, and lunch for a much famished crew. That night we talked into the wee hours of the morning. We all agreed that unlike the upper class *Rabinal Achi*, the "Dance of the Baskets" had undoubtedly been popular entertainment in pre- Conquest times.

Sad to report, years later I learned the film of the performance was destroyed in a fire. All I have of this truly remarkable event are Maud Oakes' wonderful color slides and the recordings. But even more lamentable, the ballet has not been performed again. In 1979 I returned to Nebaj, again invited by Carlos Gordillo to see the annual fiesta. That year Guatemala was in the midst of violent

157

guerrilla warfare. Sr. Arriola, now retired in Guatemala City, warned me that dead bodies and dismembered limbs regularly floated down the river nearby. Although aware of danger beyond the capital, I felt reasonably safe with my friends. With me in Carlos' car was an anthropologist who had worked in Chajul for years. "Tell me," I asked, "have you ever seen the Dance of the Baskets?" "No," she replied, "nobody has ever mentioned it to me. Don't be surprised," she continued, "Indian culture is in great danger of being wiped out." "How so?" I asked. "Well," she said sadly, "It is government policy these days to recruit young Indian boys into the army. While in boot camp they are fed a constant stream of propaganda disparaging their own culture. Unfortunately, when they return home on furlough, they make fun of their parents' traditions. Rather than face their children's ridicule, they give up their Indian ways. Besides, the Ixil villagers, more than others, have been systemically dispersed into so-called 'model towns,' where they are taught 'civilized' ways, meaning those agreeable to the military clique. I am sure I've never seen the ballet because the people of Chajul don't want to be laughed at by their children."

Rabinal and Chajul were the high points of my journey there; everything else was anticlimactic or of passing interest, nor did I have time to explore each dance or ceremony I saw along the way. Sometimes I saw truly inferior performances, mainly because of interference by "educated" folk bent on "civilizing" the Indians. My dairy records my impressions of one such experience: "...The dances were something out of this world. Those poor kids must have had stones tied to their feet and arms. I had to congratulate the dame who produced this wooden, boring thing. *Muy original,*' she told me. '*Muy original*,' I said, echoing her words, and biting my tongue..."

I have spent many years learning about Indian culture, but I would be remiss if I did not mention their extensive knowledge of herbs, plants and medical practices. One sight remains fixed in my memory: in a deep ravine Maud and I chanced upon a group of men and women, stripped to the waist, splashing about in hot sulfur baths. On seeing us, the Indians beckoned us to join them: "It's healthy," they said, "the waters here will cure any illness you have." We hurriedly withdrew, I'm not sure yet whether from modesty or fear of the black water. Having no medical training or expertise in such matters, I can merely point out the medical profession has come to respect Indian knowledge. Today there are several Mexican hospitals where native healers and scientifically trained doctors work side by side and trade knowledge. "But does it work?" I asked a young doctor. "Yes, it does," he said emphatically. "For one thing, it helps heal the breach between two branches of medicine, folk practice and new science. Indian shamans have firsthand knowledge about many drugs unknown to us."

Then one day our comfortable, untroubled world was shaken to its core. We took off to see the market in the town of Solola, situated along the banks of the beautiful, serene Lake Atitlan. For hours we cautiously traveled through low-hanging clouds, the narrow curvy highway almost invisible two feet ahead of us. Even the marketplace, silent and mysterious, was shrouded in clouds; Indians in somber-colored woolen ponchos suddenly appeared, and disappeared in the mist.

Suddenly we saw the Mexican flag flying at half-mast at the police station. The captain came out to greet us. "I'm sorry to tell you," he said with tears in his eyes, "but we have just received news over our wireless that your president has died." We Americans were

159

in a state of shock for the rest of the day. Our thoughts turned to home, to Roosevelt, to the war that was still raging. What kind of a man was Mr. Truman? Was he capable of winning the war? We knew nothing about the vice-president and were sorely troubled. Later on, we heard about the spontaneous demonstrations of grief and remembrance all over Latin American. Like the Americans, they wept and honestly mourned his passing.

The last week in Guatemala was a whirlwind of events: farewell dinners for Arriola, concerts, and preparation for the lecture I was to give for the Ministry of Education. I shall never forget it, Edith, Salvador, Ernestine, Maud and myself working together. I was the center of attention; so many young men fawned over me I felt like a Hollywood star. Besides, I had endeared myself to the Guatemalans by making copies of all recordings for their archives.

My diary says: "They said goodbye with flowers and candy, kisses, hugs and tears, and promises to see each other again. At the airport I had my last look at them peering over the railing -- Farnsworth, Chamberlain and Webb from the Embassy, and Salvador, Edith and Ernestine (no dog or boy) all waving as I boarded the plane. When shall I see them again, those dear lovable companions of my golden years?"

***

Chiapas -1945

It was already spring when I left Guatemala for Chiapas, the last leg of this extended recording expedition. I met Juan in Salina Cruz, the Isthmus Pacific coast port, where we spent a long weekend at the only *pension* in town. Less than elegant, I remember it for one incident only -- we bought a three-pound lobster, the biggest I ever saw, for one dollar. We dug out every scrap of luscious meat, leaving nothing but the empty shell. A half century later I still consider that lobster a once-in-a-lifetime bargain.

We swam, drank, took leisurely walks along the long, sandy beach, noted the U.S. ships docked in the harbor, the only sign of the war raging in the Pacific. Never were we as happy as during those few sunlit, carefree days, the last we would enjoy together. The 17 years difference in our ages, my independence and long absences, curdled our relationship. The breakup was yet to come, but saying goodbye that day in Salina Cruz was painful. I resolved to finish my work and return to Mexico City as soon as possible.

Upon arrival in San Cristobal, my Chiapas headquarters, I was thrown into a whirlwind of activity, and my personal life faded into the background. When Edith Hoyt joined me a few days later from Guatemala, I was delighted; feeling at that moment vulnerable, worried and confused about the future, I was grateful for her warm friendship. In this quiet colonial city high in cool mountains, I walked along ancient cobble-stone streets lined with whitewashed, balconied houses; only a red neon sign flashing in the dark of night reminded me of the 20th century. Later, after travels in Spain, I realized that San Cristobal was a faultlessly preserved replica of countless Spanish towns. While houses, cathedral, and plazas looked like Old Spain, the resemblance ended there: San Cristobal was the largest Indian trading center of Chiapas. The market in those years (before Americans moved in) was thronged with bronze-skinned Tzotzils and Tzeltals, the local tribesmen. Definitely in the minority were mestizos and pale-faced Spaniards. Sharing space with humans were sheep, donkeys and yapping, skeleton-thin dogs foraging for food, always underfoot.

San Cristobal's market was a miracle of native handicrafts, but my attention was caught by the unusual male costumes: high-backed *huaraches*, natural-colored ponchos, and strange hats. One day, I asked Señor Clemente, a director of the local Indian Affairs Departments, soon to become friend and guide, to tell me about them. He laughed, "It's a long story. Those high-backed *huaraches* are pre-hispanic. The rest we owe to the Spaniards. They brought sheep; now the Indians have warm woolen ponchos. Second, they assigned each village a special feature -- a particular brim, weave or color. That way they could identify the Indians especially during tribal revolts -- and there were many." When I remarked that women's clothes were more colorful, more artfully designed, Clemente replied, "That's because they try to please their men, isn't that so?"

Suddenly I remembered an incident from my first visit to Chiapas: One day, as I picnicked with the Governor and his party on a grassy knoll, an Indian woman walked by. From her bulky figure it was obvious she was wearing several *huipiles,* the top one shabby and frayed. The Governor, however, suspected it was worn on top to protect new ones underneath. He called her to his side and most graciously asked, "Will you sell me your *huipil*, the nice one?" Embarrassed by attention from someone clearly upper-class, she thought for a moment and shook her head. "No," she said shyly, "I'm taking this to my sister who lives ten leagues from here." "I'll give you 50 pesos," he said. "With that money you can make another one for your sister." But no, she kept on shaking her head. Obviously, nothing could change her mind. I shall never know why she wouldn't sell it, but I do know that weaving has special meaning for Indian women; it is the one skill which gives them status otherwise denied, as well as artistic satisfaction and control. Weavers belong to a declared guild with unwritten rules -- and they jealously protect their territory from male intrusion.

I once discussed the subject with my friend, Dr. Daniel Rubin de la Borbolla in Mexico City, who added another unexpected dimension. Borbolla, Latin America's most distinguished folk arts authority, was a mine of information. "I'm going to tell you something that will surprise you," he said, " I have always believed that women were the first mathematicians." "Now why is that?" I asked, my eyebrows raised in disbelief. "Think of it --" he said, "weaving, one of the world's oldest skills, is generally a woman's art; she has to count every stitch. Unless she can add, subtract and multiply, nothing comes out right. Of course, I can't prove it, but you will admit it is a possibility -- right?" What an intriguing thought!

Like my first expedition in 1942, technical problems dogged my footsteps -- heavy equipment (my albatross), no electricity, muddy, slippery roads, and wasted days waiting for people and equipment to show up. To solve the problem, we invited the Indians to come to us in San Cristobal to record their music. This way, I lived in comparative comfort with a good bed, decent food, and saw an occasional movie at the local cinema. True, I saw the same Tarzan movies I had seen the week before in Tuxtla Gutierrez, but that was better than nothing. I did notice, however, that whole scenes were lifted from one Tarzan film to another, a really cheap way of making movies.

But soon the recording sessions began. Away from home, the Indians had a wonderful time, a respite from backbreaking work in the fields or feeding animals. They played guitars, violins and harps (which required hours of retuning after each piece), sang songs, drank plenty of *comiteco*, the local firewater, and spent the money I gave them in the market.

We often think of rural cultures as regional, or tribal. Here in Chiapas I became aware of village culture. Just like their clothes, each song, each instrumental style belonged to a particular place. It was considered wrong to sing someone else's song. When they did sing them, it was with a guilty air, like being caught with stolen goods. One day I found an accordion in Chamula marked "Made in Germany," probably left there by some European visitor; I also heard someone yodel in Swiss style in Zinacantan, but never found this elsewhere.

Just as we finished an entire week of recording, our long-delayed gasoline motor arrived from Mexico City. Almost at once, the chief religious authority of the nearby town of Chamula invited me to record music there. Clemente and I loaded the equipment and a few gallons of gasoline into the Department truck and drove a few bumpy miles to the village. Little did I know then I was to make another important musical discovery. On our arrival, the fiscal, a kind of judge, a dignified Indian official, took me on a tour of the dusty village streets lined with thatched, whitewashed huts. Far off in the distance, blue mountains shimmered in the bright sun. We readied our cameras. "Don't take any pictures," he warned us, "Those mountains are our ancient gods and we don't permit pictures." Next we stopped in front of a row of huts picturesquely situated. Again he warned us, "They are sacred, too."

Finally, the fiscal explained: "We worship many Christian saints in this village. To honor them, we build each one a special house with things that remind us of their lives." I was particularly charmed with the house of *El Niño Jesus*, the Baby Jesus, furnished with a cradle, toys and baby clothes. I thought, that baby is a real baby, just as the Virgin of Guadalupe is a real mother. No wonder Indians easily accepted Christianity; the saints were fallible and vulnerable just like them, and more forgiving than the old gods, so remote and impersonal, and too often, cruel and bloodthirsty.

The fiscal continued: "We have something else to honor our

saints, a special song for each saint. We don't sing them in church or on the street, only inside. Come to my house and my wife and I will sing them for you." Doubting Thomas that I am, I suspected they would be like those banal tunes choir-masters teach their choruses everywhere in the Christian world.

We entered a long, narrow room, the darkness pierced by a single candle, bare except for a long wooden table with benches on either side. I set up the equipment and placed the motor outside to dampen the sound. Soon the fiscal's wife, a short, portly woman wrapped in a long *rebozo* quietly entered and sat next to her husband, facing us on the opposite bench.

I placed the microphone between the two singers, put the needle down on the acetate disk, and signaled them to begin. Darting glances at us now and then, they sang first quietly and then with more confidence. Suddenly, I realized I was hearing something that resembled what I had first heard in Guatemala, multi-part music. Unlike unison singing found in the north, these songs resembled our canon, or round, much like "Frère Jacques" or "Row, Row, Row Your Boat".

At first hearing, I wondered whether it was accidental. But when song after song was sung in the same way, I realized I had stumbled on a real discovery. Later I found instrumental music with the same polyphonic characteristics: a trumpet played the main tune, the flute improvised on the melody, and a drum brought everything together with a dramatic rhythm, like a third voice. Later on when I described this music to European ethnomusicologists, they dismissed it saying, "No doubt they learned it in church." Actually, people all over the world, Africa, Asia, the Americas have created many kinds of multi-part music; claims of European origin simply fly in the face of facts.

After the singing I asked the fiscal for a translation into Spanish. "The one I just sang, " he said, "is a prayer to *San Pedro* (Saint Peter) who protects us on our travels. We say

> Father San Pedro
> Do me three favors
> And give me three blessings
> Don't abandon me on the road
> Now I go home to sleep
> So please
> Don't let anything happen to me
> And if I wake tomorrow
> I will thank God.

Ancient traditions are like truffles that, hidden from view, have to be dug up to be savored. To the casual observer, Chiapas is Christian country, yet, underneath lies a secret vein, a devotion to a past recalled through song and ritual. In Chamula I heard a perfect mix: pre-hispanic music with an appeal addressed to a Christian saint, in reality a thinly disguised Maya deity. Afterwards, upon questioning authorities in San Cristobal I was met with blank stares; no one had ever heard them then, or 20 years later during a return to Chiapas. Are they still alive today? Those songs are the most tangible survival of an ancient past; long before the European invasion, village religious authorities were singing these remarkable songs. They are as much a treasure as the Maya ruins scattered throughout the state.

The purpose of my 1945 visit was to document traditional Indian music. However, I also observed Indian efforts to join the contemporary world. When I arrived, a literacy campaign was in full swing to teach the Indians to read and write Spanish. One day, I was invited to a village class. The teacher said, "We don't have a schoolhouse, I hold classes outdoors under the trees. My desk is a

166

wooden table and my students sit on the ground." I was really impressed with what I saw: old and young came, even a few women, people who had never held a pencil or a book in their hands before. With a shortage of rural schoolteachers, those with rudimentary skills taught those with none at all. It was the gateway to a better life. I still remember their eager faces as they listened to the teacher and wrote their first words in the little lined notebooks the government gave them.

I came to appreciate Indian intelligence and humanity. One day, a village elder invited me to take a walk with him. "Come, niña," he said, "let me show you our town." He led me to the pride of the village, a tiny plaza shaded from the hot sun by fragrant flowering bushes. Pointing to an enormous tree in the plaza, he said, "You see those roots? That is the center of the world." I understood his meaning, "We are rooted to this place, just like that tree." But it also means "wherever I am is the center of the world." What could be more provincial than that? However, upon reflection, there are provincials in New York City, London and Paris. Anyone who thinks he is the center of the world, that his way of life is the best, the wisest, the smartest, the only way, is a provincial in my opinion.

When my acetate disks were used up, I closed up shop. Edith, Clemente and I set out on horseback to visit the villages of the Chiapas highlands. *Sans* equipment, just carrying enough clothes and one luxury, a bottle of rum, it was a real holiday. We roamed through cornfields now grown high above our heads, the horses munching along the way. The valleys were green and verdant from the rains; everything growing with tropical frenzy. Edith taught me French and I helped her with Spanish. At one point my horse stumbled and I tumbled to the ground unhurt. Too young to be afraid, I mounted the mare again and on we rode to our first stop.

For the next few nights we were plagued by murderous fleas. With no hotel or *pension* anywhere in sight we slept on a bed of pine needles on the Town Hall floor. What a night! At three in the morning Edith shook me out of a deep sleep. "Henrietta, this place is full of fleas and they are eating me alive!" Half drugged with sleep, I had a random thought: maybe rum will kill the little pests. I sprinkled half of our precious liquor on the pine needles, a needless sacrifice, for they nipped us more viciously than before. I spent the next hour crushing those I could catch between my thumb and index finger. If Edith hadn't awakened me I would have slept through the night without stirring. My ability to withstand attacks by bloodsucking insects is the secret of my survival in the Mexican wilderness. Finally, the fleas wore themselves out, or passed out in a drunken stupor, and we went back to sleep until daybreak. That was not the end, however, for we spent the next night in much the same manner.

On the third day, red-eyed and irritable, we proceeded to our next destination, a village five hours away. Late in the day we realized the impossibility of returning to the previous village. The Indian authorities came to the rescue; they dispatched a messenger to bring back our sheets from the previous town. Just as night fell they returned and gratefully we spread the sheets out on the pine needles. By this time we were beyond exhaustion, and fell asleep instantly. But horrors! At three in the morning Edith nudged me again: "They brought the sheets, all right," she complained, "and the fleas, too." Now fully recovered from their *crudo* (hangover), they mercilessly attacked us again. That was the third night with no sleep. I was ready to head back to Mexico City; I had had enough.

The activities of the next few days I remember through a thick haze. We visited a cave with ancient drawings etched on the walls, noted shrines to the saints, their glass-enclosed images surrounded with white lilies and sprigs of purple orchids, and finally, an inaugural ceremony for a newly elected authority of the village Chenaljo. Bedraggled, down at the mouth, and tired, we came to the entrance of town. There, awaiting us, was a delegation of town officials; the band played, banners waved, and people clapped and blew kisses as we were escorted into town. A royal welcome!

I have made many references to the Indian love of theater -- it is not only entertaining but provides a harmless way to poke fun or insult authority. Because most mestizos don't understand Indian languages (more than 50), Indians feel free to express their feelings without fear of censorship or punishment. In Chiapas I was told of one such event: It seems, in response to a revolt in Chamula three Mexican generals arrived with great pomp and circumstance (trumpets, drums, cannons, fireworks) to intimidate the Indians. During their stay, the general and his mistress went off to the hills to make love, returned a few days later, and left, to the relief of the villagers.

Since then, every year at Carnival time the event is dramatized to ridicule their Mexican rulers; they reenact the sexual act (permitting only the Indians to see it): two male Indians, under blankets, play the lovers with appropriate actions and insulting dialogue. As described to me, this brings on laughter and derision. The fiesta ends with a bizarre dance; the plaza, strewn with straw in a checkerboard form, is set ablaze, and dancers hop from one square to the other   One day, I shall go back to the village in disguise to see the whole thing!

Returning to San Cristobal, the day dawned cloudy with promise of rain. Clemente went on ahead, with Edith and me trailing behind. Just as we came in sight of Chamula, the last town before San Cristobal, the heavens opened up and, in a matter of minutes, we were drenched to the skin. Our rain capes were useless; the rain poured down our necks in a steady stream. As we were about to follow the path around the mountain, an Indian came by and seeing our dilemma said, "Let your horses go on ahead and head straight down the hill on foot; that will save you lots of time." We followed his advice. Gingerly, we inched down the hill but soon realized the soil beneath was pure clay. We slid all the way down, holding on to thin branches for support, stopping to scrape the sticky soil from our boots. At the bottom of the hill we found another obstacle -- a high fence surrounding the town. We tramped around in the mud looking for an opening. Just as we gave up hope, Clemente came by and helped us over the fence. The Indians waiting for us in a nearby hut under the eaves howled with laughter, no doubt delighted to see white folks so wet and bedraggled. An hour later, the sun shone through the thick clouds, and we headed back to San Cristobal.

***

Return to the United States - 1945

Suddenly, I was recalled to the States. One day, Gamio received a letter from Charles Seeger, then head of the Music Division of the Pan American Union, requesting my presence in Washington for consultation on the radio programs written some time before. My stay in Washington was brief, I paid a visit to the Library of Congress and the Pan American Union, and had a taste of Washington in wartime. I saw my family briefly in New Haven. They were no richer than before, despite money earned by both parents in wartime industries. My brother was away at war in the Pacific, and my sister was working on a Yale University project.

I spent a few days in Cambridge with Chenk hoping to salvage our tottering marriage. What I recall of that brief visit was getting to know his teachers and the houses they built for themselves. Walter Gropius, the charming Marcel Breuer and Richard Hudnut had all come from Bauhaus, that German citadel of modern architectural design. Yet, each one professed his own esthetic. Gropius' house was comfortable, cool, informal with a rumpled lived-in air; Breuer's house, on the other hand, was doggedly modern, like a Mondrian painting, full of bright colors and angles. Much as we tried, it was no use -- Chenk and I parted company that fall of 1945, and I returned to Mexico.

But my relationship with Juan was coming apart at the seams as well. As we approached the airport I was truly confused. Well, I thought, you've broken up with Chenk, but to spend the rest of your life with Juan would be stupid. He's not for you; he's a dry academic, unimaginative, stuck to his books, churning out boring articles, and you belong in the world of the arts. No, this cannot be. Little did I know that my future was being decided for me -- for Camille, in a drunken moment, had taken up with Juan while I was in the States. Waldeen, who knew about the affair, tried to stop me from seeing Juan. I paid her no attention, did not hear the warning note in her voice and blindly rushed off to his place. Then one day Camille came to see me. "I'm sorry to cause you any pain, but I cannot undo what has already been done." And that was the end. I rushed back to my own apartment, my heart broken, my tears spilling over. Why hadn't I been told; why didn't my friends tell me the truth? I was distraught for weeks; depressed, ate nothing, distracted myself with concerts and dinner parties. But I heard a voice in my head, which said, "Don't despair, you will live again, work and love again. Juan was not for you anyway." I listened to that small persistent voice and survived.

***

171

Tarahumara – Yaqui - 1946

A few months later I took off for what was to be my last trip before returning to the United States -- Tarahumara and Yaqui territory in the states of Chihuahua and Sonora. "Everything is signed, " said Jose Luis, "you can leave whenever you like. Come by the office tomorrow morning." Bright and early I tore down to the Department of Education. Jose Luis was beaming. "Here are plane tickets for you and Agustin to Chihuahua, and your ticket to Hermosillo, Sonora, as well as travel expenses, and an official letter for the authorities."

"Wait a minute!" I cried. "Where's Agustin's ticket to Sonora?" "Oh," he said with obvious embarrassment, "the Minister only approved his trip to Chihuahua." I was crestfallen and immediately complained to Dr. Gamio. "How can you expect me to go to Yaqui territory alone?" I pleaded. He smiled, put his arm around my shoulders, and said, "You'll be perfectly all right. You know how to take care of yourself." Such confidence, I thought. Here I was, going into unknown territory, loaded down with 200 pounds of equipment, armed with only an official letter from the minister of education. Suppose the Indians didn't trust me? "Okay, I'll go," I said, "but I don't like the deal."

A few days later, Agustin and I flew to Parral, the jumping-off point for our journey into the mountains. With the help of the Department of Indian Affairs, we found a truck heading to Baquiriachic, slept the freezing night in the car, and arrived at our destination after nine grueling hours on what might laughingly be called a road. "You are in the wrong place," we were told as soon as we got there. "This is mestizo territory. The Tarahumaras live further on in Guachochic." A truck is scheduled to go there in four days and they can take you. Or you can go by horse. Besides, maybe you're on a wild goose chase; we never heard the Indians sing." I let that one pass; it was not the first time I had heard such a claim.

From my diary: "April 19-20. I'll be damned if I'll get on another horse. I fume the rest of the day and decide I have no choice but to wait for the engineers. Surprise at sundown: Some politicos arrive from Chihuahua City, on their way to Guachochic, and promise to take us there. There must be a God or something! We load as much equipment as the car will hold and send the rest by pack animals."

Another entry from my diary: "The road is nothing but a nightmare! Up the mountain, down the mountain, around the mountain! Gives me the creeps just thinking I have to return the same way. Four hours later we arrive at our first destination, Baquiriachic, to find the whole town decked out for a celebration. Indians dancers, their faces, legs and arms painted in white zigzag streaks stood around listlessly waiting for a signal to begin. What luck, I thought, I've come just in time to see a Holy Week performance. Was I ever wrong! They had been hired by the politicos to advertise their election campaign."

Again from my diary: "April 23rd. Guachochic. I wish I could be content as I have been on other trips. I just want to finish my work and head home. Thoughts about Juan and our breakup haunt me; I keep thinking of my brother, my family, Chenk, and it makes me nervous and anxious. I have moments of great loneliness, in spite of all the people and activity around me.

"The wind blows like fury across the plains of Chihuahua, and the rain clouds gather. Everything is dry and arid now at the end of the dry season, yet the trees are in bloom with delicate pink and white flowers. At sunset the mountains turn a deep, misty blue and

173

the dark green pine trees ring the wide meadows like sentinels on guard. Just outside town there is a cascading waterfall, which sends sprays of cool water into the air. The other day, Indian girls brought me a bouquet of white and purple irises; they only arose my longing for home.

"April 24th. The sight of the cascade reminds me I haven't taken a bath in days. I summoned up enough courage, walked over slippery rocks with the help of one of the girls, and plunged into the water. It was freezing, but I sure feel better for it.

"April 30th. The nights are so cold, like Vermont in the dead of winter. I wear a long-sleeved nightgown, sweater, socks and a hot-water bottle at my stomach and still shiver. What a pretty sight I am! Sitting near the fireplace in the hut where I live, I wondered why the wall around the hearth seems to move. I bend a little closer, trying to focus my eyes in the near darkness. To my horror I found that, yes, something was moving -- hundreds of roaches, marching like soldiers on parade. Ugh! The sight turns my stomach and I go to sleep hungry. I have visions of blueberry pies, ice cream and doughnuts. At the end of the dry season there is nothing to eat but tortillas, frijoles, thin slices of potatoes fried in rancid oil, dried apples, and dried, stringy beef. There is no milk because the cows are let loose to forage for grass wherever. When you see them wandering on distant slopes they are so thin you can count their ribs, every single one. So, what do the Tarahumaras eat? They eat squirrels and field rats, anything with meat on it. How repulsive, but maybe they taste good. After all, I have eaten iguanas in Tehuantepec, and surely they are the world's ugliest animals. Extreme poverty was visible everywhere. I am told the Tarahumaras never have enough food to last the year out because of insufficient arable land and storage facilities. Several songs I recorded describe the hunting of field rats when the corn gives out."

One day, Agustin appeared with a small pitcher of milk. "I begged it from the Lopez family," he said. "Here, it's for you." I drank it down to the last drop. It tasted like nectar of the gods. The cow that so generously had provided me with a delicious drink belonged to a mestizo family who kept their cows on the farm, despite the shortage of water and forage. That pitcher of milk immeasurably improved the black mood that had overwhelmed me since arrival.

Guachochic was an unusual Indian town; there were no signs of government or religious authority. I spent my leisure hours with the town schoolteacher, a mine of information about Indian life. "Things are better here than before, "she said, "For years the Jesuits had educated the Indians. When the federal government set up its own schools they reacted violently, they were not about to give up peacefully power they had wielded for centuries. My husband was the district inspector and for years they made his life a hell. He paid no attention to their threats, knew they were following him as he made his rounds. But one day their *pistoleros* cornered him in the woods and shot him in the back." I sighed. "But Maria, why did you stay here?" I asked. "I had become so used to the Indians, I couldn't leave. Besides, I wanted to continue my husband's work. I am their teacher, they have no other, and I will stay until I die."

Then she continued, "The Tarahumaras are not Catholics in the true sense of the word. You won't find altars, pictures of the saints or Jesus on the cross in their houses." One day, she took Agustin and me to the old ruined colonial church on the outskirts of town. "Look at it," she laughed, "it's falling down. When the priest comes here every now and then he crosses himself, and says, *Ni las moscas se paran aqui* (Not even flies stop here). None of the Indians come here, they worship God in their own way, and ignore the priest. The Jesuits rarely come here either; they say it is

175

possessed by devils. No wonder! The Indians no longer pay their tithe, and education is no longer in their hands."

A few days later we watched a Tarahumara council meeting. The outdoor courtroom, held in the shadow of the schoolhouse, was quiet and solemn. The petitioners sat in a semi-circle around the tribal governor and his assistants, and presented their cases. At that moment I wished I understood their language. What were they talking about? What kind of justice was meted out here, with no lawyers or jury? Maria told me that most complaints are about land divisions and family squabbles, and sometimes drunken brawls after too much drinking during fiesta time.

The mystery of Tarahumara life deepened as Agustin and I got to know the youngsters, who followed us everywhere we went. However, the relative calm of the village hid some startling facts, if we were to believe the children. According to them, suicide was common; they said that some children preferred to die than suffer their parents' disapproval. Apparently, Tarahumaras had little tolerance for lawbreakers, even the youngest among them.

As the days slipped by, Agustin and I became aware that the Tarahumaras lived a double life, half pagan, half Christian. Yes, their language was committed to writing, they had a federal school, politicians courted their votes and they were connected by road to cities. Yet, they were semi-nomadic, migrating during cold winter months to warm lowlands, hunted with bows and arrows, dammed the rivers and caught fish with their hands, and made beautiful pottery and baskets. Even their wooden cabins and stone storage bins were unchanged, and many still lived in caves. To mark the seasons and for curing ceremonies, they practiced pre-Hispanic rites, used peyote, sacrificed animals, sang ancient songs, played ancient instruments, all presided over by singing shamans.

As Christians, to celebrate saints' days and holy days they played violins and sang songs, like the Mexicans, in two-part harmony; during Lent they wandered the countryside playing drums, the sound dampened with cloth coverings as penance. Two religious systems, each with its own rituals, lived side by side in what appeared to be complete harmony.

Indian festivals all have a religious motivation -- to appease the gods, to ask for help, for better crops, good health or more children, etc., but it is also cut-up time. Once the rituals are over, the fun begins. "There is plenty of sacrificed meat to eat," I was told. "They dance and sing to violins and drums for days, get drunk on *tesguino* and forget the rules. Yes, couples even run off to the woods and do God-knows what." I pretended to be shocked, but secretly I thought, everybody has to blow off steam, kick the laws in the face, even if only for a minute. Apparently, nobody is punished for misbehavior, or at least they didn't tell me. Like everywhere else, sex is a well-guarded secret.

Agustin had a wonderful time taking pictures of these handsome people. Once renowned as long-distance runners, the men are strong-featured, tall and athletic-looking, and invariably wrapped in woolen blankets as a poncho. Mexicans say the blanket is placed on the Indian's back at birth and he wears it even to the grave, for at burial the body is wrapped in it. Like the Seris and Indians on the American side, men wear their hair long with a band around the forehead.

One morning, Agustin and I were tinkering with the recording machine. We were at our wits end because the mike cord had snapped in two. Just as we had figured out a way of holding it together manually, a group of youngsters came by. I don't remember exactly how it began, but within two hours we had recorded a dozen songs. One of the boys, Edubijis Loya, acted as

177

prompter, reminding the singers of the tune or the words. From that day on, we had a constant stream of singers offering a song or two. An unexpected treasure, they were little ditties about ordinary everyday life, just like the ones recorded in Huichol country. "Everyone knows a few," said Loya, "but a lot of young people like the Mexican songs better. But," he added with a smile, "you, Enriqueta, have given us a good reason not to forget our own songs. It isn't every day that we have a purchaser (*marchanta de canciones*)." There's nothing like money to keep the creative juices flowing!

On the last day, we gathered together to translate the Tarahumara songs into Spanish. I shall never forget the intelligence the Indians displayed. Today, 50 years later, I look at Agustin's wonderful photographs and I relive that Spring of 1946. Just last year, a group of Tarahumara children sang in Mexico City at the annual fiesta organized by the National Indian Institute. I heard the children sing just as they had so long ago; they haven't forgotten.

The trip back to Parral by truck was more walk than ride. Every few miles we were ordered to get out and push the truck through endless breaks in the dirt road. Sometimes the truck veered so sharply on its side I thought it would surely keel over. However, the gods must have been with us; I arrived with nothing worse than a raw back from the constant shaking of the truck. I shouldn't complain -- ten hours by truck was better than three days on muleback.

Agustin and I parted company in Chihuahua City, his last trip as my photographer. For a few days I was courted by city officials, a dinner in my honor at the Lion's Club, and a radio interview at the local station. I waved goodbye at the airport; I was not to see him again for 40 years.

Trouble soon awaited me from an unexpected source. My next destination, Hermosillo, in the state of Sonora, is directly west of Chihuahua City, a short distance as the crow flies. I had to take a circuitous route: first, north to the United States border, and then south down Mexico's west coast to Hermosillo.

The flight to the border was short, landing me at an obscure airfield on the U.S. side. When I tried to retrieve my equipment, I was told it had been impounded and would be held until permission to release it was received from the Mexican Department of the Interior. I was flabbergasted. I showed them official letters explaining my mission, but they were adamant. I was within the jurisdiction of the border control and would have to follow the rules. For the next few days I stormed the customs offices. I pleaded for help from the English consulate, then from the American consul, a bumbling idiot who spoke no Spanish. Finally, the customs clerk, who reeked of liquor, offered a "solution": Pay the customs fee and you can have your machine. "You understand," he said, "unless I sign the order, they won't let your machine on board." The fog in my mind lifted. I was being held up for a *mordida*, the bribe that moves everything in Mexico. "How much?" I asked. "12 dollars," he said, bleary-eyed. I paid, received a receipt. The next morning I drove to the airfield, an unpaved, grassy meadow. The taxi driver hauled out my stuff and put it in the small, bare customs office. The genial customs officer eyed me with interest. "Didn't I see you last year in Guatemala? He asked, "I inspected your equipment then, if I am not mistaken." "Yes," I said, "I was there." He smiled and said, "Go ahead, I don't need your papers. I'll see your equipment gets on board."

An hour later the little nine-passenger Boeing landed at Hermosillo. An hour on the train took me to the principal Yaqui town, Vicam, in the middle of the desert, dry and hot, with unpaved streets. The Yaquis are a tall, beautiful, terribly proud people, famous warriors with a history of bloody encounters, first with Spaniards, and then with Mexicans. To appease them the Mexicans once recruited many of them into the Mexican army, but hostility continued, and occasionally rears its head even today. Besides their warrior reputation, they are immensely proud of their music and dance. Even today the Deer Dance (*Baile del Venado)* is the most brilliant dance of the Ballet Folklorico's repertory, Mexico's world-famous folk dance group.

Like the Tarahumaras, the Yaquis live in two worlds, pagan and Christian. But, unlike their neighbors, the two worlds merge: Both pre- and post-Hispanic arts are performed for Christian holy day fiestas. So, at any saint's day celebration you can hear both pre-hispanic music for the Deer Dance, as well as European violins and harps for the *pascolas*, the characters representing the coyote, the deer's enemy.

The Deer Dance is one of the most fascinating spectacles of Indian Mexico. The dancer dramatizes the plight of the deer as he grazes peacefully in the meadow, then his fear and anguish as he is cornered and killed by coyotes. Bare to the waist, the deer dancer wears an actual deer's head as a headdress, and below his knee-length pants, rows of dried butterfly cocoons emit a crackling sound as he whirls around. While he dances, the singer, seated on the ground, accompanied by wooden rasps and a water drum, sings poetic verses, warning the deer to seek safety. This water drum is a tin wash-basin partially filled with water in which a half-gourd floats; struck with a thin stick it makes a doleful, bass sound. Though this is a serious theme, the Yaquis inject fun wherever they can. The masked *pascolas* imitate the coyote's movement, howling like wild beasts as they run through the crowd. The following verses are fragments of the story:

The mountain grass moved
With the gently blowing breezes
And whistled softly.
It grows on the mountain top
And blows with the wind.
Deer, deer, deer,
Coyote is hunting you.
Plunge into the water,
He will not follow you there.

As I listened to the music and watched the lithe movements of the dancer, I once again thought how privileged I was to witness an enactment of an ancient art, a dramatization of perhaps ancient millennia-old mythology performed with skill and passion. For me it was a living document, one with a human face, more revealing of their culture than bones and pottery shards found in archeological mounds.

My fondest memory of the Yaquis is the final session before leaving. That evening, after the devil sun had descended behind the horizon, the entire community assembled in the town hall to help with translations of the texts. The governor explained: "We want to make sure everything is correctly written down." For hours we discussed the meaning of each song. As the night wore on, the temperature in the huge room rose to unbearable heights; the children fretted in their mothers' arms, and I thought I would suffocate. But not the Yaquis. They went home only after the last song had been put to rest. And I still have the original translations in my files, exactly as they dictated them, on the same (now yellowing) paper. The next day I boarded the Southern Pacific line to Guadalajara, slept the night in my bunk, caught the National train to Mexico City the next day, and despite a Jesuit's (very intelligent) futile attempt to convert me, arrived home safe and sound.

181

Those were to be my last weeks in Mexico until the 1960s. I stayed with Dasha and Paul Kirchhoff, was scared out of my wits by an earthquake, and said tearful goodbyes to my friends. The atom bomb had exploded, the war was over. My brother was safe and sound but it was news of my mother's illness that hurried my departure. It was June 1946, I had spent five years in Mexico and now I was going home to stay. Chenk met me at the Washington airport; we would try reconciliation.

***

Return to Mexico - 1960s

Shortly after return to New York from North Africa and Spain, *The New York Times* reported that Daniel de la Borbolla was in town for the Metropolitan Museum's inauguration of its newly-refurbished salons. As director of the Mexican Museum of Popular Art, he was among many foreign dignitaries invited to celebrate the reconstruction.

I immediately called the Mexican consulate. "How can I reach Dr. Borbolla?" I asked, and left my telephone number. Within a few hours Daniel called me. "I'm leaving for Mexico tomorrow morning," he said in his usual half-mocking tone. "Not before you see me," I almost shouted. Placating me, he said, "Well, I have an hour at five o'clock. Can you make it?" At five I was at the hotel; needless to say the hour stretched to four, the norm for any appointment with him. "Humph," he grunted disapprovingly, "Spain. What were you doing there?" "Research," I replied. "I'm not paying court to Franco." "But, you left your work half done in Mexico," he chided me. "Maybe I'll go back," I teased.

And I did, in the summer of 1964 with my sister Ruth, and my husband, Irving, my first trip there in 17 years. As the plane neared the Valley of Mexico, I could hardly see the land below for the entire area was shrouded in a huge yellow-gray cloud. "What is that?" I asked the stewardess in alarm. "Just the pollution", she said calmly and walked away to attend to more pressing problems. As the taxi sped us into town along the *periferico*, a new highway circling the city, I caught my first view of modern Mexico City, enveloped in murky fog and ringed with tall skyscrapers. I felt lost. The city was too big, too impersonal, too, too busy (soon to grow to gigantic proportions -- 20,000,000). But there, in the murky sunlight, were my old favorites -- the marbled Palacio de Bellas Artes and the graceful blue-tiled Sanborn's -- and it gladdened my heart. How wonderful to be back, how wonderful to wander once more down familiar streets, saunter leisurely through Alameda Park, and marvel at Cortez's elegant palace and the Cathedral, its facade as ornate as ever.

My friends were still there: Dasha, stunning as always, now married to handsome Raul Ugalde; Olga Costa and her husband Jose Chavez Morado, both fine painters, and many others. Borbolla and his wife Sol Arguedas invited me to dinner at their new house in San Angel, a spacious home furnished with the finest Mexican folk arts, and which was to be my home for decades to come. Only Waldeen was missing, gone to Cuba to form a modern dance group there.

We all got together at a party. We sang, ate and drank, as we had in the old days when we were all so young, when every day was an adventure, a time to flirt, to risk the dangers and pleasures of love. Most of all, I remember that party because I rediscovered a favorite song, *La Llorona*, about Mexico's legendary weeping woman. I had sung it for decades, its melancholy air haunted me, but one day it was gone; I couldn't remember a thing. I had heard it in 1942 sung by Chabela Villaseñor, a beautiful and gifted woman, the heroine of Serge Eisenstein's film "Thunder Over Mexico" and collector of songs from her native state Jalisco. "Chabela died a few years ago," said Dasha, "but ask Olga Costa, she knew all her songs." That night, Olga sang it just as I had heard it so long ago. This time I recorded it on my small Sony cassette recorder. I could have saved myself the trouble: years later I discovered I had recorded Chabela's singing *La Llorona* in 1942, and had forgotten all about it! I have honored her memory by including it, and three others, it in a recent CD of Mexican love songs. The voices in the last verse conclude with these unforgettable lines:

Cinco sentidos tenemos	We have five senses
los cinco los precisamos;	Five we are aware of
y los cinco los perdimos,	Those five we lose
cuando nos enamoramos.	When we fall in love
Ay, ay, ay, ay, ay, Llorona	Ay, ay, ay, ay, Llorona
Lloroncita, cielo lindo.	Lloroncita, heavenly beauty.

I had one more ghost to lay to rest: Juan Comas. It was with great trepidation that I went to his office in the Department of Anthropology at the National University. He greeted me at the door, probably as nervous as I was. I asked him about Camille, whom he had married; he asked about my family, what I was doing, how long was I staying, and then the visit ended. He walked me to the bus, apologized for not taking me home, and we said goodbye. As I left, I wondered how I could have fallen in love with such a dry stick. Nothing remained of my old feelings for him. What demon had possessed me in the first place? I never saw him again I was in Mexico in 1979 when he died, and I briefly renewed my friendship with Camille, but it never flowered: it simply withered on the vine. That part of my life was over.

I turned my mind to my own interests. My old friends --now the older generation-- filled me with dire rumors about the demise of folk and Indian cultures, and the baleful influence of American rock and roll, etc., etc. True, their teen-age sons were listening to Bob Dylan, the Beatles, and the Rolling Stones. But in the 1960s rock was more than entertainment; it was an expression of rebellion against society. Mexican university students, like our own and others in the world, were embroiled in political turmoil. Besides, and perhaps more important, while there had always been music for adults and children, rock was the first created specifically for teenagers; it did not displace any other music but simply filled a vacuum!

I toured the Folk Arts Museum with Borbolla. The museum was crammed with an astounding array of textiles, toys, furniture, jewelry, ceramics, copper and silver objects. "But Daniel," I said, "I was told the folk arts were in a terrible state, so how come this incredible array in your museum?" Borbolla looked perplexed. "Don't believe everything you hear," he said, "Since you've been here the government and banks have revived industries we thought dead and gone. On the other hand, that support has encouraged all sorts of new designs, new materials, new forms, new techniques." I noticed the museum was filled with buyers. "How's business?" I asked. "Very good," he said. "We even sell their things around the world."

"OK," I said, "I can see the folk crafts are flourishing, but what about music? Remember all the work I did in the 1940s, is it still alive? " "Now you've come back," he said, "that's what you'll have to find out for yourself."

Years before I had promised to return to the state of Michoacán, the scene of my first recording trip. It was there that I heard the music of the Purepecha Indians that inspired me to work in Indian areas. As soon as possible we boarded a bus, headed down the same highway I had traveled 22 years before, a narrow two-lane road with twisty hairpin curves that revealed breathtaking views of distant mountain ranges. My first sight of *Mil Cumbres* (the Thousand Peaks) with its layers of high peaks filled me with wonder. Arriving in Morelia, the state capital, we caught a second-class bus headed for Patzcuaro, loaded with Indians market-bound with huge baskets of produce and chickens. Halfway there the engine sputtered and died out, but a passing taxi picked us up and delivered us safe and sound to Patzcuaro. I had last seen it in 1942 and there it was unchanged -- mysterious, serene, cool and gray in the fading daylight.

Bits of history came back to mind. Five centuries earlier this lovely lake had been the center of the Purepecha empire, one of the great Mexican civilizations. It is said that the Aztecs, besieged by Spaniards, had sent envoys to Tzintzuntzan, the Purepecha capital, pleading for help; they were turned away. The Aztecs were everyone's enemy and Purepechas, like other tribes, were not disposed to rush to their rescue. But once Tenochitlan the Aztec capital fell, so did all the other minor civilizations.

Had the town changed since 1942? My first few moments were reassuring. Not even the cobblestones had been removed! In the market, seated on the ground were women selling their wares as in the past. How beautiful they looked in their black-and-blue-striped *rebozos*, gleaming coal-black hair braided with colored ribbons, their voluminous skirts girded at the waist with colorful woven belts. As of old, vegetables and fruit, freshly caught silvery whitefish and golden trout were attractively arranged in little piles around them. Nearby vendors were hawking woolen ponchos, black and green pottery, and finely-woven hats made from the lake's dry reeds. I wandered happily through the crowd. Yes, everything was the same!

I paid a visit to the new folk museum, a lovely colonial building with spacious exhibition rooms around a gracious patio. Teresa Davalos, the director, assured me that transistor radios, as well as the plethora of plastic items I had seen in the market, did not signify the death of folklore. "Look at this wonderful work," she said, guiding me to an exhibit of shining, hand-hammered copper articles, "They are made in the town of Santa Clara. Until a few years ago, it was a barren village, today it has a flourishing industry -- and that's only one example."

"But what about music?" I inquired. "That too is encouraged, continued Teresa, "there is more music, more dance groups, more composers than ever before. Every year we have government-sponsored festivals with rewards and prize money for the best performers. Everyone loves the money, of course, but it's also a matter of pride. Just to make sure I'm not imagining things, why not go out to Jaracuaro Island and see for yourself?"

A few days later, we hired a taxi to take us along the dusty, bumpy road around the lake, and then by dugout canoe to the island in the middle of the lake. The singers, instrumentalists, and composers I met there convinced me that I had stumbled upon a musical bonanza never imaged, not even in my wildest dreams.

That visit in 1964 was just the beginning. For the next few years I spent my summer and mid-winter holidays with my City College students recording in every Purepecha region. With no money of my own I was fortunate enough to get grants from the American Philosophical Society and help from the Governor of Michoacán, Agustin Arriaga. Of course, without the support of the people, mestizos and Indians alike, I never could have done a single thing. In the city of Uruapan, the entrance to the mountain-dwelling Purepechas, Arturo Macias, an architect and dedicated folklorist led me to musicians of the area. Every day they would come to Arturo's house to record their music, a gentle blind harpist, who earned his living in the marketplace playing for a peso ($.08) per song, a string trio that sang in a strange falsetto. The best by far was a trio of mestizo girls, the Pulido Sisters and their aunts, the Solorio Sisters, who sang Indian songs, and with whom I formed a long and affectionate friendship.

On my own, I found musicians schooled and unschooled everywhere in the area. For instance, the Bautista brothers, Joaquin the guitarist, and Francisco, the violinist, a graduate of the National Conservatory of Music, came from a family of musicians dating back to the 19th century. At that time their native town Paracho, famous for guitar manufacture, had a highly respected music school. Although the school no longer exists, the Bautista family still recalled with pride their musical past. I don't know exactly when the two most popular Purepecha song forms (the *pirecua* in 3/4 time, and the *abajeño* in 6/8 time) were created or by whom,) but I suspect no earlier than the 20th century; the form hasn't changed since then, just gained new words and music based on the old structures.

For years I had been recording music of the past, so-called traditional songs and instrumental styles reaching back into history. In Michoacán music was of the moment, old songs forgotten, new ones on everyone's tongue. The area's most prolific composer, Juan Victoriano of San Lorenzo, a village near Uruapan, expressed the principle clearly and succinctly: One day I said, "Juan, every time I come here I record your latest songs, but never those you wrote years ago. How come?" He looked surprised. "Señora," he replied, "why should I sing them? They've been sung already, even by the Pulido sisters" (the mestizo girls mentioned earlier). Although I admit there was some logic in his attitude, scholar that I am, I wanted to, record all his songs from the first to the last. I finally convinced him. Reluctantly, he disappeared into his house and returned a few minutes later with a sheaf of ruled notebooks. There, in those little dog-eared books, he had written the words of his songs in his own Indian language. He recalled the melodies by playing them on his violin, with the help of his friend on the guitar.

As weeks slipped into months, I realized that music in Michoacán was a full-fledged industry. Wherever and whenever we set up our recording machine, we were besieged by seemingly endless numbers of singers and guitarists eager to sing their own songs or somebody else's. Since we were the big show in town, the entire village turned out to watch. Everywhere we found dedicated performers, fussy, exacting, and disheartened when they gave a poor performance. Sometimes they sought us out at our headquarters and asked to be recorded again. "I sang badly yesterday when you were in my village," complained one singer. "Would you record my songs again?"

Of course, my students, university-trained, had to get used to principles different from their own. Sometimes they tuned the guitars for the Indian musicians, thinking to help them. "Oh, that sounds wonderful," they'd say admiring the students' know-how. Yet, as the recording session progressed and instruments went out of tune, they never bothered to retune. One day my student, Jody, tried a violin in what seemed to be a sorry state. "Nobody can play this thing," he said, struggling unsuccessfully to play a tune on it. Pretty soon its owner appeared, put the violin under his chin, drew the bow across the strings; it sounded just fine. Jody scratched his head. "Well, I'll be damned," he said, "I'd never have believed it if I hadn't seen it with my own eyes." At that point we decided not to improve Indian musicianship, and left well enough alone.

Like us, their composers vied with one another; "borrowing"

tunes from each other; or copying instrumental arrangements brought accusations of plagiarism. One day, as we prepared to leave Jaracuaro, I heard shouts behind me. I waited for a small group to approach. "Señora," they said, "we are from the family of Nicolas Suarez. Perhaps you have heard of him?" "Of course, "I said. "He was a famous songwriter in the 1920s, wasn't he?" Suarez had become quite well-known for his romantic songs. Invited to sing in Mexico City, he took fright at the noise of the city and hurried home, never to venture forth again. Wreathed in smiles at my knowledge of their relative's fame, they lodged their protest. "Do you know," they said accusingly, "that most of the songs sung at Antonio Cruz's house belong to our family? They robbed us of our property". I could only offer sympathy and assurance that proper credit would be given, now that everything was recorded on tape.

As I have described elsewhere, Mexican Indians love the theater, and Michoacán had its own variety. Juan Macarios Santos, a local school teacher from Jaracuaro, recounted the following incident: "The story is told," he said, "that many years ago, and who knows exactly when, the people of a certain town near Lake Patzcuaro were celebrating Holy Week with a Passion Play. One of their number was chosen as the Christ, and the onlookers acted out the part of the mob. They were so carried away by their part in the drama that they literally stoned to death the Christ-actor. It was a terrible thing, I tell you. The man's family complained to the authorities but they could do nothing. After all, they couldn't prosecute the entire village. The relatives were partially appeased when it was suggested that the man had died in a state of grace. It happened long ago, but people still talk about it."

Like elsewhere in the Spanish world since the middle ages, Patzcuaro celebrates the Nativity in a pageant called Pastorelas. As described by Macarios it is a pageant, a mixture of Bible stories, even sketches from The Thousand and One Nights. "On Jaracuaro

190

Island," he said, "where I was born, the Pastorelas is presented as a struggle between good and evil -- on one side adoring noble shepherds, on the other, seven black devils in black masks with fangs, long red tongues and red eyes, realistic enough to frighten the children out of their wits. "

Macarios' narrative, merely descriptive, avoided voicing a deeper meaning. However, one day, at Juan Victoriano's house in San Lorenzo, I witnessed a scene from the Pastorelas, revealing an unexpected side of Indian attitudes toward authority. First, three shy girls sang the special songs composed by Victoriano, then he recited the formal Spanish text, reading from a rented printed manuscript. Suddenly, the audience was convulsed in laughter. And no wonder; instead of taking the stiff, pompous lines seriously, he made fun of them, mocking upper-class manners.

One more event tickled my fancy. I have always noted the tact with which the Catholic Church deals with persistent pagan beliefs. Although Purepechas are more modern than the remote tribes I visited in the 1940s, they still cling to some truly pre-hispanic customs. In 1966, we arrived just in time for the festival of *Corpus Cristi,* a moveable Christian holiday which coincides with the onset of the rainy, i.e., planting season. One day, Indian authorities of the Island of Pacanda invited us to their celebration. On a bright Sunday morning in July, the community-owned launch picked us up at the Patzcuaro dock. With us was the officiating Catholic priest from Patzcuaro and a bevy of young girls from his parish, out for a good time. Upon landing, we went immediately to the incense-filled church where men and women kneeled on the cold stones of the church floor; dogs wandered disconsolately among the worshipers. Soon the priest, who had made the journey in shabby jeans rolled at the cuffs, appeared at the flower-bedecked altar, dressed in regal white satin and gold vestments for the Mass. Outside, the huge bells tolled, rockets swooshed aloft, while within

191

the church *alabanzas* (praise songs) were performed by high-pitched singers to the accompaniment of a harmonium.

When the Mass concluded, we all filed outside to witness a prehispanic planting ritual. Teams of bulls adorned with flowers and ears of seed-corn pulled ancient wooden plows around the earthen atrium, plowing furrows to plant symbolically, stalks of seed-corn. A hunter wearing a Hitler mask darted in and out of the crowd, acting the clown and grimacing at the children. Every now and then he would point his rifle at an armadillo shell dangling on a string.

As the pageant was taking place, the priest appeared from the church and led the procession along the furrowed lanes. Behind him walked the Indian women, solemn and barefoot, carrying lighted candles. Men carrying giant tissue-paper fish joined the line, and we brought up the rear. Rockets rent the air, and lines of fireworks, strung between trees, crackled in rapid-fire sequence, culminating in ear-splitting booms. Three bands played simultaneously, each one playing his own tune, oblivious of the others. And, of course, church bells tolled. Throughout the entire proceedings a basketball game was in progress on a nearby court. The boys paused for a moment, looked at the ceremony with disinterested eyes, and continued their game.

When the procession ended, I asked the young priest for an explanation. "First, let me assure you, the church doesn't interfere with these ancient rituals. Before the Spaniards, the Indians petitioned pagan gods for rain; today, as Catholics, they ask the Virgin." "And that hunter with the gun and armadillo shell, and the Hitler mask? What about him?" The priest smiled: "He's the entertainment, a dual character -- evil and comic at the same time; the armadillo he 'kills' is the embodiment of evil. He is the one dramatic personage of the fiesta; he is the philosopher, the commentator on life." "What kind of comments does he make?" I asked. "I don't know for sure because I don't understand the language," he concluded. Well, I'm still in the dark, but I imagine that the philosopher's targets were right on target, poking fun and laughing up his sleeve at authority.

While Indian culture has absorbed most of my attention, I have never lost interest in the songs and games of children -- all children, whatever their color or ethnic background. Adult songs are so serious, but the children -- they sing, they run, they jump, they dance, and make believe. No matter where I have traveled, I always recorded their songs and games. In Uruapan, I met the Illsley family, Americans who had settled there after World War II. Bundy, a tall rangy woman, and Walter had six children, five born in Mexico, and ran an excellent business of handwoven fabrics. I loved their house, an informal place where the children slept wherever they pleased and took their meals at odd hours, a kind of 24-hour, mostly self-service restaurant. Walter had been in China after the war and followed the route of Mao Zedong's triumphant army routing the Japanese. Bundy was the practical member of the family, and kept the household and business a going concern.

One day, Bundy suggested I record the neighborhood children who came to the house every day after school to play games and sing. Cathy, her 10-year-old, volunteered to be my assistant. The day I arrived with my equipment, Bundy went out into the street, blew a long whistle, and within 10 minutes the children came running. The bigger girls carried their younger siblings in their arms, all eager to sing. My heart melted at the sight: The girls were so pretty with their velvety brown skin, glistening black hair and snapping black eyes. Then I heard them sing. I couldn't believe my ears! Such perfection, such faultless ensemble! Had they rehearsed? "No way," said Bundy with finality, "that's how they sing every time they play together." We weeded out the tiniest girls and recorded the 10- to 12-year-olds. Cathy, proud of her authority, bossed them around. Later on I released an LP of their songs, which became very popular in New York schools.

The 1966 trip was the last recording expedition, but my relationship with the Purepechas has continued. In 1994, as I finished a lecture in Mexico City and was acknowledging applause, suddenly I heard my own recordings wafting through the auditorium. Down the center aisle came the Pulido Sisters, older by 29 years, but immediately recognizable. There they were, dressed in the same costume of years before, long skirts and white blouses, their long black hair braided with colored ribbons! I was stunned; it had been a complete surprise. They came on stage, we embraced, and the audience went wild with applause. Oh, how Mexicans love drama, the emotion, the embraces, the tears of joy! The sisters sang my favorite songs and I joined in, if not with the words, at least the melodies.

Since then I have returned to Michoacán many times, to lecture and to be honored at official ceremonies arranged by the National Indian Institute in Mexico City. "You will see all your old friends," I was told on one trip as we sped north on the highway to Michoacán. "We have an invitation for dinner at Juan Victoriano's house in San Lorenzo." My heart beat faster. How wonderful, I thought, I will be seeing him again, 30 years later! What will he look like, will we recognize each other? Questions just tumbled around in my head. A few hours later, we walked into the patio of his modest house and there, just inside the entrance, was Juan, his face wreathed in smiles. I later learned that he had spent a sleepless night in anticipation of my visit. We embraced like old friends; then we were surrounded by his children -- Cecilia and Pedro, now married; their spouses and their brood of children -- all wishing us well, waiting to embrace me too.

But suddenly Dominga, his beautiful wife, stood in front of me. Without saying a word she looked straight into my eyes, folded me in her arms, kissed me, and the tears rolled down her face. I cannot remember ever being so moved. In the 1960s, during the many recording sessions in her house, she had hovered in the background, sullen and resentful, maybe jealous. Now she was a presence to be reckoned with. During my entire stay in the region she attended every public event -- concerts, lectures, and ceremonies in my honor -- a dignified woman in full command.

My friendship with Juan and Dominga has spilled over into the next generation. One day, when I was in Uruapan, their son, Pedro, came to see me. He has ambitions to become a journalist, and is a most intelligent young man. "Pedro," I offered, "how would you like to be my assistant?" He practically glowed with excitement. "What do I have to do?" he asked. "In your childhood," I said, "who told you stories, say, about your family, about the village?" Pedro paused, thought a moment, and with his eyes twinkling, said, "I understand what you're saying. It was with my mother that I spent most of my childhood. She told me those stories." I pressed on: "What about sayings and proverbs?" "Heaps of them," he replied." "Well," I said, "Just set up your recording machine and your video, and go to work." For all I know that's what he is doing now.

Soon I discovered other women like Dominga, with a new attitude towards life. Years before, I had heard from a social worker stationed in a Purepecha village stories of sexual abuse of women by their men. Finally, the women threatened the men with violence if they didn't stop. I don't know the consequences of their act, but in the mid-'90s there was evidence of change; Indian women were starting their own enterprises, very determined to succeed.

Radio has invaded Indian communities. The National Indian

195

Institute has established more than a dozen radio stations in selected Indian districts. In the village of Cheran, half the station's staff were women. At a ceremony in my honor, a young Indian woman, the MC, translated my Spanish remarks instantly into Purepecha. Run by Indians, the station broadcasts not only news of community interest, but serves as a musical archive; composers record their new songs there. In addition, the young broadcasters open their listeners to the outside world. I even found some of the latest hits from the Caribbean, the Beatles and other 60s favorites.

While my research in those years was so successful, I cannot forget that the 1960s was a time of political turmoil everywhere in the world, as well as in Mexico. I was in Mexico both before and after the terrible events of 1968, when hundreds of students were mowed down at the National University, and hundreds more imprisoned. I arrived one day at the airport, only to be told that several of my old friends were among those jailed, and charges were never brought against them.

My friend Waldeen returned from her long stay in Cuba torn in her feelings (like so many Mexican artists and intellectuals) about the situation on the island. Although she had had signal success as the choreographer of "mass modern ballets," she was most distressed by the influence of Soviet advisors on Cuban cultural life. One story clings to my memory.

At a policy meeting of dancers, the Soviet representative made the following statement: "The modern dance is a creation of capitalist imperialism; the classical ballet is the true expression of the proletariat." "I couldn't believe my ears," Waldeen said. " The classical ballet was created originally for the pleasure of Russian royalty. Even today women are still depicted as dolls, and men are effeminate macho figures. Not my idea of a worker's ballet!"

196

Isthmus of Tehuantepec

1971-72, 1992

I next promised myself to return to the Isthmus of Tehuantepec. Twenty-six years later I was on my way, this time with two City College students, Jennifer Sookne and Meryl Gordon, and my son Peter, now in his first year of medical school. We went by train to Oaxaca City, and then by taxi along a new highway to the Isthmus. After hours through cool, spectacular mountain country, the road gradually wound down to sea level. How familiar it all looked -- the palm trees, the pineapple fields, the women in their long skirts carrying enormous baskets on their heads, the dust and the heat.

But wait! It wasn't the same. First, in the town of Tehuantepec we found a comfortable hotel with -- glory be -- a swimming pool and a decent restaurant. A walk into town revealed a sanitary new indoor market, an air-conditioned bank, and a record store blaring forth jazz, the Beatles, rock and roll, and the latest music from the Caribbean. Even the old train, El Tehuano, that crossed the Isthmus from Atlantic to the Pacific, wasn't in use any more.

I had a rush of memories. How could I forget that old, rattling train, the bustling, aggressive female traders and the strings of crawfish swinging from coat hooks. I recalled the conductor's frustration with the market women clogging the aisles with enormous baskets of produce. I can still hear the cries of women hawking their wares at every whistle-stop. All that cacophony of

197

voices, the pushing and shoving, the colorful disarray was nowhere to be seen in the 1970s.

Why am I so fascinated by this flat, dusty, hot, piece of land? I've seen more dramatic country elsewhere, yet it has a hold on me. Perhaps I am fascinated by the imposing archeological wonders, Monte Alban and Mitla, just outside of Oaxaca City. No, it's their songs that made me return. I could never forget that young girl in Tehuantepec in 1942 crooning *La Sandunga* and *La Llorona* as she rocked that little baby in her arms. On this trip, however, I recorded the songs in full, sung by Pablo Castañejo, a young man from Juchitan, to stunning guitar accompaniment. Surely, they are among the melodic treasures of the world, unforgettable love songs so sensual, so poignant, so filled with desire, yearning, and guilt. Yet, music is a male province, they are the poets, composers, and performers, but most of the songs are about love, love that is difficult to obtain and hold on to. Women know the songs but don't perform them in public; their musical sphere is within the Catholic Church.

I was obsessed by the words of *La Llorona:* who was this weeping woman, why the tragic words? I don't remember who told me the following story about the song's origin but I wrote it down in my diary. Here is my English translation of the tale: "A rich young man sets up a *casita* (a house for his mistress), for a simple poor girl with whom he shares his life. She has three children by him. However, his family marries him to a rich society girl, and the affair comes to an end. Maddened with grief, she stabs her children to death and then runs wildly through the streets of the city. To this day, people claim to see her as she wails for her children, and takes revenge on men.

Although a story of colonial times, there is a striking resemblance to a pre-hispanic tale. In that story a goddess dies

198

after the birth of her first child, and returns to earth to assault adults and children. Actually, none of the versions of *La Llorona* make reference to the legends, but the name has remained as a symbol of the tragic aspect of love, and of life itself. Here is one stanza from a version from the state of Jalisco, sung by Chavela Villaseñor in 1942:

Yo tenía una barca de oro	I had a golden boat
Para irme a la Havana	To take me to Havana
Y por seguirte, mi tesoro,	Because I followed you, my treasure
Perdí mi Guadalupana	I lost my Guadalupana

That last line means she lost the protection of the Virgin of Guadalupe, the patron saint of Mexico.

The next one is from the Isthmus, a rare verse sung for me by Pablo. It says:

Dicen que no tengo duelo	They say I do not mourn
porque no me ven llorar	Because they don't see my cry
hay muertos que no hacen ruido	The dead don't make noise
y es mas grande su pena.	But their sorrow is greater

But the people, they were as fascinating as the music. First of all, they didn't look like the rest of Mexico. Scattered among the brown Indian faces were blue eyes, blond hair, fair skin -- visible signs of traffic with other people. In the 19th century the French were there when Napoleon's stooge Maximilian ruled Mexico, then other Europeans and Americans came with hopes of building the canal there. That never happened, investors pulled out, as the canal was ceded to Panama.

199

But, it's the women of the Isthmus that catch the eye. They are easily the most elegantly dressed women in Mexico. Like Japanese ceremonial kimonos, their holiday clothes, fashioned of embroidered satins and velvets, cost a fortune. But, to this day, the most treasured item is the necklace of American gold coins, obtained at the beginning of the century, for God knows what price. Like Lorelie Lee, they believe that diamonds -- or gold in this case -- are a girl's best friend.

The most distinctive part of their costume, however, is a spanking white headdress fashioned of a child's starched and pleated lace dress believed to have originated in China. The Tehuanas put their heads through the open neck and the starched lace forms a halo around the face; or, they arrange it on their heads so that the pleats fan out in a sweeping cascade down their back.

Those women are also powerful figures in the economy. They are the chief vendors in the market. There is nothing unusual about that; women the world over run the marketplace; however, in the Isthmus they own their businesses. Some are wealthy landowners and run profitable cafes. What a contrast from the rural women I have known, endlessly patting out tortillas, always pregnant, always with a baby on the knee.

Isthmus women waste no time on pleasantries. One day, as I walked among the stalls in the Tehuantepec market, I was hailed by a vendor. "Come buy my *calabazas*" (squash), she urged. "I can't use them," I said, "I don't live here." She bristled. "*Jodete*" (go fuck yourself), she said, dismissing me with a wave of her hand.

One hot afternoon my students and I were invited to a dance mainly attended by women and children. Under a canopy shielded from the blazing sun, the orchestra blared forth all the songs I remembered from the '40s: La Sandunga, La Llorona, La

Petenera. The women danced with each other, their hips swaying from side to side, gliding effortlessly across the dance floor, ignoring completely the rhythm of the music. On our arrival the dancing and music stopped, and everyone crowded around us, plying us with questions: "Are all these young people your children?" one old woman asked me. "Are you going to live here, wear our clothes, and learn our language?" Unlike the kids in the center of town, anxious to earn pennies from tourists, these women had no interest in learning English. A moment later, a toothless old woman was teaching us our first Zapotec words: "*Tu lalu?*" (What's your name).

We exchanged views. "Do you know," I asked, "about the women's liberation movement in the United States?" "We've heard," they said, "and it's about time we had one here." Another woman explained the life of women exactly as most lived it: "Sure," she said. "We all work together, men and women; in the morning we prepare breakfast, do the washing." She flexed her emaciated arms. "Then comes the ironing and sweeping." Here she jumped out of her chair, swinging her arms to show the broom sweeping across the floor. "Then comes the night," she continued. "That's for...." She grinned, leaving the sentence dangling in the air. Crooking her finger, she poked each child in the navel.

Unlike other Indians, the Zapotec women I met spoke openly about their intimate lives, about men, marriage, even sex. "What month are you in?" I asked innocently of a woman with a swollen belly. She smiled and shook her head, obviously embarrassed by my question. "No, no, she's not pregnant," one woman broke in. "It's her husband. They've been married for seven years, and she's got nothing to show for it. He's got no balls!" She laughed, showing her pink gums, until a fit of coughing stopped her. The other women looked sympathetically at the young woman and shook their heads. In this society, a woman without children is on the bottom of the social ladder.

So, here I was in a part of Mexico where women are not housebound, but in the market earning a living, and sharing household tasks with their men. Yet, sexual relationships were exactly like the rest of Mexico: in the weeks spent in the Isthmus I heard enough stories about unfaithful and irresponsible men to fill a book; women are expected to be monogamous, while men are free to sleep with whomever. However, sex before marriage is common, and illegitimate children are not stigmatized.

One night after a long recording session, as we cooled off in the hotel garden, I asked a young musician, Benjamin Betanzas: "What about *machismo* in the Isthmus?" "Yes," he admitted, "it's here because a man has to have respect. If a wife runs away, the husband finds her, beats her up, and sometimes even kills her. What other satisfaction does a man have?"

What came as a real surprise, however, was women's attitude towards homosexuality, something I was to learn on my last visit to the area, 20 years later. Once more in the Isthmus, with Mexican friends, Victoria Eugenia Landeros, a gifted young fashion designer, and Joaquin Huerta, an economist and photographer, we were invited by the Juchitan Cultural Center to a lunch in my honor. We met the leading poets and musicians, and received tapes of their most recent songs. As we dined on the Isthmus specialty, roast iguana (which tastes like chicken but is bonier), the talk turned to women. "Oh," said a young musician, "our women are remarkable, strong, intelligent, so smart." Without raising my voice, as innocently as possible I asked, "Then why don't your women have the same sexual privileges you men have?" I may as well have dropped a bomb. Later, back in Mexico City, Victoria Eugenia gleefully described their response to all her friends, "*Se quedaron con la boca abierta y no dijeron ni una palabra*" (They remained with their mouths open and didn't utter a word).

Until recently homosexuality was a taboo subject, something to sweep under the rug. I don't remember it as a topic of conversation in Mexico until one day at wedding ceremony in Juchitan. Tehuanas wearing their gala clothes were seated in row of benches under a huge tent; the men were scattered here and there, most of them in the back row, more like onlookers than invited guests. The band was playing and the dancing was in full swing. Suddenly, a beautiful ornament hanging from the rafters opened up like the petals of a flower; a live dove flew out, flapped its wings and flew off into the blue sky.

Later I learned that the designers of these lovely effects were the homosexuals of Juchitan. Marinella Miamo, an Italian anthropologist, a long time student of the Isthmus, explained: "They are the artists of the city. They design everything from the wedding decor to *huipil* embroidery. Some are poets, some composers and musicians or painters; they're a very talented lot." "How do people feel about them?" I asked, totally perplexed. "It depends on who you talk to," Marinella said. "Mothers of homosexuals have no trouble; they are a woman's security. Some marry and have children of their own, but most stay at home, take care of their siblings and their mothers when their husbands leave them, get sick, are too old to work, or are widowed. We know they introduce young boys to sex, but even this doesn't seem to bother the women. I don't know what will happen now that AIDS has come here; maybe people won't be so accommodating."

"How about lesbians?" I asked. Marinella shook her head. "Oh, no. Women don't like them at all because they don't have children." She continued: "There is plenty of tension here between men and women. Women complain because men spend their time drinking in the cantina with their pals, or fooling around with other women." She paused, sipped her coffee, and said, "Much as they love their homosexual sons, they really want girls. I've seen mothers take their five-year-olds to market. By the time they're 10, they know all the tricks of the trade."

"One more question, Marinella, " I persisted, "With all the economic power women have here, why I haven't seen a single woman in local government? They're all men." She laughed and shrugged her shoulders. "Well, I always tell them they should run for office but they say politics is an ugly business, so we let the men run it." "But suppose they have complaints," I asked, "what do they do then?" "Plenty," she said, "When a man beats up one of them, they all go to City Hall to protest. You can imagine what happens when a gang of angry Tehuanas storms City Hall demanding their rights; the politicians do exactly as they are told. I don't know how long that situation will last, but that's the way it is now."

Not the least of my activities on my last visit to the Isthmus was renewing some old friendships. Soon after arriving we located the home of Milo Cortes, the leader of the area's best band, one with a remarkable marimba player. Yes, that was his house, his name was outside on the door. I knocked, and a young woman answered. "Please," I said, "does Milo Cortes live here?" She looked hard at me. "I am Henrietta Yurchenco -- I was here many years ago and recorded his band."

"I remember you," she cried, throwing her arms around me, "You came with your son and your students!" In a moment, Milo and the rest of his family came rushing in, his wife, grown-up children, their spouses and assorted grandchildren. We were drawn into the house. They asked a million questions: Where we were staying, and wouldn't we all stay there with them, they have enough hammocks for all of us to sleep in, and we could go on picnics together, and how was my son? "Oh, you have two grandchildren, how wonderful, will you bring them here soon?"

It was the kind of welcome one only dreams of. They had remembered us as a happy time in their lives. What more could I ask of my life and work? Though we didn't stay with them, we ate together, went on a picnic, swam in a swimming hole ringed by lush tropical growth, broiled freshly-caught fish and seafood on an old-fashioned brazier, and enjoyed their warm affection and genuine concern.

It was now time to leave. On our last day, Victoria Eugenia, Joaquin and I headed out to nearby Salina Cruz, a town on the Pacific coast, now bustling with activity, an ugly, industrial city. We searched for the little restaurant where I had eaten an incomparable fish stew, a kind of Mexican bouillabaisse, but it was gone. It looked like any of our contaminated towns back in the States.

Victoria Eugenia, Joaquin and I sauntered along the long, sandy beach that stretched for miles along the coast. In the distance we could see shadowy freighters. The three of us stood silently at the water's edge, our arms around each other, and watched the rippling waves as they broke on the beach. Then, slowly, we walked back to the waiting taxi.

***

12-In native dress, on a trip to Oaxaca City, Oaxaca, Mexico. *Photo: Basil Yurchenco, 1942.*

13-First recording trip to Patzcuaro, Michoacán, Mexico.
Photo: Bill Miller, 1942.

14-Close friend Seki Sano, actor and film director, Mexico, 1944.

15-Close friend, Waldeen, dancer. *Photo: Foto semo.* "For Chenk: With much love -- and a Merry Christmas!...also many happy New Years yet to come...Waldeen, Mexico [City], December 11, 1945."

16-Friend and mentor, Dr. Daniel Rubin de la Borbolla. Mexico, D.F. 1944.

17-First field grip to record Purepecha Indians. Young boys and girls being recorded. Michoacán, Mexico. *Photo: Bill Miller, 1942.*

18-Benjamin Apan and his wife Alicia; Sol Rubin de la Borbolla, Director Museum of Popular Culture, Mexico; D.F.; Henrietta Yurchenco; unknown person; and Pedro Victoriano, Mexico, 1996.

19-A friendly *gobernador* of the Cora playing a drum and 3-holed reed flute. Jesus Maria, Nayarit, Mexico. *Photo: Agustin Maya, 1944.*

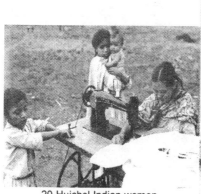

20-Huichol Indian women learning to use the sewing machine. Jalisco, Mexico. *Photo: Agustin Maya, 1944.*

21-Huichol Indian. Jalisco, Mexico, 1944.

22-Henrietta Yurchenco, Señor Bonilla, Chief, Dept.of Education Mussion; Huichol shaman; and Agustin Maya. Huilotita, Jalisco, Mexico. *Photo: Agustin Maya, 1944.*

23-Morning after an all-night singing session presided over by the Huichol shaman and members of the small mountain community. Huilotita, Jalisco, Mexico. *Photo: Agustin Maya, 1944.*

24-Community photo after Huichol curing ceremonies. Includes members of the Mission of the Department of Education of Mexico. Henrietta Yurchenco seated in front, second from right. Huilotita, Jalisco, Mexico. *Photo: Agustín Maya, 1944.*

25-Henrietta Yurchenco and the only mestizo family family of farmers living adjacent to community of Seri Indian fishermen and hunters. Desemboque, Sonora, Mexico. *Photo: Agustin Maya, 1944.*

26-Henrietta Yurchenco, Agustin Maya (holding camera), and Maria Luz, a Seri woman who sold marihuana but very smart. Desemboque, Sonora, Mexico. *Photo: Agustin Maya, 1944.*

(Above) 27-Two Seri sisters. Desemboque, Sonora, Mexico. *Photo: Agustin Maya, 1944.*

(Left) 28-Tall beautiful Seri woman. Desemboque, Sonora, Mexico. *Photo: Agustin Maya, 1944.*

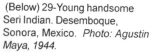

(Below) 29-Young handsome Seri Indian. Desemboque, Sonora, Mexico. *Photo: Agustin Maya, 1944.*

30-Tarahumara country scene. Chihuahua, Mexico. *Photo: Agustin Maya, 1946.*

31-A Catholic church in Cora territory. Jesus Maria, Nayarit, Mexico. *Photo: Agustin Maya, 1944.*

32-Tarahumara Indians on a mission on behalf of candidates seeking political office. Chihuahua, Mexico. *Photo: Agustin Maya, 1946.*

33-Landscape -- mountain area. Tarahumara region. Guachochi, Chihuahua, Mexico. *Photo: Agustin Maya, 1946.*

34-Tarahumara Shaman with rattle.
Baquiriachi, Chihuahua, Mexico. *Photo:*
Agustin Maya, 1946.

35-Tarahumara Indian drummer.
Guachochi, Chihuahua, Mexico.
Photo: Agustin Maya, 1946.

36-An Ancient bow and arrows used by Tarahumara
Indians. Guachochi, Chihuahua, Mexico.
Photo: Agustin Maya, 1946.

37-Tarahumara Indian maize planter with plow. Baguiriachi, Chihuahua, Mexico. *Photo: Agustin Maya, 1946.*

38-Lake Patzcuaro, Michoacán, Mexico. *Photo: John H. Greene, 1942.*

39-Notable Purepecha composer, Juan Victoriano, San Lorenzo, Michoacán, Mexico, 1965.

40-Juan Victoriano, San Lorenzo, Michoacán, Mexico, 1997.

41-Henrietta Yurchenco with Juan Victoriano and his wife Dominga. San Lorenzo, Michoacán, Mexico, 1985.

42-Henrietta Yurchenco, Juan Victoriano, and son during recording session. San Lorenzo, Michoacán, Mexico. *Photo: Joaquin Huerta, 2002.*

43-Peter Gold, Henrietta Yurchenco, and musicians during a recording session. San Lorenzo, Michoacán, Mexico. *Photo: Paige Lyon, 1965.*

44-Henrietta Yurchenco broadcasting at radio station IMER, Mexico City. *Photo: Joaquin Huertta, Fall 1998.*

45-Henrietta Yurchenco with the famous Pulido Singers, performers of Indian Purepecha songs, with their brother. Uruapan, Michoacán, Mexico, 1997.

46-Musicians from Oaxaca, Mexico participating in a National Festival in Mexico City, 1992.

47-Henrietta Yurchenco and a friend with a Flamenco singer. Granada, Spain, 1953.

Chapter Four – Spain

1953-54

I had always admired Chenk's considerable creative gifts. He was a superb draftsman, a fine painter and sculptor. Unfortunately, he drove me to distraction. Ever since his espousal of Wilhelm's Reich's theory of the orgasm and its unmistakable aura of male supremacy, I felt imprisoned, my every word and action dissected. As my desperation increased I knew I had to escape. Once again I acquired some piano students and taught at several nursery schools. Finally I saved enough money to make my move.

Peter and I sailed for Spain in the summer of 1953 when he was five years old. Five days later we stood on the deck as the ship sailed up the long stretch of the Portuguese coastline leading to Lisbon. The sight of fishermen in their gondola-like boats, the porpoises that frolicked alongside the boat, leaping out of the water like graceful dancers, set my heart racing. It was all so different, so new, so fascinating. But when we approached the dock where hundreds of people awaited our arrival, I was sorely disappointed: they looked just like us Americans, the same faces, the same clothes. What had I expected, anyway, two-headed humans with webbed feet?.

The next day we disembarked at La Linea, the Spanish port near Gibraltar. I hired a taxi to take us to a nearby coastal village for a week of complete leisure. We spent the long sunny days on the beach hiding from the fierce Mediterranean sun in our rented cabaña, watching the Spanish men saunter along in their pajamas, the accepted beach attire, and swimming in transparent waters now green, now blue and purple. Nights Peter and I wandered to the town square to watch the girls do circle games. Sometimes we joined in, for they were like those in Mexico, sometimes we went to the movies at 10 p.m. and treated ourselves to ices at 1a.m. And then to bed. I will confess it was a novel schedule for us brought up on "early to bed, early to rise makes a man healthy wealthy and wise" but we adjusted easily. We also had to adjust to a new eating schedule, not our customary three meals a day, but many little ones: an early continental breakfast, a late morning snack, a 1p.m. aperitif served with shrimp fresh off the broiler (Peter had a strawberry milkshake, a big comida at 3, a post-siesta 5 p.m. coffee and pastry, a light supper at 10 or 11, and at 1a.m. the ices mentioned above. Yes, this life agreed with me.

But one week of leisure at the seashore was all I could take. The itch to explore, to look below the surface was still with me. My first gesture in that direction was a trip to Granada, whose defeat by the Catholic Monarchs in 1492 brought the end of Islamic rule in Spain. Happily, we wandered up the tree-lined path of the Alhambra, the hill that leads to the Moorish palaces. Except for the tinkling sound of rushing water from twin streams on either side of the road, a deep silence prevailed. The tall leafy trees formed a canopy high above us, rays of sunlight filtered through the darkness. Surely it is an enchanted place; I seemed to hear the sighs and whispers of long departed poets and lovers who, like us, had wandered along its paths. In our ascent we passed Manual de Falla's house and I was reminded of the sensuality of his "Nights in the Gardens of Spain". We stopped to rest at the fountains, *El Pimiento* and *El Tomate*. Later I was told, "Ah señora, it is the most romantic place in the world; everyone falls in love here. "

But nothing had prepared me for my first sight of those ancient monuments. Unlike ornate European facades, the outer walls were unadorned flat surfaces. Yet within, there was opulence

208

beyond compare, the walls carved with lacy designs as intricate as Persian rugs. Even more luxurious and voluptuous was the Generalife, the summer palace. Once these rooms had been decorated with damask, silks, carved furniture and exquisite pottery, once the music of ouds and melodious pipes filled the air. Though empty and silent now, the bubbling fountains and sculpture were still there, testimony to a world now gone forever.

Presently Peter and I stopped before a plaque attached to a palace wall: Washington Irving had lived there in the early 19th century while writing "Tales of the Alhambra." Legend has it that Irving found the Gypsies encamped in the old rooms, surrounded by rags, the walls blackened from their charcoal braziers. Years later the Spanish authorities chased them away, and restored the rooms to their original splendor.

But our attention wandered from the Moors to the present. We spent four delicious days at the former convent of San Francisco, once occupied by monks, now a government-operated hotel. No sign of poverty and sacrifice here, the monastery had been a paradise of polished woods, terraced gardens, spacious patios, gushing fountains, and an incomparable view of the Valley of Granada. Though once a Christian retreat, its brass ornaments, luminous pottery and rich hangings were reminders of Granada's Moorish times. And best of all, the hotel kitchen served the finest cuisine in the country, delicate crayfish, broiled fish in almond sauce, and aromatic red wines. Our stay was short-lived because a few days later the son of the French president claimed our rooms, and we found rooms in a modest *pension*.

As our first sally away from tourist sites, we saw our first performance of flamenco at "El Albaicin", the gypsy quarters. It was dreadful, a mediocre show presented before unknowing tourists. The second performance, this time at a cafe, La Chirimia, on the edge of town, only slightly better, at least was down to earth, and eye opening. La Chirimia, famous since the last century when flamenco was in its apogee, was now dark and dingy; it was also a whore house (which is why it was shunted off on the edge of town, out of sight of respectable Granada citizens). I met the chief prostitute, a handsome and intelligent woman in her 40s who laughingly claimed she had slept with everyone from the prime minister down. I returned there several times with Peter, who sat in her lap while we talked. She regaled me with gossip about her lovers, stories about the flamenco greats at La Chirimia. But she was also a serious woman. "Believe me, señora," she said, "García Lorca was murdered by the Guardia Civil in front of the Cathedral while he prayed. They hated him because he wrote the truth about them in his plays and his poetry. And then they threw his body into a common grave outside of town." She sighed, "*Ay, Federico, que poeta tan grande!*" (Oh, Federico, what a great poet.)

She went on and on. "Listen," she said to me, "if you're going to Madrid, I can give you a letter to the Minister of Culture; he'll treat you well. After all, I do have some influence with my ex-lovers." I didn't accept her offer, but I appreciated the thought. Sometimes I would see her at the main cafe in Granada; she was discreet, passed my table without even looking at me. La Chirimia and the outside world were two distinct realms, and she kept them separate.

Granada gradually became familiar, the streets, shops and cafes thronged with people going about their daily routines. But the ghosts of a past, though hidden, still haunted the city, palpably and passionately alive. I came to know Sr. Arqueada, who lived in a beautiful old house with a fine rare book library and several vintage

210

string instruments, among them a few Stradivarius. Later I was told he had acquired this fortune when, as tax collector during General Franco's dictatorship, he imposed heavy fines on the wealthy with taxes in arrears; they bought him off by giving him their treasures. When I met him in 1953, he was a respected citizen, lending his instruments for the yearly music festival. People whispered about the nasty ways he acquired his booty, but left him alone, letting bygones be bygones. Despite his questionable past, Arqueada was an admirer of García Lorca. While his wife plied Peter with sweets, he led me to the garden wall, overlooking the magnificent Valley of Granada dotted with slender cypress trees and meadows of myriad shades of green. "This was Federico's favorite spot," he said pensively. "He came here often, and when he spoke, it was sheer poetry." He sighed and shook his head. Like Arqueada, I met many that year in conflict about the Civil War and its aftermath, the dictatorship of Francisco Franco.

After weeks in Granada, armed with letters of introduction, Peter and I, now joined by Maga, an American architect, left for a trip to the Alpujarra, the southern mountain range. Just as we approached Orgiva, the end of the line, I spied the only other passenger on the bus, a pleasant-looking man in his 30s. "Do you know this man?" I said pointing to the name on the envelope. "Madam," he said, "that letter is addressed to me." That was the beginning of a wonderful friendship with the town doctor.

Orgiva, a one-horse town with no hotel or restaurants, had only one claim to distinction: a beautiful tower built by Moors escaping Granada after its defeat in 1492. Life was uneventful, one day like the next. Daily, the old men gathered at the town's only cafe for *jerez* (sherry), a game of checkers, and gossip; it was a closed circle, outsiders excluded. The doctor, however, saved our lives. His house became our auxiliary hotel; we showered there, ate there, and spent evenings with his friends, like him, intellectuals with a job to do but bored with provincial life.

From them we learned some local customs: mornings we breakfasted at the cafe, each day we were told our bill was paid, but not by whom. We never saw the faces of the men who daily had their coffee at the bar because their backs were turned towards us. But one day, one of them, a friend of the doctor, turned around, and bowed to me. I nodded my head in thanks. That night I asked the doctor. "Why the secrecy?" "Señora, it's a delicate matter," he said, exploding with laughter, "like going to the bathroom. You don't announce it, you just go."

But more was to come, an unexpected journey. One day, the chief engineer of a power plant under construction in the nearby mountains invited us to visit him at the site. The next morning a company official picked us up in his car, and we took off for a bumpy trip through the mountains. As we climbed and climbed, we passed several neat tree-lined villages. "Who are these people?" I asked. "They don't look Andalusian." Ah," said our genial guide, "so you noticed. After victory at Granada, Isabel and Fernando allowed the remaining Moors to settle in this area. A few years later, they changed their minds, pushed the Moors to the coast where boats took them to Africa. Then they brought down peasants from northern Spain, gave them land, and they've been here ever since. That was common policy after the Reconquest."

Finally, we arrived at the campsite. Good heavens, I thought, it looks like the surface of the moon, nothing but bare hills, not a tree, not even a bush in sight! David, the engineer of the works, awaited us. "First we'll take you to the mountain top to see the work in progress When you come down we'll have lunch." We hopped into a cable car and were instantly lifted upward at an alarming angle. Soon we leveled off, and now on a lesser incline, we rose higher and higher. In the distance, we could see Mulhacen, the highest peak in Spain, not as high as the Alps, but impressive nonetheless. At the top, after viewing the construction, refreshed by a cold drink we headed down to the campsite.

David led us up the stone steps to his house. The spacious terrace was a garden, lined with potted plants -- fragrant jasmine, dwarf lemon and orange trees, long-stemmed carnations and ivy clinging to the walls. The cook served a delicious meal with wine for every course. Peter and Maga, spirited away by the workmen, spent the afternoon eating sweets and playing games while David and I had coffee on the terrace. "Tell me," I said, "how did you do it? Yours is the only house in this barren wasteland." "There was nothing here when I arrived," he began. "For six months I lived in a tent just like my workmen, we brought food up here, and did the best we could. Meanwhile, this house was gradually carved out of the rock. Gradually I brought my books, my easel and paints, my guitar, record player and radio, all the things I love. In the winter I often spend months here by myself." He paused. "Of course, without my housekeeper and her husband," he continued, " I couldn't have survived. "

We drank our coffee and brandy in silence, my gaze constantly wandering to the barren landscape. "Would you like me to read some poetry, perhaps *El Romancero Gitano*?" he asked. "Yes, I would love that," I said, and sank back on the cushioned sofa and surrendered myself to the magical words of the great, tragic poet. Now I was to hear Lorca's words in his own territory, read aloud, and in the original Spanish. As I listened I realized what had seemed obscure and abstract in the English translation in New

York was suddenly clear. Lorca was rooted in the Spanish earth, especially his native Granada; he knew its folklore, history, its customs -- and its blemishes. No Spaniard has written about Gypsies, or women, with more compassion or understanding. I shall never forget that afternoon on the stone terrace of this obscure place in southern Spain.

It was in a reflective mood that I came back to Orgiva. The following week we spent exploring the little Alpujarra villages where stark white houses huddle together on high mountain cliffs. Lorca himself had once collected songs there, and now I collected them again. In one village I rounded up the children to sing, setting up my small battery-run recording machine in the middle of the street. Peter, my able assistant, shouted at those who had only come to watch with, "My mother is recording." And they all quieted down though they understood not a single English word. They sang these suggestive lines:

De los cuatro muleros (3)	Of the four mule-drivers,
Mamita mia	Mother mine,
Que van al rio (2)	Who go to the river
El de la mula torda (3)	The one with the gray mule
mamita mia	Mother mine
es mi mario (2)	Is my husband
Ay, que me equivocao (2)	Sorry, I made a mistake
Que el de la mula torda	The one with the gray mule
mamita mia	Mother mine,
es mi cuñao	Is my brother-in-law

The recording sessions ended abruptly when a few days later I met some of the girls on the street. "We can't sing for you anymore," they said, "our parents think it wrong for us to sing for strangers." Being in a hurry I had regrettably not asked their parents' permission. Reluctantly we returned to Granada.

A few days later we headed for Fuengirola, a coastal village known for its fandangos, Spanish dance-songs popular with Gypsies. The blue-green Mediterranean was a soothing sight after the rugged bone-dry Alpujarra. At City Hall we presented a letter of introduction to the mayor. "Welcome," he said, "we don't have hotels, but there is a *pension* we can recommend." He motioned to his assistant, an unsavory character who looked like a *pistolero*. "He'll take you there." We followed him to a tall structure situated on the beach. "This," he informed us, "was once a hotel, but now the only tenant is Isabel, who runs a *pension* on one floor."

Happily, the elevator worked, and took us up to the eighth floor. A knock on the door, and in a moment, framed in the doorway was an enormously fat woman surveying us with ill-disguised hostility. "The mayor says," our guide began apologetically, "he would be grateful if these people could stay with you for a few days." She glared at us, not very friendly, but asked us in. "I have only two rooms," she said firmly but politely, "and I warn you, there is little in the marketplace, so meals will be very simple." I assured her that the arrangement was most satisfactory; Peter would sleep in my bed, and Maga could have the other room.

The first day passed without incident. The next morning I awoke to find Peter gone. Hurriedly I searched for him. No, he hadn't escaped down the stairs. Finally, I found him in the dining room, a lovely glassed- in terrace that looked out to sea. Seated atop pillows piled high on an armchair, a bib around his neck, his face and hands squeaky clean, Peter was eating his breakfast,

215

totally in the clutches of Isabel. She sat opposite him, regarding him sternly. "Eat your breakfast," she said, and Peter obeyed, not understanding a word of Spanish. "You see," she said accusingly, "he obeys me; his hands and face are clean, and he eats what I tell him to eat." It was a claim I couldn't make; if I tried the same tactic, I would have heard screams of protest. I acknowledged her superiority in these matters.

Isabel and her husband lived a quiet life and made a meager living running the *pension*. Once a successful businessman, he gave it up because, according to Isabel, he could not bear the long periods away from her; he retired and they moved to Fuengirola. His days were as predictable as the rising and setting of the sun, spending most of the day with his male friends for coffee, a brandy, and a game of cards. I never saw him vary that schedule, day in and out.

But the outward calm hid a real tragedy; Isabel could not bear children. To add to her misery she suffered from a painful liver ailment. As the days stretched into weeks, Peter became her surrogate child, her solace during the frequent attacks of pain. She smothered him with kisses and embraces so fierce they fairly took his breath away. He knew she loved him, and he obeyed her without complaint.

Isabel's warning about her poor table was a gross exaggeration. A magnificent cook, she transformed even the most insignificant ingredients into gourmet delights. Her vegetables a la vinaigrette and meat-filled squid in a saffron sauce are a few creations still remembered with particular relish.

The beach was a friendly place and we easily made friends with a group of vacationing girls from Madrid. Part of the fun was sharing mid-morning snacks with them. Though fishermen sold most of the daily catch in the market, they kept the fat sardines for themselves. Over small driftwood fires they broiled a half dozen sardines at a time, wrapped them in brown paper, and sold them to the vacationers. Our fingers dripping with fat, we ate even the delicate bones, and washed them down with cold, pale *manzanilla* wine. It was culinary heaven.

Sometimes we hired a boat, and rowed out to distant beaches to hunt octopus. I watched with admiration as our strong-armed friends speared them to death, and then beat them to soften their powerful muscles. Even when properly broiled, the meat was too tough for my tender gums. Nevertheless, I loved swimming out to sea to see schools of tropical fish in rows beneath the water's surface -- pink fish on top, yellow and black striped below them, lower yet, speckled brown and yellow, and even lower, luminous ivory fish.

Later, after lunch and a siesta, the girls would assemble in my room. On the beach I offered them cigarettes, always refused. In my room everyone accepted them. Within minutes my room looked like an opium den, dense with smoke. And then the confidences began. "Why do all the women wear black?" I asked. The girls explained: "In Spain you wear black four years when a mother or father dies, and less time for all the other relatives. Since the periods of mourning run consecutively, a woman can wear black most of her life, if she's unlucky." "How come you girls don't wear black," I asked. They laughed. "That's because nobody knows us here. The same thing goes for smoking."

In Fuengirola I had my first opportunity to see flamenco in a country setting. Unlike the commercial Gypsy entertainment in

Granada, the Fuengirola dancers were ordinary people having a good time. The recording session began quietly enough, guitarists accompanied the singers. The dancers, their arms upraised in graceful curves, did simple steps and intricate *taconeo*, the rhythmic heel and toe typical of flamenco dance. As the hours sped by they forgot about me, I don't think they even noticed my departure. The next day, I heard the party lasted the whole night long. Poor Peter, he fell asleep in someone's arms, and finally I carried him home.

We returned to Granada. It was autumn, the first rains had fallen and nearby mountains were now snow-capped. In the evening we sauntered through the streets stopping at sidewalk push carts to buy fresh roasted almonds, and the huge, bright orange, juicy persimmons found only in Spain.

But my life as a tourist soon ended as I settled into the life of the city. I began to notice the underfed, undersized orphans on the streets, heard stories about families torn asunder by political differences, all consequences of the Civil War and its aftermath. "My father," said a friend, "was a Republican, but I was on the other side. I was a young hot-head and really believed Franco would save us from Communism. When I was 18 I joined the Blue Battalion, fought on the Russian front, and lived to regret it. The Spanish soldiers were so brutal, so murderous, I was completely disillusioned. I returned to Spain, and never got mixed up in politics again. My father and I, though we lived in the same house, didn't talk to each other for 25 years."

Then I had a disturbing encounter with a local doctor. Peter had a fall, and when his knees became infected I took him to a local pediatrician. The cruel treatment he prescribed, alcohol on open sores, turned me against him. Finally, he gave Peter a penicillin shot, and I calmed down somewhat. I decided on a frontal attack. "I hear you are a staunch supporter of the present regime, " I said. "Oh no," he protested, "you have it all wrong." And then he told me his story.

He had been an army doctor, an open Republican even after Franco came to power. "There were hardly any doctors in Spain after the war, and since they needed me, I was left alone. I make no secret about my opinions either; everyone in Granada knows exactly how I feel."

A moment later, his anger surged against the United States, because it had just signed an agreement with the Pope. "*Una porqueria*" (a stupid act) he shouted, slamming his fist down on the table, "it will be your fault if World War III breaks out!" A moment after this tirade he lifted Peter tenderly in his arms and cradled him, once more a doctor. I never understood the alcohol treatment, or his hesitation to give Peter penicillin -- a mystery to this day.

I was soon to learn more about Spain on a personal level. In 1953 life seemed so peaceful, so orderly, everyone so polite and kind. But I soon discovered Spaniards live a double life, one an orderly public life, the other a turbulent private one. Even their provincial streets reflect this division: on a typical street, the long line of smooth, undecorated, windowless walls is broken only by doors leading indoors. (Remember the walls of the Moorish palaces?) Once inside the door, however, the patios sparkle in the sun: flowers, lemon and orange trees, cages of singing birds and pet crickets, and bubbling fountains belie the austere exterior.

A love affair brought me to a head-on collision with entrenched tradition, and a threat to my life. Paco, a painter of sorts, lived like other Spanish males, a wife and children at home, and mistresses on the side. This little fact I did not know until much later. His wife knew about her husband's extra-marital affairs but, like other Spanish women, did not consider them a serious threat to her marriage. Only when she realized her husband was in love with me did she take action: she threatened not to kill me, just maim me. For a few days I dodged her, ate meals indoors, and ventured out only when the coast was clear.

Soon I became the focus of gossip, our relationship discussed in every cafe; what I did, what I ate, where I shopped, every conversation was reported to Paco. Jealousy reared its ugly head after Peter and I had lunch one day with an 80-year-old man. "Why are you jealous of someone with one foot in the grave?" I asked. "He's a man, isn't he?" he shouted. Such arguments were beyond my American understanding. But we were young, and love absorbed our lives, though I knew it would be short-lived. We plotted every moment together; how to escape for an afternoon drink, how to invent pretexts for his late homecomings.

It was a hopeless situation, and the idea of living in Granada as Paco's mistress in some *casita* on the edge of town never occurred to me. I booked passage on the first boat leaving Gibraltar; I was ready to go, though with a heavy heart.

My last night in Granada was a disaster. Peter and I waited hours for Paco at our favorite cafe, but he never showed up. At 6 in the morning he appeared at the *pension*, disheveled and distraught, having spent the night in jail imprisoned and periodically beaten on his wife's orders. Finally, tired of the game, the police let him escape.

Spanish men are the last of the romantics. Life in the

220

provinces is so dull, so uneventful, so circumscribed by impossible rules that a love affair, particularly an illicit one, becomes all-consuming, and marriage a bore. Here is a salty Spanish proverb (collected from men) that confirms the sentiment: *"Casamiento, consamiento, y el arrependimiento en su sequimiento"* translated reads: "Marriage, boredom, and regret in that order." They plunge into romantic escapades like starving men grasping for each morsel; a man without an amorous past is no man at all. While the same might be said for provincial life anywhere, the Mediterranean is one place where it thrives at its maximum.

I have only one proverb given to me by a woman: *"El estado perfecto de la mujer es la viudez."* Translated it reads: "The perfect state of womanhood is widowhood." And I have always added, preferably with a hefty bank account!

***

Upon return from Europe, Chenk and I parted for good. Peter started his education at a nursery school, and I received a research grant from the American Philosophical Society. Early in the spring of 1954,I sailed for Europe, leaving Peter with his father. I spent a few months in Italy, was dazzled by Rome, Florence and Venice, and left for Spain for a second visit, this time on a recording trip. For the first time since the 1946 Yaqui expedition in Mexico, I was alone, lugging my new tape recorder (10 pounds instead of 200) and my own luggage.

Being by myself gave me the leisure to explore Madrid. I spent days at the Prado completely absorbed by the works of Velasquez, El Greco, and the brilliant Zubaran, whose paintings of women are unsurpassed. While I marveled at the sensuality of Goya's *La Maja*

221

Desnuda, his royal mistress, the Duchess of Alba, nothing sent me into peals of laughter more than Goya's mammoth-size paintings of the royal family. Unlike Velasquez' idolized portraits of his royal patrons, Goya saw them as they were -- human, ordinary, and quite ugly despite silks and jewels. Most days I walked to the National Library, passing exquisitely dressed children at play, watched over by lace-capped nanas, and old men peacefully reading newspapers on rented park benches.

I read books on Spain's popular theater, folk music, and dance, and received advice from leading musicologists. Armed with a few facts, about to leave Madrid for the provinces, I realized I still lacked practical advice like where to go, and whom to contact. Help came from an unusual source: *La Seccion Feminina,* the women's section of the Falangist party. Folk culture was their province, they were the organizers of a chain of regional folk song and dance ensembles known as *Coros y Danzas* (Choruses and Dances), one of which I had first seen at Carnegie Hall in 1953. My visit to their headquarters was cordially received, and I was given helpful lists of members to contact around the country.

For the next few months, I recorded music in villages and hamlets from north to south; now I had evidence of the diversity of Spanish folk music the experts in Madrid had told me about. It was not just castanets, guitars, and snapping fingers but a variety of styles acquired over millennia from peaceful settlers and conquerors alike -- Celts, Greeks, Romans, Visigoths, Muslims, Jews, and lastly Gypsies. In addition, I heard echoes of church music, 19th century popular songs, all kinds of music that willy-nilly drift from the city to the countryside.

For the first time in my career, village women became my collaborators. They arranged recording sessions, kept me company

222

until bedtime. Because I was a stranger and therefore unable to reveal their secrets, they plied me with confidences about their private lives -- of humiliation, unrealized dreams, love gone awry, in other words, their life in a male dominated society.

I don't remember everything, so I'll recount the few that left an unforgettable imprint on my mind. In the northwest village of Zamora a lively intelligent young woman, whose name I have forgotten, became my constant companion. We took walks to view the countryside outside of town dotted with trees in fresh shades of green and yellow. Lazy, gentle flowing rivers intersected the patches of land, and vineyards stretched out as far as the eye could reach. In this peaceful atmosphere, she worked as a social worker. The outward respectability of the village, she said, was only a smokescreen that hid unpleasant truths. "Ah," she sighed, "this life is all wrong. The parish priest has seduced a dozen girls. He's a prowler, everyone knows it and does nothing. No girl is safe when he's around. My life went wrong when I fell in love with a darling Portuguese boy. I wanted to marry him but my parents said no, he's a foreigner, it's not right. I was brokenhearted, I loved him so dearly. Then my parents picked out a traveling salesman. What kind of life will I have with him? He's gone most of the week. What shall I do when he's not around? Nothing but take care of the house? I'll die of boredom! Being a married woman around here means you have to stay home, and spend your time with relatives. I don't like him, either, but I'm going to marry him because my parents say so." She paused after this outbreak, and then quietly said, "I don't understand our ways at all. Do you know, señora, when I go to a dance, and am having a wonderful time, suddenly I think I will pay for this pleasure in heaven. Imagine, I can't enjoy myself without feeling guilty."

In another town my contact was a young married woman with a child. She was a genuine beauty, a face like the Virgin Mary in medieval Spanish paintings. In her living room, sparsely furnished with uncomfortable, straight-back chairs, commonly found in provincial homes, we talked over coffee and cake. "I'm so glad you are here," she said. "I have no one to talk to since my husband left me seven years ago. My life is a shambles. I have asked the Holy See for a divorce, or I should say, an annulment." "How can you get an annulment," I asked, "when you already have a child?" "The Church only gives annulments," she replied, "they pretend the marriage was never consummated."

Then she continued: "Seven years ago, after our son was born, my husband ran away with another woman. They live in a town near here and have two children." By now her eyes overflowed with tears. "People avoid me, as if it's all my fault. But one day, I had coffee at a cafe with a man I know only casually. I forgot about it until a week later when I received a letter from my husband. It said, 'I know about your rendezvous. You are still married to me, and you have disgraced my name.' How long do I have to wait for the Holy See to make up its mind?" she asked. "And when you do get your annulment," I asked, though I knew the answer, "will you be able to marry again?"

She shook her vigorously. "Oh no, there is only one man for each woman." "And for each man...?" I asked. She shrugged her shoulders. "That is the law of nature." And she said it without bitterness, stating a fact, one she believed in. Only a widow has the right to marry a second time!

As weeks stretched into months I began to notice the numerous spinsters I met along the way. As we sat around the table on chilly autumn evenings warming ourselves near the charcoal brazier (which warms the feet and leaves your back cold), the women spoke of the past. They are the old maiden aunts, the family drudges who take care of the children, cook, embroider, and clean the house. A typical tale went like this: "Yes, when I was young I had many suitors, I was very pretty then. We went to dances and parties; we had a wonderful time. But I decided not to marry because, to tell you the truth, I didn't want to take orders from a man, I didn't want to be his servant. I'd rather work for my family than for a man, even though I work just as hard, or maybe even harder."

Then one day, I had a rare opportunity to hear some frank opinions, this time from men talking about women. One lazy afternoon relaxing over coffee with several hotel guests, the following conversation took place: Said a man from Madrid, "I have complete trust in my daughter; she is free to do and go where she likes, but I know she will do nothing wrong." The man from Seville, however, disagreed, "I am sure if you gave women their freedom, they'd be pregnant in an hour!"

Was the first man really sure his daughter would never consider sex without marriage, or did he merely hope so? As for the second man, was he paying tribute to the virility of Spanish men, or the wantonness of Spanish women? Though they appeared to disagree, in actuality, they both agreed on the cardinal point: women shouldn't have sex until marriage. It is not only immoral but a blot on the family honor. Woe to the young girl who has illicit sex or an illegitimate child. Although I know of no incidents in Spain, recent reports from Eastern European countries indicate that young girls, even today, are murdered for illicit sex by their own families. However, Spain's past history has not been forgotten: its double standard has been documented in the *romancero*, the medieval ballads still preserved today by Spanish Jews, and about which I will speak later.

Recommended by *La Seccion Feminina* to a remote village with ancient ways, I took the bus to Puebla de Sanabria in Northwest Spain, the last stop on the line, and pitch dark when I arrived. Not knowing where to go, I asked the only other passenger, a young priest, for help. "Is there a hotel or a *pension* here?"   "Come," he said, guiding me to the lone taxi, a vehicle of ancient vintage, "I'll take you to a lady I know. She'll put you up for the night." As we lurched through the darkness, I told him my mission. "Don't worry," he said, "we have plenty of good singers. I'll get my sister to help you."

Finally, we were in town. Dimly visible was a stone stairway leading to the upper level. Not a soul was on the narrow streets, not even a dog. At the top, we walked to a huge house barely visible in the darkness. The priest knocked on the huge wooden door, and a minute later it swung open. A woman, holding a lantern, beckoned us in. We walked through a big empty patio, up a flight of stairs to a corridor lit by a single naked bulb. "Come in, she said, "I don't have any luxuries here but you're welcome to stay." I was ushered into a spacious room, furnished only with an enormous bed, a chair and a little wash stand; another hanging 20-watt bulb barely penetrated the darkness. I was tired by this time and the room was bone-chilling cold. Soon my hostess appeared with a steaming cup of hot chocolate, some biscuits, and a bottle, an empty glass liquor bottle filled with hot water. She placed it in the bed between sheets and quilts. "That should take the chill away," she said smiling at me, and left me for the night.

The next day, awakened by the morning sun, I rushed to the window for my first glance of the town. Surely, I thought, this is the most primitive place in Spain. Stretched out before me were cobblestone streets lined with two-story white-washed houses, their balconies hung with peppers, tomatoes and tobacco ripening in the sun. The empty space I walked through the night before was a barnyard now filled with clucking hens and chicks, pigs and goats wandering in and out from the street. Out on the street I encountered dogs, sheep, and cats everywhere; apparently the villagers were quite comfortable sharing space with their four-legged friends.

The señora indicated that I could take my meals across the street at her neighbor's house. Since Puebla de Sanabria was a stone's throw from the Portuguese border, I was not surprised to find customs officials among the breakfast guests. Not only were they pleasant men but also good hunters. For the few days there I dined almost every day on their catch, aromatic stews of grouse and other fine birds.

Soon, the priest arrived with his sister, who squired me around town. "Be careful," she said with a knowing laugh. "Don't walk under those balconies. With few sanitary facilities here, at night, rather than walk to the outhouse, people do their business through a hole in the balcony." I took the warning seriously.

My second morning at breakfast I found visitors waiting to see me. "We have heard," they said, "that you have come here for the music. You are a musician?" "Yes," I said, not bothering to tell them I hadn't touched my instrument in decades. "We, too," they said, "are musicians, like our mother and grandmother before us." At that point I noticed they were carrying some old newspapers. They spread them out for me to see, and said quietly, "Perhaps you have heard of our relative, Victoria de los Angeles? Here are pictures of her in these newspapers, and we know she has sung in your country." For a moment I was speechless. "Victoria de los Angeles?" I burst out when I recovered my composure. "Why, she is one of the most famous sopranos in the world." On and on I babbled about her singing, her fame, etc, etc. They listened to me in silence, and then said "Ay, señora, but you should have heard her mother sing." What modesty, I thought, or is it that the child must never be superior to the generation before?

Victoria's mother, like other family members, sang in the local church before moving to Barcelona where Victoria was born. Victoria had come back to Puebla de Sanabria once to sing in the church to fulfill a vow, to the everlasting pride of her aunts and cousins. I saw them every day during my stay there; I was always greeted with bows from the men, and embraces from the women.

The priest was good as his word; every day singers appeared to sing. Some of my best Spanish recordings came from that village. When the initial shyness wore off, the songs flowed in a constant stream, the singers urging each other on. One session held in the back of a grocery store, hardly large enough to hold the singers, the bagpiper and his drummer, soon filled to overflowing with curious villagers. Suddenly, a few spectators detached themselves from the crowd and began to dance. The crowd pushed back to give them space; men and women twirled around in tiny steps, oblivious to everything; the bagpiper and drummer played like demons possessed. Suddenly, one villager said, "Stop, why are you dancing? What kind of fools are you, don't you see the señora doesn't have a camera?" For a moment the dancers looked at each other sheepishly, and then apologetically at me. Within a few moments the crowd spilled out into the street headed by the musicians, the dancing began anew and continued until exhaustion brought them to a stop. "Thank you, thank you," they said as they headed home, "we had a wonderful time. You will come again, won't you?"

One day, I had a session alone with the bagpiper. Always the Western-trained musician, I asked the piper, "Will you play the scale for me?" He shook his head, not understanding my request. I tried to explain. "Would you please play each note in succession from the lowest to the highest?" A theoretical principle like a scale was entirely foreign to his way of making music; he played airs, or dance tunes, but single notes, never! After a long while, he did play a scale and was delighted to have discovered something new about his music. Besides, he had pleased me, a musician like himself.

Leaving Puebla de Sanabria was difficult for me but also for the villagers. A respite from routine, my visit was an opportunity to dance, sing and tell stories. But I had to go. I headed south to Plasencia to visit the brother of Garcia Matos, a leading folklorist I had met in Madrid. I don't remember their house particularly but when the door opened I was surrounded by children of all sizes. Later when wife and husband met me for coffee at the town cafe, I asked, "Were all those children yours?" "Yes," said the lovely blond mother looking approvingly at her husband, "we have ten now and I wouldn't mind having another. We are so happy when we hear the children's voices." I stared at her in disbelief, and said, "With so many children how do you manage?" "Oh, my dear, the servants take care of them; when they cry there is always someone there to take them off my hands. It's easy that way."

What a life, I thought, every year another baby, the weekly visit to the beauty parlor, coffee at four, fittings at the dressmaker's, visits from the family, and a staff of servants. No wonder she looks handsome, young, well-groomed and without a care in the world. Is life really that perfect? And what would she think of mine? I dared not tell her, I'm sure she would have thought me insane.

I returned to Madrid and decided to spend my last few days in a small town of the province of Avila. My hotel was an ancient farmhouse where meals were still cooked over an open hearth. The bed, which I had to climb up to, was covered with exquisite embroidered and crocheted coverlets, just like descriptions I had read of 18th century costumes. Most of all I remember I ate an enormous shimmering flan all by myself.

I contacted the town's best singer but was disappointed to learn she was leaving town to visit a sick relative. "I am going to Avila," she said, "but I will be back the day after tomorrow." "How can I be sure?" I asked. "Don't worry," she said affectionately embracing me, "I'll be back. If you had asked me to cry, I wouldn't come, but you asked me to sing, so I will return." She was as good as her word, and sang all the songs she knew, helped out by her friends and relatives.

I packed my bags, put the recorded tapes in my suitcase and left for America, but not before receiving a few words of advice: "Please," said one man, "tell everyone in America that Spain is more than flamenco and bullfights." I promised, and never forgot.

Come to think of it, I never paid any of the singers. Not that I didn't try; they just refused. I still remember offering money to one imperious-looking singer with enormous eyes and long black hair. "Señora," she said, drawing herself up to her full height (she was almost six feet tall), "*Aqui canto por gusto no por dinero*" (I sing for pleasure, not for money).

***

Chapter Five – Morocco

1954

My interest in the Sephardic Jews began in 1954, when I met Jews in Madrid on a visit from recently liberated French Morocco. Although they had lived quite comfortably under Moslem rule for centuries, there was a growing hostility in the air. They had come to Spain to test out the waters: could they return to the land that expelled them almost 500 years before?

Among them was a sophisticated and charming man in his late 40s, with whom I formed a cordial friendship. He had been the private secretary to El Glaui, the sultan of Marrakesh. "A Jew as private secretary to a Muslim?" I exclaimed. "Yes," he assured me, "El Glaui is an intelligent and tolerant man, pro-French, pro-Western, and friendly to the Jews. Why are you surprised?" he chided me. "Remember, we Jews have lived with Moslems in Spain long ago, and afterwards in North Africa, and under the Ottoman Turks."

One day, at a local cafe, he said: "Let me give you some advice. You came to Spain to record their old songs, right? You would do better in Morocco. Don't you know Sephardic Jews, even today, sing the old Spanish ballads? Every Jewish family knows a few, even my own unmusical family." "Come now," I said with disbelief, "they still sing ballads from a country that kicked them out?" "You don't understand," he said patiently. "They are our umbilical cord to Spain. We still are attached to Spain. After all, they didn't annihilate us like Hitler, they gave us a choice -- become Christian, you stay, otherwise you go. As you know, most Jews left, scattering to all parts of the world. Now, some became true converts to

Catholicism, but others were Christians in name only, practicing Judaism in secret." He shook his head sadly. "They were the ones, called *marranos* (swine), persecuted by the Inquisition as heretics."

"What about your own family?" I asked. "Like many others, very sentimental about Spain," he replied. My family, from Burgos, kept the keys to our ancestral home as a *recuerdo*, a souvenir, for almost 400 years. In 1907 my father returned them to the Mayor of the city. And even more important -- all of us still speak Spanish, and, as I told you, still sing the old ballads."

That same year, I heard another intriguing story. In the northern town of Toro, I met the local music master, a fine old gentleman of the old school, who told me about a chance visit years before from a friend, Manrique de Lara, a Spanish army official, also a ballad scholar and avid collector. One day, to pass the time away, the two friends sauntered through the dusty streets of the village. "Soon we came upon women sitting outdoors," the music master recalled, "at their afternoon chores, mending, embroidering, and chatting among themselves. Manrique stopped to talk to them, just casually about this and that. Finally, he came to the point: Did they, by chance, know any of the old ballads? 'Ay, no, señor,' said one, 'my grandmother used to sing them but we don't any more.' Well,' he asked, 'in that case, do you mind if I sing one?' " They listened politely but sat in stony silence. Undaunted, he sang another, and then another. Halfway through the third ballad one of the women cried out in exasperation, "Señor, that's not the way it goes," and without further prodding, sang it from beginning to end. That ballad Manrique de Lara had heard years before in Istanbul, sung by a Sephardic woman. "And," added the music master, "he filled three notebooks with ballads that afternoon."

That story, like those heard in Madrid, was engraved in my

mind. Upon return to the States I applied for an American Philosophical Society grant. A few months later I received the news, Glory be! It had been accepted. In March, 1956,1 waved goodbye to family and friends as my ship sailed out of New York harbor. I knew little about the Spanish Jews, except they were descendants of those expelled from Spain in 1492. Unlike thousands of Sephardic Jews from the Balkans killed by the Nazis, they had miraculously escaped the Holocaust.

I was jittery on the trip across the Atlantic. A few days before sailing, *The New York Times* had reported riots in Tetuan, my destination in Morocco. Every day I listened anxiously to the ship's bulletins but heard nothing further. Our embassies in London and Paris, and finally Madrid assured me there were no riots.

"You've come just in time," they said, "Tomorrow Franco returns Spanish Morocco to King Mohammad; there will be a big parade in the center of town." The city was charged with excitement, the streets thronged with people. Every building looked newly washed, newspapers carried huge headlines, banners and flags waved, brass bands blared marches and *pasodobles*. Even the streetwalkers suspended business, and, for once, the cafes along the Gran Via, Madrid's principal thoroughfare, were empty.

Like everybody else, I watched the parade as it wound its way up the avenue. What a spectacle of oriental splendor! I lost count of the horses, maybe a hundred prancing white Moroccan steeds adorned in glittering gold and red velvet. The king himself rode in a black 18th-century rococo carriage, the kind used for coronations, drawn by four horses snorting and high-stepping elegantly along the Via. I forget where Franco was, that corseted, overfed military stiff, but who cared about him! All eyes were on the Moroccan king!

233

The next day I left for the south, stopping a day in Cordoba to see the famous Mezquite. From there I caught the overnight train to the Spanish border. Four hours later we arrived at La Linea to await the Trans-Mediterranean boat for Tangier. Dragging my luggage and recording machine with me, I found an empty table at the dockside cafe and ordered coffee. I sat in bored silence. Soon a man stopped at my table and politely asked, "Do you mind if I join you?"

"No," I said, "go right ahead." Before long we were deep in conversation. "Where are you going?" he asked. "To Tetuan," I replied. He smiled at me. "I'm from Tetuan. Do you have family there?" "No," I said, "I don't." He pressed further: "You have friends there, perhaps?" "No, I don't. I'm going to do a study of Sephardic music." "Oh," he said, "you are a Jew?" "Yes," I answered. "Well so am I!" he exclaimed. "Welcome, perhaps we'll see each other there." Later events proved he didn't believe a word I said. As I have reported elsewhere, decent women don't travel alone unless they're visiting relatives, or going to a wedding or a funeral. The rest are whores looking for clients. I'm sure he put me in the latter category. After all I was still young and attractive.

I may add here that, as expected, when I had coffee with him later on at a cafe in Tetuan, within a few moments I had an offer. First, he described his financial state, which wasn't much, but enough to rent a small apartment for me. I could continue to "amuse" myself, perhaps volunteering my services at the local radio station, and he would visit me from time to time. I laughed to myself: the chutzpah of the guy! I put on a good face, and said as sweetly as I could, "Thank you so much, but I'm here to work, and nothing else." He stood up, bowed, paid the bill and walked out. Although I passed him many times on the street after that, he never acknowledged my presence.

Arriving in Tangier was a real test of my stamina. I was all but overwhelmed by the deafening cries of competing child-porters and hotel agents, sometimes three pulling my arm, begging, "Take me, take me, I'll be your guide." The children, smart as whips, spoke a smattering of languages, learned from a consortium of European nations that once ruled Tangier. They switched from Arabic to German, English, Spanish and French in a matter of minutes.

Everything was on sale from hashish to sex. Everyone, it seemed, had relatives to lead you to the best, the cheapest, the most. Once I selected a guide, or several, and they had my luggage in tow, the wheedling began: "Madam, my cousin can get you *kife* cheap;" or, "Would you be interested in a 'discreet house' for ladies to watch couples...," and leave the sentence dangling in the air. Most women favored a voyeur house over a brothel. But men, I found out later, had more choices, same sex or mixed, sadism/masochism. For decades, Moroccan boys had serviced European homosexuals, but also their own. With women secluded and untouchable, sex with boys was the only outlet. "But only until they marry," Moroccan men assured me. Maybe!

I found a modest hotel in Tangier's native quarter, owned by a Portuguese communist and his Spanish wife. Carmen became my constant companion and guided me into the labyrinth of Islam, seen, of course, through her European eyes. "I don't understand them," she would say despairingly. "Every week poor country girls line the market streets looking for work. When they don't find any, they come to the hotel begging for food, and a mat to sleep on. "Help them," I say to my girls, "we always have extra food, and they can sleep on the floor of your room." But they refuse. "That's their fate, *es su suerte*, they say, and turn their backs on those poor girls."

Occasionally, we would go to the market. Especially on Friday, the Muslim Sabbath, I would see those countrywomen about whom she spoke. There they were, sitting on the curb waiting to be hired for a weekend's domestic work. Beggars, along with maimed and crippled children, lined the streets with hands outstretched for the coppers that assured the devout Muslim his entrance to heaven. And then there were the men who passed their day of rest in a shady corner smoking *kife*, totally in limbo. I shall never forget my first glimpse of a blind and crippled leper, his nose completely eaten away. It was so horrendous I ran from the sight.

The place I really loved was the bazaar -- with its leather goods, soft as silk, handwoven rugs, textiles, and mounds of mashed dates, figs, chirimoya and other tropical fruit. Then I began to notice a curious fact: Most shoppers were men, the few women always accompanied by servants, all wearing long djellabahs and head-shawls, though seldom veiled. "We protect our women," Moroccans explained when I asked for a reason. That struck me as strange. "From what and from whom?" I asked. The only "answer" I ever got was "It's our custom." I concluded that the women had to be protected from their very own men.

Later on, during visits to Muslim Kashmir, the Indian province bordering Pakistan, I saw women in the suffocating summer heat covered from head to foot in heavy black garments with only a few slits around the eyes to see through. In Tangier things were better: here and there I caught a glimpse of women sporting expensive European leather bags and wearing stylish high-heeled shoes. In private, I was told, many women wear western clothes, make-up and hair-does at private parties, but never in public.

More and more I began to notice the women. In Mexico and Spain I had been aware of machismo (as well as in my own country), but Morocco was different; here it was institutionalized, although not necessarily written into law. One day I found an intelligent young man, a museum guide, who talked to me with unusual frankness. "You don't understand," he said. "We Muslims are different from you Europeans. Your women do everything to attract a man into marriage, makeup, sexy clothes, lewd dances, and flirtations with everyone." I didn't contradict him, so he continued. "Our women are protected; parents choose their husbands, but not without their consent. Once a woman is married she uses all her wiles to keep her husband interested. She makes their home beautiful, and entertains him with songs, dances, and exotic food." "But," I protested, "why do this when she knows he'll take another wife soon enough? " Our conversation ended without resolution.

Later on I listened to a woman's point of view on polygamy: "I like our way of life," said a young girl from the Atlas mountains. "If I don't want to sleep with my husband, he goes to another wife; I don't have to put up with him like you European women." She continued, "*Cuando sale el rojo, y cuando se pone grande la barriga* (When I menstruate and when my belly grows big with child), I am left alone." "But suppose you are in love with your husband," I asked. "Aren't you jealous?" She looked at me sadly and said no more, but I noticed the resignation in her face.

I soon learned that cameras and recording devices in the Muslim world were generally regarded suspiciously. Being aggressive or sneaky was a losing game; the Moroccans had eyes in back of their heads. One day, with the help of a friend, I ventured into the market with my small recording machine. When he hid

237

the microphone in this pocket and carried the machine (which looked like a small suitcase), the connecting cord was almost invisible. Within a few minutes we were spotted and surrounded by a hostile crowd. "What have you got there?" they demanded angrily. "Nothing," we said, and took to our heels as fast as possible. I was afraid not for myself but for my machine. If that were wrecked I could pack up and go home.

The one person I could count on for advice in this strange new world was Paul Bowles, the composer now turned novelist. I had known him briefly in New York at WNYC and later in Mexico. Paul had lived in Tangier on and off since 1934 (with a few years in Sri Lanka) and was a mine of information. We took walks around the old city, the fortifications, and the market where the children tossed stones at our feet. Waiters were often downright nasty. One evening, at a rooftop cafe, Paul ordered tea in Arabic, which he spoke fluently. "Speak your own language," said the waiter with a hard edge to his voice. "I understand it, and leave mine alone."

"I've lived here a long time and I've seen a lot," Paul told me. "One day, I noticed a crowd standing around in a circle. In the center a man was beating a woman. I mean, he kicked her, hit her with his fists until blood ran down her face. Nobody stopped him; they just looked on and did nothing. After a while, the man, apparently her husband, walked away. A minute later someone else beat her some more. When I asked why the men said, 'If her husband beat her, she must be a bad woman and deserves to be punished.' 'But, who is this one?' I insisted, pointing to the second man to beat her. 'Nobody,' they said, 'just a stranger.' "

Paul continued: "Don't think the women are entirely passive. Occasionally, they take revenge on their husbands. In a household with two wives, sometimes there is peace, and sometimes not. So, it's no surprise to read newspaper reports about a husband's death by poison or ground glass in his food. On the floor above my apartment I always hear singing and dancing -- it sounds very gay but I wonder if the husband really knows what his wives are thinking?"

It was Paul who introduced me to hash. For years he had used it. It helped him hear things in music, he said, he couldn't hear without it. Besides, he suffered from jaundice and couldn't tolerate liquor, so hash was a satisfactory substitute. One day he suggested I try it. Always game for a new experience, I agreed. That evening at his apartment I had my first taste of "jam," so-called because it is often mixed into a paste of figs and dates. After eating a considerable amount and with me feeling absolutely nothing, we decided to go out for dinner. We sauntered through the streets to the hill leading down to the restaurant in the *zoco chico*, the "little plaza" of Tangier. I was perfectly conscious and noticed the usual pick-pockets who waited day and night for unwary prey, nothing unusual.

We started to descend the hill; we walked and walked and walked. What's the matter, I thought, I come down this hill every day in five minutes; how come it feels like I've been walking for hours and haven't moved an inch? Suddenly, we were at the bottom of the hill! Next we followed a circular road and again the same sensation -- like being on an exercise bike.

We climbed the stairs to the restaurant, and as usual talked seriously about everything, music, his friends, like Tennessee Williams, the world, etc. As we spoke I began to feel very strange: I could barely understand what Paul was saying, and my own words were more jumbled with every passing moment. "Paul," I said apologetically, "I don't know what you're saying. I don't know what I'm saying, either."

"Wonderful!" he cried. "Now you're having a hash hangover! It's really working; I had almost given up hope." Finally the meal was over and he escorted me back to the hotel. "As soon as you wake up in the morning," he instructed me, "call me and tell me your hallucinations." I went back to my room, couldn't keep my eyes open for a minute, and fell sound asleep. I woke up the next morning feeling fine. Then I called Paul. "I'm sorry," I said, "I haven't a single thing to report; you must have given me a sleeping pill instead of hash." "You're hopeless," he said, and that was the end of my one and only bout with hash.

For the next few months, Tetuan, an hour out of Tangier, became my home and research center. After settling into a dark and dingy *pension*, all I could afford, I explored the city. Tetuan was a cosmopolitan city, with a huge mix of Europeans, Middle Easterners, and Spaniards doing business with the Moroccans. At noon, like them, I would gravitate to the cafe in the shadow of the elegant, tiled tower to drink Moroccan-style tea, black tea poured over fresh mint. In the blustery early spring, the hot tea was a blessing. No wonder Tetuan is called *la novia de los vientos* (the sweetheart of the winds). "Ah, señora," the waiter would greet me, "I know you want your tea without sugar." I was perhaps his only client to refuse the sugary brew everyone else preferred.

One day, I engaged the waiter in conversation. To tease him I said, "Did you know that New York has a building much higher than your tower? It's called the Empire State Building." He took the news gravely, stood quietly for a long moment, and then said, "Well, it must have been built by a genie." For a moment, I had a glimpse of another world. Those *genies* and *afries* in the "Arabian

240

Nights," those magical figures that create palaces filled with gold and jewels in a flash were real beings, not inventions of Sherazad, the great story-teller.

I soon contacted the Sephardic colony, mostly descendants of Spanish Jews expelled from Spain in 1492. For almost 500 years they had lived in comparative peace with Muslim neighbors, even though in segregated communities. I heard many stories about Jewish and Moroccan cooperation, but the one I remember most vividly was told to me by an 80-year-old woman, a member of a wealthy family. "My family were good friends of the king and his family," she recalled. "We often ate together at his palace. But because we were kosher we brought our own dishes, our own food, and our own servants to prepare everything. The king respected our religion, and we respected his. There was never any problem about it. And now there is plenty of trouble after so many years of friendship," she said, tearing welling up in her eyes.

Despite the despondent atmosphere I hoped my visit would not be interrupted by political mayhem. I proceeded with great caution, stayed away from public places I deemed dangerous, and listened to the advice of friends I quickly made. My entrance into the community was via the Jewish school, established by the enterprising Alliance Francais in the 19th century. There I met the dynamic Ester Benchimol, the intelligent head of the Spanish department, who became my guide and counselor. She was a goldmine of information on Jewish history, folklore, and customs. Because of our friendship I was invited to weddings, bar-mitzvahs, to the *mikva* (the ritual bath). Most important, she introduced me to the best singers.

A stranger, I was politely but firmly questioned about my Jewish roots. My first bout was with a wealthy octogenarian. Like

241

all Tetuan Jews, she was of Orthodox faith and considered Americans borderline Jews. We tilted swords from the first moment. "How do I know you're a Jew?" she asked suspiciously. "Everybody who comes here says they're Jewish." Well, that was a new one on me. I tried to convince her by describing family celebrations at Passover and Purim. Finally, she accepted me into the fold. "I believe you are a Jew," she said, embracing me, "because you speak such beautiful Spanish." (When I told this later on to Yiddish-speaking Jews in New York, they looked at me in complete bewilderment.)

In my second bout, this time with the poor women of the community, I had to prove that I could do womanly things like cook, sew, make a bed, clean the house, etc. I would join them in the bare, cement patio of their tenement building when household chores were done and children off to school. I got low marks almost immediately. They couldn't understand why a Jewish woman like myself would leave her young son and husband to travel to a foreign country in search of songs. They had a healthy respect for the old ballads, to be sure, but family came first. They were also convinced that, as an American, I was hardly a Jew at all. According to tales they had heard, American women never go to synagogue, never stay at home, got divorces, and had careers, like men. I qualified on all points, but I kept it a secret.

They put me to the test. "Here," they said, thrusting a basket of jasmine flowers in my lap. "Remove the petals." These were later cooked in honey and spices. I passed that test, the only one; depetaling jasmine blossoms was a small plus, but a plus nevertheless.

Soon my days became routine. Each day I hurried through the narrow alleys of the *mellah*, the Jewish quarter, on my daily visits to the singers who lived in humble, crowded flats. I pushed my way through streets lined with stalls of silversmiths, shoemakers and craftsmen of all kinds, and crowded with black-robed men, the Jewish elders, men and women shoppers, and children in their school uniforms.

My first encounter with Alicia Benassayag, the most prolific of the Tetuan singers, began with these words, "How can you expect me to sing in these terrible times!", referring, of course, to the volatile political situation. But sing she did. I filled tape after tape with incomparable melodies. There were the ritual wedding songs (actually love songs in disguise), songs for the Jewish holidays --and finally, the *romancero,* the old pithy, turbulent ballads from medieval Spain. She sang them simply, without affectation, in a voice clear and pure, just as her ancestors had done for centuries untold. As she sang in her cramped dining room, she bounced her feverish, whimpering baby in her arms (those cries are duly documented in my recordings).

When she tired of singing, we would drink tea and eat her homemade cakes. "Ah, señora," she would shake her head and say, "again we'll be wandering Jews; again we'll be scattered around the world. Thank God, thank God for Israel, we have a homeland!" And she lifted her eyes heavenwards in thanks. Years later, I would meet her in Israel, but I will tell that story later on.

Then, there was Ester Cadoch Israel, a rotund, dark-skinned woman who earned a living in the market selling *churros,* those delicious cruller-like pastries eaten with morning hot chocolate throughout the Spanish world. She would come to my room to record her songs. In her passionate renditions, the ballad characters and their twisted and convoluted circumstances sprang to life; she sang as if the terrible events had just happened the night before, and she had witnessed them herself. The tragic fate of these medieval women became her own personal reality. But she always assured me that, in the end, villains would be punished; the innocents, always women, vindicated, and the world set on its proper course again. She, herself, had divorced a husband who tried to take on a second wife. When the rabbi refused to grant her a divorce, she found someone else to dissolve the marriage. Apparently, Jews sometimes copy their Muslim neighbors.

When I met her numerous family, all singers, I thought they were from different sets of parents they were so unlike one another. One night the family assembled for a recording session. All Ester's sisters had beautiful ringing voices; they clapped the rhythms, played the tambourine, sang sometimes solo, sometimes in chorus. It was not only a wonderful spontaneous evening of music but a way of connecting with the past, a reminder that once long ago their ancestors were the great physicians, poets, and philosophers of medieval Spain.

Then there was unforgettable Flora Benamor, a delicate and tender young woman, blessed with a mellow, sweet voice. Her modest apartment was an oasis of calm and peace. Singing was the one outlet for her musical talents. At my arrival in the afternoon her house was immaculately clean; if she had any children I never saw them. Every day she prepared a new repertory, so that when I finally left Tetuan I would have all the songs she knew. She sang the ballads, and especially the wedding songs, masterpieces in words and music, with inimitable tenderness and poignancy.

Fuérame a bañar a orillas del rio (2)
allí encontrí, madre, a mi lindo amigo
el me dió un abrazo y yo le di cinco

Fuérame a bañar a orillas del claro (2)
allí encontrí, madre, a mi lindo amado
el me dió un abrazo, y le di cuatro

I went to bathe at the river's edge
There I found , mother, my handsome friend
He gave me one embrace, I gave him five

I went to bathe at the clearing's edge
There I found my handsome lover
He gave me one embrace, I gave him four.

During the months in Morocco I would travel frequently to Tangier. On one of my visits I met Abraham Laredo, a scholar and member of a wealthy tea merchant family. Over a fragrant cup of tea, he said, "I know you are interested in the *romancero*, but please come to the synagogue this Friday night and listen to our cantor; he's a great singer and knows hundreds of ancient religious songs." That evening I sat in the balcony with the other women, and listened while the rabbi cantillated the traditional Biblical text. But, as Laredo had promised, my attention was riveted by the songs of the cantor, Solomon Siboni -- here was music totally unknown to me. At Laredo's suggestion I invited Siboni to record his songs. A gracious man, Siboni came to my hotel many times to sing. "Tell me about these songs, who composed them, where did you learn them? " "Ah," he said, "they have a long history. Jewish poets have been composing religious verse (called *piyyutim* in Hebrew) for centuries. When I was a young cantorial student in French Morocco I learned 600 songs from a master singer." "What about the melodies?" I asked, "who composed them?" "Nobody wrote them down, but I'm sure you will recognize them as Spanish or Near Eastern melodies." All in all, I recorded 40 *piyyutim*, some by such great Sephardic poets as Judah HaLevy and

245

Ben Gabirol (whom Christians call Avecenna); Siboni sang them from well-worn little booklets acquired in the bookstalls of Fez during his student days. "Tell me, " I asked, "What purpose do they serve in the synagogue?" Siboni laughed. "Well, you have to have some way to relieve the boredom of hearing the same Torah readings, week in and week out, year in and year out."

While I was occupied with music, Muslims were on the attack; one terrifying night they beat Jews in movie houses, threatened to burn their houses down, and robbed homes and business establishments. King Mohammad called on the Spanish police to quell the rioters, but the Jews soon realized the end had come. They petitioned the king for permission to leave en masse. Afraid a mass exodus would disrupt economic life irreparably, he refused. Just as I was leaving, he rescinded the order. Years later I learned that most Jews sold homes and possessions for a pittance, and fled, the poor to Israel, and the rich elsewhere.

I was not to return to Morocco for 27 years.

***

Return to Spain and Morocco -

1983

The intervening years were busy ones; full-time teaching at City College of New York, broadcasting again at WNYC, return to Mexico, new research in Puerto Rico, and travel to Eastern Europe and the Orient (India, Japan, Nepal) time and again. However, my university students swung into action. "You must release the material from Morocco," they insisted. "You can't just let it sit around and gather dust!" Finally, I found a few empty hours and prepared an LP for Folkways Records. Though I hadn't listened to those voices in many years, they sounded as vibrant and pulsating as when I first heard them. I wondered what had become of Ester Benchimol, Solomon Siboni, and Alicia Benassayag. Were they alive, were they still in Morocco? Do something!, I said to myself.

The person who really convinced me to make a second trip to Morocco was Sam Armistead, the great scholar of the Spanish ballad. Soon after meeting him I received two grants, one from the City University, another from the National Endowment For the Humanities. In March of 1983 I flew to Spain, the first stop en route to Morocco, and finally Israel. Unlike previous trips, I now had two companions, Allen Cooper, a former CCNY student, and Paige Lyons, an anthropologist and editor of the *American Record Guide* for whom I wrote folk music reviews.

In Madrid, Iacobo Hassan, director of the newly formed Sephardic *Arias Montano Institute* had discouraging words. "There are only a few Jews in Tetuan," he said. "Most of them left after 1956; some went to Canada, some to the United States, and others to Israel. But, I'm sure you'll be surprised to know that many Moroccan Jews settled in Spain, yes, and were welcomed back by the government with open arms. There are now fourteen new Sephardic communities here, scattered all over the country. Then he added these puzzling words, "You're determined to go to Tetuan, aren't you? Well, good luck. I have no intention of going there myself!"

A few days later we were on our way south. First we spent a few weeks in Malaga, a beautiful Andalusian city on the Mediterranean coast. As Hassan had described, I found a prosperous and thriving community, a fine synagogue, social services, both girls and boys attending university, girls holding jobs, and enjoying the same

247

freedoms enjoyed by their Christian friends. What a change from what I had seen years before in Morocco!

I immediately sought out the rabbi, who was also the cantor, and a former student of Solomon Siboni, whom I had recorded in 1956. We immediately tilted swords: as in my first visit 22 years ago, I had to prove I was Jewish. That proven, I next had to admit that Paige was not Jewish. But I stretched the truth about Allen. A generation before, his family had become Christian converts. Technically, he was Christian, but I told the rabbi he was Jewish and, like other Americans, he was not religious. "Did he ever have a bar mitzvah?" he asked. "I don't think so," I said, and the conversation ended there. Little did I know that the rabbi had plans to rectify the situation.

One Friday night, Paige and I stayed in the hotel while Allen attended services. When he had not returned by 11p.m., we began to worry. Finally, there was a knock at the door. There was Allen, with a big, sheepish smile on his face. "I've just been bar mitzvah'd," he announced, to our utter astonishment, "and then the rabbi took me home for dinner. So now I'm a Jew." Well, maybe, in a manner of speaking.

A few weeks later Allen, Paige and I crossed the Mediterranean to Ceuta on the African coast, one of two cities still under Spanish control after independence in 1956. Ceuta is a huge market of little shops selling electronic equipment. The two recording machines I bought, however, worked for a few months and then fell apart. I am convinced Ceuta is where big companies dump their defective equipment on unsuspecting bargain hunters. It has probably earned its reputation as a smugglers' town.

A few hundred Jews live in Ceuta; a small, modern synagogue

serves as their social and religious center. One Friday night, Paige and I sat in the women's balcony while Allen joined the men below. I gave him instructions: "Remember, turn the pages of the Bible from right to left. Watch the other men and turn when they do." We took our proper places, and the cantillation of the Torah began. Pretty soon, I heard "Psst, psst." I paid no attention. "Psst, psst," again. I looked up and saw the synagogue caretaker in the corridor, unmistakenly beckoning me. I walked out to speak to him. "Your friend downstairs," he said, "is he really a Jew? He's got the wrong page open, and turns at the wrong time." I reassured him. "Of course, he's Jewish," I said with a straight face. "He's had his bar mitzvah, but in America not all the boys learn Hebrew." Shaking his head he walked away muttering, "What kind of a Jew is that? Bah!"

A few days later we took a taxi to the frontier, the first lap of our journey to Tetuan. To our dismay, hundreds of people were lined up at the customs booth awaiting visas. It was a scene of total chaos. Disconsolately, we wandered among the indifferent multitude. Suddenly, a young Moroccan tourist guide appeared, like an angel from heaven, and within 15 minutes we were through the gates, in a taxi with all our gear, and speeding down the highway towards Tetuan. "Where do you want to go first?" he asked. "To the tea shop near the tower," I replied.

Finally, the taxi stopped in front of the beautiful tiled tower where I had spent so many pleasant hours years before. But where was the teashop? It was gone; there were no tables, no people, nothing, only a few Moroccan men observing us with less-than-friendly eyes.

Tetuan had changed almost beyond recognition. The beautiful Plaza de España was still there but, except for the bazaar, it was a ghost town, bereft of people and activity. We paid several visits to the almost empty Jewish social center, sat in silence for a while in the hidden synagogue. I asked the social worker about the people I had known; Alicia Benassayag had fled to Israel, and the others, Flora Benamor, and Ester Cadoch Israel, had died. Gone were the scenes of so much gaiety, the family parties, bar mitzvahs, and weddings, and no one was singing the old songs any more.

On one of my visits we met a bright young social worker with whom we spent many hours of recollections of times gone by. One day she made a startling statement: "Did you know," she said, "that Franco saved the Jews from the Holocaust?" "What?" I exclaimed, "that Nazi collaborator? How could that be?" "Yes", she said, "early in World War II, Hitler and Franco met at the Spanish border. Hitler proposed his army march through Spain to capture Gibraltar. Now, you know, señora, that whoever controlled Gibraltar controlled the Mediterranean." Having made a strong point, she paused. "Franco turned him down, he was not about to let the Nazis overrun Spain, and then seize his African colonies. So, inadvertently, whether Franco's intention or not, the Jews were saved from annihilation." On my return to the New York I checked out her story; it was true, every last word.

One day, at the social center, a young boy came to see me. "My grandmother wants to see you," he said urgently. "Yes, yes," I responded, without the foggiest notion who he was referring to. "I'll come when I can." He insisted: "She says that you should come this afternoon at 4 o'clock." Completely mystified, Paige and I went to the address the boy had given me. As I rang the bell, I suddenly realized who had summoned me, no, commanded me to come -- my old friend Ester Benchimol, the Spanish teacher of the Jewish school. When the door opened and she enveloped me in her arms, the tears ran down my face. Dear, sweet woman, there she arms, the tears ran down my face. Dear, sweet woman, there she was, and totally blind. "I am 80 years old," she said, to which I gallantly replied, "You will always be young to me." Her table was piled high with pastries and sweet breads she and her daughter had made for my visit. "Do you remember the bottle of green Cointreau you brought me on *shavouth*?" she asked, recalling the gift I had given her to celebrate the Holy Day after Passover. I had bought a bottle of yellow Cointreau for myself and a green one for her. "I just recently threw the empty bottle away," she said. "Ah, Ester," I said, "we must have been thinking about each other. I just threw mine out this past summer."

And then she recalled her youth, experiences of a Jewish girl in a Catholic world. "I was educated as a teacher in a French convent. The priest in charge had fallen in love with me. He used to put his hand on my knee, but I would have nothing to do with him. We had endless arguments on the merits of our religions, but I think I won them all. Judaism was superior in every way." I left her feeling sad beyond words, knowing I would never see that gentle loving woman again.

The next few days in Tangier were depressing. Now I understood why Hassan in Madrid didn't want to come to Morocco. I visited the old people's home and saw those who, because of old age or infirmities, had been left behind while the others fled. Allen entertained them playing a few ragtime tunes on the piano, but won their hearts with a *paso-doble*, the favorite dance of their youth. One man, only in his 60s, left behind because of blindness, sang for us the old ballads and popular songs of his youth in a sweet, lovely voice, and we recorded every one.

Most distressing were the signs of growing anti-semitism and anti-Western attitudes, which seemed to fester despite their king's tolerant attitude. With tourists on group tours, Moroccans were polite and attentive. But not to us: we traveled by ourselves, and obviously hung out with Jews. "Don't mention the word Israel in the street," we were warned by newly made Jewish friends. One day, as we emerged from the synagogue, a replica of the Alhambra palace in Granada, Allen, who "looks Jewish" (whatever that is), was spit upon and insulted. In the hotel shop I was treated contemptuously, even telephone messages were never delivered.

The few remaining Jews in Tangier were divided about their future. A few businessmen were on excellent terms with the new king, Hassan II, the son of Mohammed V. While we were there they celebrated Moroccan Independence Day on the king's yacht, moored in the harbor. But others were pessimistic. "We must leave or we will be murdered in our beds," said the remaining member of the Laredo family, whose older brother had helped me in 1956. (Years have elapsed since 1983 but I hear that Jews are once again returning to Morocco.) Paige, Allen and I gave up in despair. Hurriedly we returned to Spain, and from there flew to Jerusalem.

***

Chapter Six – Israel

1983-84

Israel was at peace upon our arrival. We felt a tremendous sense of relief from the anxieties and hopelessness of Tetuan and Tangier. Little did we know then it would be short-lived. We wandered happily through Jerusalem's old city, ate delicious arabic salads, succulent stuffed pita, blinzes, and delicate, flaky pastries in small bars and restaurants. What a magnificent city, every stone, every alleyway, every mosque, every synagogue, was steeped in thousands of years of history. Within a five minute walk we heard Yiddish, Arabic, Spanish, Romanian, Italian, and other languages I couldn't recognize. Friday night we watched in awe as thousands of black-garbed Hassidim marched to the Western Wall in military formation, like an army. We talked to Muslims, ex-soldiers of the British army, and mingled happily with a crazy patchwork of people from every corner of the earth. We toured nearby archeological sites, observed on route that the Israelis, to illustrate their claim of making the desert bloom, had planted crops on one side of the highway, and left the other side barren.

Through my colleagues at the Hebrew University Fonoteca, I finally located Alicia in the biblical city of Ashkelon, where the legendary Delilah had cut off Samson's hair. Alicia shared a tiny apartment with her daughter, whom I remembered as a baby, fitfully crying in her mother's arms during our recording sessions in Tetuan. Now I heard the story of their harrowing flight from Morocco: each member of her family had fled in panic by a separate route, sometimes with help of friendly Moroccan police, sometimes rescued by Jewish organizations. Finally reunited in Marseilles, they proceeded to Israel. Though life was a constant struggle to make ends meet, they were grateful to live in a Jewish state, despite the Palestinian threat.

The talk with Alicia finally turned to the present. Within a few years of her arrival in Israel Alicia became quite famous for her recordings of Sephardic ballads, but never appeared in public. As we chatted, mother and daughter, an Israeli woman with a university degree, began to argue. Soon their voices, louder and more strident with every passing moment, turned into a shouting match. Alicia said, "Men are smarter than women and should be obeyed and respected. Woman's place is in the home, and she should work for money only to help her husband." "Never!" shouted her daughter. "I'm as smart as any man, and I want the same rights as men. Stay at home -- like hell!" "Only prostitutes parade themselves in public," said Alicia, slamming the door on any further discussion.

Our last week in Israel was interrupted by violence. It was already Hanukkah, and everywhere choruses were singing holiday songs. We ate potato latkes in the coffee shop of the King David Hotel in Jerusalem (we stayed at the cheaper YMCA across the street). Then we moved on to Tel Aviv, enjoying cool winter breezes at the seashore as we ate at beachfront restaurants. The Mediterranean glistened in the sunlight. Suddenly, our peace was shattered: A bomb had exploded on a local bus in Jerusalem, the first in years. Apparently, the Palestinians were on the attack once more. The American Embassy across the street from our hotel hurriedly constructed protective scaffolding around the building; security tightened everywhere. For the next few days we were glued to the TV for the latest news.

It was time to leave. We hastened our departure by a few days, and flew back to New York.

***

In 1984, a few months after return from Israel, I took the spring semester off from the university to work on my Sephardic collection in earnest. It was to be a new adventure in my life; not my customary wanderings to outlandish places but quiet, studious work at my own apartment in downtown Chelsea. First, with the help of assistants, I transcribed and translated into English all the Spanish texts.

Then I discovered some interesting facts. Though I knew the Spanish ballads were the popular songs about the Reconquest, the wars that finally toppled Muslim rule in Spain, and their heroes, the songs the women sang for me were about the intimate lives of the Spanish nobility, the so-called *crimenes de passion* (crimes of passion). Many were gruesome tales about male violence against women, but a surprising number were tales about female violence, like cannibalism and mass murder! My favorite, and popular everywhere in the Spanish world, is *La Gallarda,* a prostitute who kills a hundred lovers, and hangs their heads from the nearby olive trees. She gets her come-uppance in the end. The most dramatic by far is *La Infanticida* , the Child Killer. An unfaithful wife kills her son, afraid he will reveal her secret, murders him and serves him in a stew to her husband. But the meat speaks up, and before the husband can kill her, she turns into a green bird and flies away. Whether fact or fantasy, we will probably never know, but they offer an intriguing glimpse of the moral climate of medieval Spain.

One question intrigued me: Why did Jewish women preserve songs about Christian aristocrats for 500 years? I've been often told that they are reminders of their distinguished Spanish past. But surely, there is another reason. Since these old ballads are sung by women, they are a pleasant way to teach their daughters a proper code of sexual behavior, particularly the dire price a girl pays for the loss of her virginity. Without that precious hymen she loses not only her chances of marriage, but also dishonors her family. In any case, I still remember with what gusto and relish Alicia, Flora, and Ester sang them. They were, in a time before radio, TV and movies, the only family entertainment.

I continued to track down everything bearing on women. Somewhere there must be evidence of women's lives, their own thinking, told in their own words. When I was in Tetuan browsing through the stalls of a bookstore I came upon two volumes of stories told by the Jewish women of Tetuan to a Spanish folklorist, Arcadio Larrea Palacin, some years before my arrival there. I translated twenty-five of them, some of which showed their practical, no-nonsense approach to life, and others which seemed to spring out of the "Arabian Nights", replete with flying princes and jewel-studded palaces.

What intrigued me most were their opinions about themselves and their menfolk. Unlike their domestic posture as obedient wives with only household concerns, in their stories they portrayed themselves as superior to their menfolk in intelligence, common sense and imagination. Only religious figures, the rabbis, were regarded with respect and admiration. So, I have learned that there are two sides to every story, a man's and a woman's, and come to think of it, maybe three sides: a man's, a woman's, and the truth.

***

Chapter Seven – Galicia

1989

In 1985, while I was lecturing on the Sephardic ballads at the University of Copenhagen, a fellow ethnomusicologist thrust a magazine into my hand. "Read it," she said. "It's an article written by Marisa Rey, a Spanish anthropologist, and a neighbor of mine." Published in an English feminist magazine, *Spare Rib*, it summed up her research in the province of Galicia, in Northwestern Spain. To my amazement, she claimed she had found matrilineal societies flourishing in many coastal villages. Matrilineal villages in patriarchal Spain, I thought, how could that be? I read and re-read the article until I had completely absorbed the information.

"I know it's shocking news," Marisa said when I met her shortly thereafter, "but both Carmelo Lisón Tolosana, my compatriot who preceded me, and I found the same conditions: The women in certain villages, not all, will their possessions only to their daughters, control all the money earned by their men, and both men and women work in the house and on public works. They even know how to abort unwanted children. Furthermore, many are skilled herbal healers, and women still consult their *sabias* (wise women) on every subject imaginable."

"What about the *miegas*?" I asked her. I had read about the so-called malevolent witches persecuted during the Inquisition. She laughed. "They're still around, but the women consider them their protectors." "What about the men?" I asked. "Men claim," she continued, "that they have seen *miegas* wandering around dressed in white, carrying candles, ringing bells and muttering prayers. They warn the men to change their wicked ways. 'Travel by day,' the *miegas* intone, 'for the night belongs to us.'" And then she added, her eyes twinkling, "I don't know if the stories are true, but I keep on hearing them."

I was intrigued by Marisa's stories and decided to see for myself. Several years later, I went to Galicia with three of my students. By this time, I had read about the discovery of early matrilineal societies in Europe by the archeologist, Marija Gimbutas, and read about ancient pre-Biblical societies in the Middle East in a book *When God Was a Woman* by Merlin Stone. But, as long as 2,000 years ago, a Roman historian had already noted that the Spanish women he met there were strong and aggressive. So I was prepared for anything that might turn up in Galicia.

Although a short visit, we soon realized that though its fascinating capitol, Santiago de Compostela, was the grandiose seat of the Spanish Catholic Church, and once the most important site of medieval pilgrimages, the villages belonged to another world, one shrouded in mists of ancient history. We set out for an exploratory trip along the chilly Atlantic coast and spent a fruitless day talking to village priests and schoolteachers. It was almost nightfall when, despondent and exhausted, we headed back to Santiago. Suddenly, I spied a group of men and women reclining leisurely under a shady tree off the highway. I jumped out of the car, with my students following me. We introduced ourselves and asked whether they knew any singers of old songs in the village. They smiled, nodded their heads at each other, and said in the most disarming way, "We are all singers here. We'll sing for you right now, if you wish." "No, no," I cried, "not now, wait until tomorrow, we'll find a *pension* and stay here for a week or so. We'll bring our recording equipment, take pictures, and videotape everything. Is that all right with you?" "Yes, yes, the children will dance for you, too, they love to dress up in holiday clothes."

We found rooms in the nearby town of Lira, and settled in. For the next few days we saw them constantly, recorded their songs and videotaped the children's dances. We crowded into the tiny living room of their best singer, a blind woman, for the recordings. Had drinks and cakes while the strong, lovely women sang like an aviary of birds, always in the two-part style I had heard everywhere in Latin America. I marveled at their perfect singing, and the ease with which they switched from one part to the other. After each song they looked at us expectantly. Had we enjoyed it? And when assured that we had, sang another, and another. Music, better than words, was their way of telling us about themselves, their strength, their optimism, their past. Occasionally they mentioned that most of their men were away working in foreign lands or elsewhere in Spain, and they saw them only occasionally. We didn't question them directly but we understood from the way they walked and talked, from the way they bonded with each other that, though life was a constant struggle, they were in control, not manipulated by anyone.

Of course, the children were beautiful; they treated us like members of the family, led us to their favorite haunts, to the old graveyard with its glass-walled niches, and ancient grain silos. They preened before our cameras in their velvet skirts and pristine white blouses, and hugged and kissed my students a hundred times.

One day, we drove into the nearby mountains along miles of empty roads. Dotted here and there were tiny, almost deserted villages that must have been old a thousand years ago, maybe even two thousand years old, as my friends in Santiago claimed. We drove up cobblestone streets hardly wide enough for a single car, saw stone houses with tiny windows, now almost empty. At one

259

point, we stopped our car at the sight of two peasant women leading their cows along the road. Tall, stately women dressed in black, wearing huge wide-brimmed straw hats, they were extremely friendly. "*Ay, niñas*," they said affectionately upon seeing us, "*de donde son ustedes?*" (Hey, girls, where are you from?). We took their pictures, bid farewell and headed back to the coast. I said to my students, "Those women don't look Spanish; those long noses are exactly like those I've seen in Ireland and Scotland. And don't think I'm theorizing! The Celts were here thousands of years ago." And to prove my point, I reminded them that we had seen Celtic ruins in Portugal, a short distance from Galicia, at the beginning of our trip.

We spent the last day in Lira. The few men in the village, fishermen, mainly lobstermen, we saw every morning at the bar of our *pension* having a drink or coffee. They never spoke to us and seemed not to notice our presence, even when we passed them on a stroll along the beach. However, as I paid the hotel bill, I was approached by one of them. Politely, with his head bowed, he said, "Thank you for coming to our village. We are proud you made your study here. I hope you will come back soon." I was flabbergasted. Unlike Spanish men, these Gallegos never once flirted with my young students or flaunted their masculinity. We shook hands all around, smiled at each other, received blessings for our families, and promised to come back. Galicia was my last trip to a Spanish province, but it left me with many unanswered questions. Was this chilly, wind-swept land a survival of ancient times when women were as powerful as men? I cannot forget that in flamenco performances, the women dancers are equals of males in technique and sexual aura, and that women dancers switch roles to perform the intricate *taconeo* (footwork) just like the men. What a difference from the classical ballet where women are like dainty dolls, constantly lifted by men into the air!   ***

Chapter Eight – Puerto Rico
1967-69

By the mid-60s I had spent years in the Spanish world on both sides of the Atlantic but never in the Caribbean. I probably never would have gone had it not been for the accusations of neglect by my City College students. I took them seriously, and over the next few years made many trips to various French, English and Spanish-speaking islands. I witnessed African and Christian cult worship, was fascinated by the wild possession dances, pulsating drums and clever political songs. I also admired their skills at mask-making, iron-sculpture and painting.

My first visit to Puerto Rico, however, so captivated me that for the next few years I concentrated all my efforts there. On my arrival at San Juan's airport I could hardly believe my eyes. Was I in Puerto Rico or some place in the States? MacDonald's logo flashed in red lights with the message "9 Million Hamburgers sold". In San Juan all the labels in Walgreen's Drug Store were in English, nor could I understand the prices. For instance, how come bananas and coffee, grown on the island, cost more than in the States? "That's because they're shipped to the States," I was told, "packaged and shipped back to us. Add the cost of a middleman, and we pay more than you do."

One day I rode the bus to Mayaguez, the city on Puerto Rico's west coast. On the way we passed the outskirts of a huge American Army post. "What are we doing here?" I asked a fellow passenger, a young American soldier on his way to join his regiment. "I'll answer your question with one word," he said: "Cuba." It was explanation enough.

Much intrigued by ramifications of international policy, I continued exploring the island. Old San Juan had once been the city hub in colonial times. Now restored, it had a romantic, old-world aura; I wandered down each street, stopped to admire the rows of small pastel-colored houses with their iron-wrought balconies. It was all so familiar; they looked exactly like those in Andalusia.

The beach front, the *Condado*, on the other hand, was new and brassy, and so crowded with mammoth Miami-style hotels the ocean was hardly visible. The beaches, off-limits to Puerto Ricans at that time, were almost always empty of swimmers because most American tourists were busy laying bets at the gambling tables. I watched the players but was never tempted myself; as a kid I played cards for bottle tops and once I won 32 cents in a poker game in Mexico City. That is the sum total of my gambling history.

Away from the tourist haunts I had my first encounters with Puerto Ricans. On a crowded bus one day, I suddenly felt someone's gaze fixed on me. When I finally located the source, a jovial black man, he rose politely from his seat, tipped his hat and bowed his head in my direction, smiled and then resumed his seat. Another time, on the outskirts of town as I waited for the bus, rain began to fall. Nearby, a black woman, observing I had no umbrella, walked to my side, and lifted hers over my head. When the bus arrived we boarded without exchanging a word.

Such were my first impressions of Puerto Rico in the winter of 1967. I soon met Ricardo Alegrias, the director of the Institute of Puerto Rican Culture, who told me about Loiza Aldea and the great fiesta of Santiago. "Come back in July," he said, "it is a spectacular event you can't afford to miss."

Mid-July and I was back in Puerto Rico, this time with students and Julia Singer, our photographer. We rented a car and sped down the highway to Loiza Aldea, a village on the island's north coast. Happily we wandered through town, but to escape the hot July sun, we sought refuge in a shady coconut grove of little huts (bohios). Each house was surrounded by potted plants, gay flowers, and spiky desert bushes, the tips of which were decorated with eggshells, painted a delicate blue. Within the grove, the children played in the clearings, naked as the day they were born, watched over by their elder siblings.

The first day of the festival dawned bright and clear, not a cloud in the sky. It began with High Mass at the church in nearly Loiza. For three successive days a procession, led by a statue of Santiago, headed down the highway to the seashore 6 miles away at Loiza Aldea. Then came open trucks with blaring brass and a steel band, and behind them, hundreds of scampering children and women (their hair in curlers) on foot. Adding to the cacophony were numerous cars honking their horns to the rhythm of the drums. But what caught our attention, most of all, were the masked dancers scattered here and there throughout the crowd. Who were these men in weird bat-like costumes and three-horned coconut-shell masks with bulging eyes and lolling tongues? Later, we found out.

In the blistering heat, Julia took photos, and Peter Gold, my student, recorded the band music. I gave up midway and gratefully accepted a ride to the end of the march. The afternoon's scheduled activities ended with horse races along the beach. How splendid the riders looked in their handsome Spanish capes and wire masks astride graceful little horses, called paso finos (fine gait) as they pranced and preened before the spectators!

263

The races over at the beach, we followed the tired and hungry crowd to the center of Loiza Aldea. The smell of barbecued *lechon* was everywhere, bars thronged with drinkers, and blue crab patties and *pasteles*, meat-filled pastries, were on sale at open kitchens. The streets were packed with children, drummers, dancers, everyone performing skits and tricks like actors on stage. Even the village homosexuals were there; in flamenco costumes and blond wigs, they preened and swished down the street snapping their fingers and tapping their feet in true Spanish style.

But there was more to come, we were informed by the villagers, you must see the *bomba*, they urged. As night fell, we found a huge clearing on the edge of town. Hundreds of people had already gathered there, from babies to the very old, to form a huge chorus. In the center, at the ready, were two young drummers. At a signal, they began to play, the sound reverberating in the stillness of the night. Soon the chorus joined in with one lovely song after another. Suddenly, a young man stepped into the light, paused before the drummers, and slowly began to dance, twisting and turning his body in graceful arcs, his feet beating out the rhythm. The *bomba* was now in full swing. The crowd cheered the dancer until, worn out, he dropped out of the circle. A moment later another took his place. Even the children were given a chance to show off their skills.

Meanwhile, we set up our recording machine near the dance circle and recorded intermittently as the chorus sang each new tune. Nobody interfered with our activities, but no one seemed to notice us either. At one in the morning, dead tired, we packed up our equipment and went back to our digs in San Juan to spend what was left of the night.

The next night we returned to the *bomba* site, and again set up our equipment. But, this time we were met by the organizers. "What happened to you?," they asked accusingly. "You left in the middle." Then I realized we had missed the cues: we had been their special guests, even without a formal invitation, and had walked out during a performance. Like actors or dancers anywhere in the world they felt slighted, demeaned by our departure. I apologized, and promised to stay until the end. That night they outdid themselves, there was electricity in the air, and they danced and sang and played their drums as never before.

After all that theatricality, and completely at sea about the festival's meaning, or origins, I hunted for someone to enlighten me. Right on the main drag of Loiza was a little shop, owned by the village mask maker and chief craftsman, Castor Ayala. He became our mentor, our storyteller, and historian. Mr Ayala spoke such colorful English that I would be remiss if I changed or left out a single word. So here it is, exactly as I recorded it. "Yeah," he said, "we feel it in the blood. This festival originated in Spain. One evening there was a great battle between the Spaniards and Moors. So they made masks with horns, like the ones in our festival, and costumes like vampire bat, like a devil, called *vejigantes*, in colors. Then they placed Spanish soldiers in the costumes and sent them at the head of the Spanish army. When the Moors saw those devils jumping around, they get afraid and run away. In the confusion, the Spanish army attack and won the battle. It was Santiago who led the Spanish soldiers to victory."

So, that's what it was, a celebration of the Reconquest in medieval Spain, the same event celebrated everywhere in Indian Latin America. Years later, sleuthing in the New York Public Library, I found the real beginning. It started out as a lavish 12th or 13th century pageant given at the Spanish court to commemorate the first Christian victories over the Moors. Later, *sans* gaudy finery, it moved to the marketplace as popular street entertainment. After the conquest of the Americas, the Catholic clergy taught it to their flocks, Indians and African slaves. I have always found it ironic that both Indians and Africans identified with the triumphant Christians rather than the Moors, like them a defeated people.

"But how did it get its start here?" I asked Ayala. "About 1832," he said, "an old woman here found a statue in the trunk of a tree in Medianias. She showed it to the priest who said it was a statue of Santiago. And every year since then, they make a festival in his honor."

"But," I said, "I saw three different statues, one for each of the three processions. How come?" "Well," he replied, "the little one you saw is for the children, the middle-sized one is for the women, and the big one for the men. That way, everyone has his own saint."

I still had one more question. "Mr. Ayala," I said, "the signs in town say your festival honors the gentle apostle, St. James, but the statues I saw were of a Spanish knight with the severed head of a Moor under the horse's feet." "Yes," he said, "but they are the same saint, only in different roles. You see, we honor Santiago as the warrior who led the Spaniards to victory against the Moors." Years later, I was to see that warrior image of St. James in the cathedral of Santiago de Compostela, Spain. There it was, an elaborate sculpture called *Santiago de los Matamoros*, St. James the Killer of Moors.

The festival over, life in Loiza came to a dead stop, everyone exhausted from the superhuman effort. In our spare hours we visited Ayala at his shop. As he whittled away, shaping cups and jars of coconut shells, he told stories about his village. We hung on every word. "The hurricane of San Cipriano was in 1932," he began. "She had winds 180 miles in speed. That night the wind blew in gusts. We had no warning, but we knew a hurricane was coming because the goats sniffed the sky at about five o'clock and were very nervous. My father say, 'You see the goats; there is going to be a hurricane today.'

"We take the goats to the yard and tie them up, but they don't want to stay, so we untie them and they run under the house. We know it by the hens, too. The hens here in this country sleep in the trees, but not that evening. Mother say, 'Oh look! They are going under the floor, one after the other, whoooop, under the floor.' Instinctively, they were searching for a safer place.

"Father say there will be a hurricane in two or three hours. We prepared everything neatly. We leave nothing loose. By six or seven o'clock, the wind strike harder. Father say, the hurricane is about half an hour away. Then father tie us with a big rope one to another, one to another. By nine o'clock the roof was stretching. I said, 'Father, let's get out of the house, it is going to fall down!' When the last one -- that was father -- got outside, the roof fell down -- crash! -- inside the house. If we didn't go out, the house would have killed us all. Till five in the morning, we stay outside. The hurricane swept over us; we see raining and balls of fire around the trees, balls of fire in the wind. We were wet and trembling with the wind and the sand that blew, with the wind that burned your face. Wow! The palm trees around the house fall down.

"When the hurricane was over, we try to go inside the house but we can't. Then we saw the lamplight. You see, when the roof fall down, it collapsed in the center of the house but left the corners standing. During all the hurricane, the lamp stay burning!

When the storm was over, I start to make breakfast for all the families whose houses fall down. After that hurricane we moved away from the seashore to where we are now. The winds of a hurricane sound like two hundred airplanes at the same time."

We never tired listening to Ayala's stories but more and more we were drawn to Loiza's musicians, family groups that we saw performing all over town. One day we chanced upon one of those impromptu concerts held under a tree on Loiza's main street. Soon my students were swapping songs with the singers, trying rhythms on their drums, and teaching them our own songs. Sofia, the lead singer, invited us to her house near the beach to meet her parents Mai and Pai and her brood of children. We sang with them, watched the children at their games, drank iced drinks on her porch -- and fell in love with each other. I came frequently during the next few years to see them. Neither Sofia, or anyone else, cared that I was from the States, or that I was white and they were black; I was a teacher and therefore deserved respect. They understood my work ultimately would be used to educate others. That was a noble purpose, for they believed fervently in education.

During the summer months when we came to visit we brought paints, crayons and reams of paper for the children. I still have their wonderful drawings in my files. When they tired we dashed to the beach for a quick swim. "Let's sing," I'd call out, and the children would gather round the table for the recording. "But where are your drums?" I asked. Without a word they dashed out into the sandy road outside the house and picked up anything that could make a sound, a rusty tomato can, an old iron tire rim, a discarded box spring, the kind of stuff found in the town dump. Some of their songs were learned in school, and the rest were hand-me-downs from Spain, Mexico, Africa and the States. To my amusement the American songs were often sung in unrecognizable

English. I finally traced one of them down: an action song which begins, "Head and shoulders, one, two, three," became in Loizan Spanglish "Erichori, very one, two, three". Deisy, Sofia's oldest daughter, followed me around, was the best singer and I loved her like my own child. With Sofia in command, the children, mischievous and smart, had to follow my orders to the letter.

Getting to know Sofia's family was a high point in my life. Though I spent hours with them I never "interviewed" them; we just talked, exchanged stories about life, hopes for the children, and swapped recipes. Mai Vargas, Sofia's peppery 70-year-old mother, jokingly calls her dark-skinned ex-husband her "blonde" husband. He comes by now and then in an ancient jalopy that barely makes the trip from his house to Sofia's. Señor Vargas is an old-style gentleman with the manners of a Spanish grandee and doesn't understand in the least, modern women's desire for equality. The only way to assuage his male vanity is to surrender on small things. Mai playfully twits him about his amours (probably the reason they split up); Pai only smiles and winks at my youngest student. When we go on an excursion in his car he pays for our refreshments, opens the door for me, and guides me by the elbow. When we offer to pay he is offended, it is an insult to his male vanity.

We sit on Sofia's porch and lazily pass the afternoon telling stories while my students and the children frolic at the beach. Mai recalls the Loiza of her youth. "You just had to be sorry for that town," she says, and these are her exact words, "there were only twenty-two houses scattered here and there and, at night, they were lit by kerosene lamps. The goats and cows came to eat in the plaza. Imagine, animals eating grass in the plaza!" She also remembers all the good things, no money but plenty to eat, and enough milk, and eggs to share with neighbors using the old-fashioned barter system. "Those who had money paid two cents for a bottle of milk, and if not, you paid with something you had from your garden. I had a nanny goat with big teats. I named her Papa and I raised a daughter of mine on her milk." On race, she was quite clear and did not believe in "purity". "They say," she mused, "there are only two races, black and white, but the hen gives birth to many-colored chickens. Sometimes you can't tell a person by his color. For example, someone is perfectly White, and his hair comes out like a Black."

About the younger generation she had harsh words, though she admitted going to wild parties and being "indiscreet" in her own youth. With fire in her eyes, and thunder in her voice she pronounces judgment: "Before we didn't have disorder among young people. Now there is civilization. Disgraceful things are happening. People fight with clubs, sticks and knives killing each other. They are so stupid. And then there are drugs." She shakes her head in despair....

One day she said something that truly surprised me: "When a child is born here," she said, "everyone cries for him and brings presents." "But why," I ask, "why do you do that? " "We cry," she says, "because nobody knows the destiny of that child, how his death will be. When a child dies we hold a *baquiné* (wake), sing songs and play the drums." To this day I am not sure what she meant. To celebrate birth with tears, and death with songs was new to me. Perhaps the tears express the natural worries of every new mother, "Is my child without blemish and, will he/she have the necessary talent and opportunities for a fruitful life?" And the songs at the wake, a send-off, a celebration of his life, however it was.

My most intimate friendship was with Mai's daughter Sofia. Sofia was a widow with six children, the first one born out of wedlock, and the rest by her second husband. Tall, stately and attractive, Sofia was outspoken about her life. She hid nothing, described the terrible treatment she suffered from her family because she had "sinned" as a young woman, the struggle to educate herself and make a living, and the turmoil of her life with men. "To tell you the truth," she said, as we had a cool drink on her porch, "I don't like to boss men around, but I want to be respected. People say I'm tough. Well, if that means I won't put up with abuse, they're right. My husband never harassed me because he knew I'd harass him back. I'm a woman of temperament." She went on to describe the fighting matches with her husband, a boxer, which ended in a draw only when each had dealt the other a black eye. But she's a generous woman. "If my husband needs help," she says, "I'll wear pants and work like a man. If my man can't feed us for some reason, I'll work for both of us, and with all my heart. But, nobody gives orders here but me," she added, "not Pai or Mai, nor my kids, nor anyone." And I believe her to this very day.

Sofia became my guide through the maze of Loiza's religious institutions. Like many villagers she was a Catholic, but one with little faith that prayers and attending Mass would solve problems like drinking and carousing. She also barely concealed her contempt for Jehovah's Witnesses and Pentecostals, the Protestant churches established in Loiza by American missionaries. To prove how ineffectual they were, she took me to a Pentecostal meeting. She sat there with a sneer on her face, disgusted as she listened to the dull sermons and testimonies on sin and salvation. But, when I refused the entreaties to join their church, Sofia positively glowed with happiness, and walked out of the meeting hall with her head held high.

She also believed in *espiritismo*, Puerto Rico's form of

Caribbean Afro-Christian cults, and considered herself a witch, a good witch with powers as a healer and benefactor. "I have all the spiritual development I need to be a medium," she said. "Other people have more knowledge, but I'm a clairvoyant. I see things simply by talking to people. In my dreams I cure crippled and sick men just by putting my hand on them. I would cure thousands of people, not with medicines, but with plants other people don't know about. They are everywhere and I have cured with them."

Despite faith in her powers, Sofia realized they had limitations. "When I feel sick I go to a doctor. If he can't help me I go to an *espiritista*. I'm not going to let myself die just like that. God has given these people understanding. Yes, one has to doubt, but one has to believe also." "Suppose it doesn't work," I said, "what then?" She shrugged her shoulders, "What can I lose, at least it won't harm me." I couldn't argue the point further.

On Sofia's suggestion I paid a visit to a San Juan *botanica*, where spiritualists buy their supplies. I was amazed at the array of herbs, plants and pills. There were printed prayers for countless Christian saints: St. Silvestre, St. Joan of Arc and St. Malta -- and for spiritual forces I never heard of -- the Just Judges and the Holy Shirt. Besides these were the African Powers, each with its own mission, and its own color -- Alegua (black), Alofi (red), Ocun (white), Shango (brown), and Yemala (red). "There are people," said Sofia by way of explanation, "who have been shot at, but not killed, because the bullet hit a button or a belt buckle; that's because of the Holy Shirt. He protects you from bodily harm."

Sofia's sense of justice rested on shaky grounds. One day Sofia herself was hauled before a judge for attacking a woman who had threatened her with a knife. Although she never told me, the injury must have been serious. Nevertheless the judge let her off

272

and fined the victim $100.00. "How did you get away with it?" I asked her. "That day," she said, preening herself, "I used a prayer that said, 'With two I see you, with three I tie you, your blood I will drink, and your heart will break.' That why nothing happened to me." I still can't see the connection.

The belief in spirits was widespread in Loiza Aldea. Ayala spoke about his talents as god-given. He believed he had an invisible protector, an Indian, who stood guard at his shop and was the source of his inspiration. "One day," he said, "the spiritualist in Guayama told me, 'That Indian was your father in ancient times, and he is by your side always. Don't you feel him by your side when you're alone?' 'Yes,' I said,' I don't see him but I feel him there.' She said, 'Everything you design is not from you; your hand is directed by him.' Perhaps she is right, because I feel something rare when I design. I have to make it the moment I see it, or I forget it." He was very proud of the household articles he made, especially the masks, one of which, he had been told, hung in the receiving room of Buckingham Palace.

I never put much stock in dreams, or the Freudian interpretations so popular in my youth; yet, here I was sitting on Sofia's porch in Loiza completely absorbed listening to hers. Years have passed since I first heard them, yet they keep recurring in my mind, because they are so vivid, so stark, so realistic. Sofia began: "Lots of queer things have happened in my life. When I was in seventh grade, my mother worked in Santurce. I brought up the children, fed them, and took care of the house. During this time I slept in my mother's room. One night, everyone had gone to bed but I couldn't sleep. I felt frightened and left the kerosene lamp burning on the dresser. Suddenly I heard someone open the front door. An old black woman entered my room. She was very thin, tall, and hunchbacked. As she came towards me, I could see her

273

stiffly starched skirt and long-sleeved jacket. I was frightened. The hunchbacked lady took off all her clothes -- kerchief, jacket, her enormous bra, a skirt, and another skirt -- and put it all on a chair. Then she climbed into my bed. I was afraid to move or scream because my little brother was sleeping next to me. Suddenly I looked at him and saw that he was dead! There we were, my brother's corpse, the old lady and me. Then she began sticking her fingers in my eyes, my ears, my mouth, everywhere she could."

She paused, and then continued her story. "At daybreak, the old lady dressed, and my brother became alive again, but the nightmare was not yet finished. I saw a tiny dwarf about as big as my finger, sitting on a bench, holding a tiny jar. He plucked my pubic hairs one by one. Every time he plucked a hair, a drop of blood fell, and he gathered it into his tiny jar. After a while, he waved goodby, put his little bench under his arm, and disappeared through a crack in the wall. By this time it was 9 o'clock and I was late for school. Miss Becerri, my teacher, came looking for me. She and my sisters entered my room, shook me, and sat me up in bed, but I was so nervous I couldn't talk. Miss Becerri understood I had a nightmare and promised to help me.

"They took me to a spiritualist, who explained everything. She said that behind my house lived an insane woman who believed my mother had caused the death of one of her children. That woman had been reading devil books, harmful books that arouse bad spirits. Since my mother wasn't home, all this happened to me instead of her. When my mother came home I told her the whole story. She told me she had the same dream in Santurce! That spiritualist knew exactly what had happened, and why."

Then one day she recounted one of her happy dreams. With her youngest boy cradled in her lap she began: "Once, when I was young, my mother said, 'Sofia, sweep the back yard.' That night I dreamed I swept so much sand away I uncovered a hard surface like cement. It had a handle. I lifted the handle and saw a path with a stairway. I walked to the bottom and saw a long table with twelve chairs. I knew it was the table of the Last Supper. Straight ahead on top of a boulder, Jesus was sitting, holding a long shepherd's hook. I felt such happiness that I stared at him respectfully. He said to me, 'I've been waiting for you. I want you to come every day and clean this place, but don't tell anyone or you won't find the door again.'

"I swept the floor, washed the dishes, and put them away. Then I said goodbye and left. The next night I had the same dream. I went back and did the same chores. But, the third day my heart was so overflowing with happiness that I told my mother the whole story. 'Mama, I feel so good when I'm down there. Outside it is hot and there is so cool. It's so beautiful, so delicious! And she said, 'Is that true?' And I said, 'Come and see for yourself.' We sneaked out of the house so no one would see us. Jesus treated us so nice and was as always, so happy. I said, 'This is my mother. You told me not to tell anyone, and I'm not going to tell anyone else, but please let my mother stay.' He didn't answer, only smiled and seemed happy we were both there. But the next day I couldn't find the door anymore."

The last time I saw Sofia she was in particular distress. I made an unannounced visit to Puerto Rico and went straight to Loiza Aldea. As I approached her house, I heard bloodcurdling screams. Sofia was lying on her bed, two women on either side, and her children standing round in obvious terror. One of the women, an *espiritista* herself, told me that Sofia was possessed by her dead husband, and they had come to help her exorcize him. Suddenly Sofia screamed again and thrashed around on the bed. "It is my fault," she said in anguished tones, "that man would still be alive today if I hadn't been so mean to him." She spoke of a man whom she had rejected and who had committed suicide. When she momentarily calmed down she noticed me. "I'm so sorry you see me in this state, Señora Enriqueta, I knew you were coming because I saw you in my dream two nights ago." Again she screamed and tossed around, this time with alarming vehemence. The two women pleaded with her to stop, "Sofia, any more tantrums like that and you will be dead, and your children will be orphans!" But Sofia continued her list of woes, especially about her sixteen-year old son's disastrous marriage to an even younger teenager. "They are two children playing grownup," she moaned. "My son hangs out all day with the married men, drinking and playing cards. And his bride stays home with me, and gets in my way, and doesn't know how to do anything." Finally, exhausted from the ordeal, Sofia stood up, walked into her tiny living room, looking calm and collected; she had exorcized her demons and was ready to resume her life. "I'm glad you are here, Enriqueta," she said embracing me, "let's work together, as always."

Sofia and I relaxed over a cool drink and then she described all that had happened since my last visit. "You know I have boyfriends, but I live alone. A man has to court me for a long time before I say yes; I don't go just for pleasure; a man has to benefit me, has to respect me for what I am. That man I told you about, he died, but I can't just cry about the past. I have a new man now. This man I have now is really helpful. Sometimes I come home and find the house clean, the floors mopped, and the rice and beans cooked. He takes care of my kids and never talks rough to them. He can give advice but if he comes with a lot of noise I'd tell him, 'Beat it, is this your house?' Food, clothing, shoes, money, I'll take those anytime, but he can't be my boss. You have something, share it with me. I have something too; here have some."

Although the new man helped financially there was a catch; he was married with children. One day Sofia's *espiritista* told her to expect a visit from his wife. Two days later, she appeared on the porch looking very angry and nervous. Meanwhile her husband hid in the house. Sofia politely received her unwanted guest. "People tell me," said the wife in a loud voice, "that my husband comes to visit you." Sofia had decided on a strategy of denial. "Listen," she said, "do I look like the kind of person who would do such a thing, me, a widow with six children? You can search my house if you like." The wife soon left, assured that Sofia had been a victim of malevolent gossip. "Why did you do that?" I asked Sofia. "I'm just being sensible," she rejoined. "If I had admitted anything, she would fight with her husband; he would be unhappy, she would be unhappy, and I would be unhappy too. This way I reassure her, and we go on as before. Anyway, I don't want marriage, I don't trust men."

I have often wondered how it all came out. In villages like Loiza, free spirits like Sofia live a tough life. Under the surface calm is a highly charged atmosphere, and it is easy to believe that malevolent spirits move about in the dark of night. One night, there was a ghostly, but real attacker in the woods outside her house threatening to burn her house down. Although she did not tell me, I'm sure he was a former lover with revenge on his mind. From then on I began to realize that even I, child of reason, and rightfully frightened by tangible things like a man with a gun, could also be scared out of my wits by things I couldn't see. That night my students were so frightened they begged me to leave. Not until we were safely back in San Juan did we breathe a sigh of relief.

Personally, I have never been drawn into religious life, but I have been an observer of many unusual systems of belief, as I have described elsewhere in these memoirs. One more religious encounter awaited me in Puerto Rico, this one in San Juan. Mita, the leader of a truly native church, born Juanita Garcia Peraza of wealthy parents, explained to me that she founded her church to serve humanity in gratitude for surviving a serious illness. In 1969, when I met her, she claimed 10,000 followers in Puerto Rico, the United States and the Dominican Republic. Her followers believed she was the Prophet of the Twentieth century, as Moses and Jesus were of their time. She called all to salvation -- rich and poor, black and white. Besides spiritual goals her church operated a non-profit cooperative, and businesses like bakeries and taxi services. While her followers were the island's poor and uneducated, her ministers were educated articulate men, and smart traders as well.

Mita was in her 60s, a big motherly figure that hid a will of iron. I visited her farm, where she raised animals and farm products. Hundreds came to see her for help; she gave each one a dollar, or paid their rent, or hospital bills. Her followers claimed she cured cancer, diabetes, heart trouble, whatever.

The congregation was ultra conservative and puritanical. One of her administrators explained, "My life was pleasures and vices -- women, dancing, gambling and drinking. My whole family suffered for my sins. But, when I met Mita, fear entered my heart. Instead of a party, I go to church and pray. I am happy, so is my family, and my illnesses have disappeared."

Mita seemed to resemble those early bluenose Americans who took hatchets to beer kegs, banned dancing and the fiddle as devil music. But she knew how to use Puerto Rico's popular music for her own purposes. Three bands were always on hand in her enormous house of worship -- a small brass band, a string trio, and a duo, which alternated during the service. Only the words embodied her vision of the world.

One day, I received an invitation to attend a service at her temple. I suspected something special was brewing because Mita insisted I be there. The immense hall was crowded with worshipers, all dressed in white. Impassioned preachers aroused the congregation to a feverish pitch, and the singing began. The people rose to their feet, clapping, stamping their feet, and swaying their bodies, many in trance, to the rhythm of the music. Shouts of joy welled up as the songs reached their climax, and a roar swept the hall. Then -- complete silence. The brass band struck up a joyous march -- and finally, Mita appeared on the platform, a bright, smiling figure waving a white handkerchief.

Suddenly, Mita fixed her gaze on me. Addressing me directly, she pleaded with me to join her crusade. Everyone's eyes were on me too, waiting breathlessly for my answer. I waited until she finished -- and then slowly shook my head, no. Mita slumped into her seat, in obvious defeat. The service over, I climbed up the stairs to the platform, put my arms around her, and said, "Mita, forgive me, but I cannot do what you ask. Please, can't we be friends?" Her answer was cold and unforgiving. Like the Pentecostal church in Loiza, Mita is in the business of saving souls. Friendships flow from commitment to her ideas, and she has no stomach for friendships in the abstract.

After the service I spoke with her ministers. "You see those three lights over the temple," one said, "they stand for love, unity, and freedom, love between members, and unity of all people in one church." "What about the third light -- freedom?" I asked. "That means we must be free of sin." I learned something new that day: a

279

word can mean whatever you want it to mean.

Thus far, I had spent most of my time on the Puerto Rican coast, without ever visiting the island's mountain villages. When I learned that Peter Hawes, a member of the Almanac Singers in the 1940s, was living in Certenejas, a mountain town, I went to visit him and his wife Ellen. We had a grand reunion. Thanks to them I met two talented guitarists, both about fourteen years old, whose playing so impressed me that I returned many times to record their music. They played and sang Puerto Rico's traditional *decimas,* *aguinaldos* and *plenas* in incomparable mountain style, one relatively uninfluenced by Afro-Caribbean music of the coast.

Pete and Ellen also introduced me to Doña Lola, an inimitable 80-year-old powerhouse! Going down the road to town, she looked like a ship in full sail. We spent hours listening to stories, told in inimitable language, about her happy youth. "O.K.," she said, "we didn't have bad times because we didn't know what bad times were. My pop wasn't really rich, but he did all right. There was a school here, but none of us older kids went. The teacher would come to round us up, and you know what we'd do? Crawl under the table. Me, what I liked to do was follow my Papa around, help him with the harvest." Then she paused, and proudly said, "Sometimes I earned 30 cents a day, and 35 cents if I worked until midnight in the tobacco fields."

Lola was no fool when it came to men. She took to heart the old saying, *mejor sola que mal acompañada* (better alone than in bad company). After a four-year courtship with a local boy she called it off. "He was a nice guy," she told me, "His only fault was that he was lazy and poor. He'd work a few days to buy cigars and shirt or two, but nothing else. Now, what can a girl expect from a man like that?"

Lola finally married Rafael, whom she met at the tobacco parties. "We danced mazurkas, polkas, *seis gambao*, *corrios* and *chorreaos* until five in the morning. And if we had fun gathering tobacco, we had more fun that night. We'd go in groups and stop at each house, do a few turns and go on to another house with our music." Her final words still ring in my ears. "I really liked the old days better! You could be garlic-ugly and strong. For me there was no right or wrong. I felt I could do anything."

Despite our different backgrounds and way of life I felt a special kinship with Lola in the mountains and Sofia in Loiza; they were women I could talk to about anything, my family, my lovers, husbands, and my children. We understood each other because we were women, and because we knew poverty. And, miracle of all, we shared a sense of the beauty of life.

In 1969 I spent most of my time in San Juan itself researching material for a book about Puerto Rico targeted for a teenage audience. Mika Seeger, Pete Seeger's daughter, and several students joined me on that trip. Unlike previous trips to villages, I now had discussions with politicians, labor and youth leaders, artists, musicians, and university professors. Most of all we talked about the overwhelming American presence on the island. "Even the University of Puerto Rico," I was told, "is called The American University in Puerto Rico. Most scientific journals and books are available only in English. So is your rock and rap. Whatever you have in the States, we have here! "

"Right now we're trying to build a Puerto Rican identity," said Antonio Martorell, a gifted graphic artist, the director of *El Taller Alacran* (The Scorpion Workshop) which teaches artistic skills to juvenile delinquents, school drop-outs, and drug addicts." We

281

must do this because we have always been put down, beginning with the Spaniards, who saw this as a wilderness."

As usual I pursued my interest in women. Were Puerto Rican women like their disadvantaged sisters elsewhere in the Spanish world? Nilita Vientos Gastón, a leading intellectual figure, was my best informant. Magnetic, eccentric, bold in her public actions and speech, she had held important posts in public life. "It's true," she said, "Women do just about everything in Puerto Rico. They are much more important in literature and politics than in the States. For example, for fifteen years I was director of the *Ateneo de Cultura Puertoriqueña* (Atheneum of Puerto Rican Culture), our oldest cultural institution. I was the first woman to hold the post, and I directed the most important literary review. I was also Attorney General for some years." Then she went on to name the posts that women occupy -- the mayor of San Juan was a woman, there were legislators, doctors and scientists, university women -- an extraordinary development of the last few years.

"Attitudes, however, towards sex and morals," she continued, "they change too, but slowly. These days a father is proud that his daughter is a lawyer or a doctor, but sex with a man she's not married to -- that's an unforgivable sin. The very rich and the very poor have always done whatever they wanted. It's the middle class woman who is condemned by the community." I didn't bother to tell her that I have long known, and admired, just such middle-class women for their skill in deception; they know all the ways to fool parents, as well as husbands and lovers.

Finally, Nilita spoke about her own private life. "The truth is," she said ruefully, "my father and brothers lay down the rules; I have to tell them where I'm going, the men I see, and when to expect me home." By the hints she dropped, I'm sure she resented her family's interference, but did she ever fight back? That she never told me.

One hundred years has passed since the United States took over Puerto Rico. Yet, like many marriages, their relationship rests on shaky ground; neither party knows if they are better off together or apart.

***

Chapter Nine –
Eastern Europe and Germany

Roumania - 1959

Over the years, sandwiched in between field trips and teaching at City College I managed to travel to many countries in the Orient and Europe, often to attend international conferences on folk music. The truly memorable ones were those in the Soviet orbit, pleasant affairs where we reported our latest findings, renewed friendships with old colleagues, and, above all, had our introduction to peasant life and culture.

Yet, invariably we felt the numbing hand of Marxist ideology-- the inability to view the arts -- or history -- in terms other than the "class struggle", the fear of innovation and "capitalist contamination", and stifling censorship. In Germany, and mostly Austria, the specter of Nazism still lurked distressingly in the shadows. While ordinary tourists could ignore politics, we musicians could not; we had it thrust upon us.

Roumania was the first country I visited, not only for the annual meeting of the International Folk Music Council, a UNESCO sponsored organization, but to attend Roumania's mammoth five-day folk arts festival in Bucharest. I flew to Vienna and there boarded a Roumanian plane for the flight. When the plane taxied out on the tarmac, I took fright, the little craft looked like a World War II relic. Would it get off the ground, I wondered nervously, and if it did, could it fly? Once on board my fears increased, for the cabin was dark and gloomy, and flew so close to the ground it barely skimmed over the trees of the Carpathian Mountains below. However, the fight attendant did her best, assuring us the airline had never had an accident. Later on, I learned Roumania's entire fleet consisted of three passenger planes, and never flew in bad weather. Good thing I didn't know that while we were aloft, but on second thought, suppose I had? It was a lovely day, not a cloud in the sky, and I was really excited about this first trip into Soviet territory, curious and a little worried about what might happen.

The first sight on landing only increased my anxiety; there we were in pitch darkness with only a red neon sign reading "Bucharest" above the airport facade. Silently the small knot of passengers filed into the dimly lit, almost empty airport. Our bags were brought in from the aircraft, and we faced the hostile glares of the customs officers. As they were about to open our bags, two young people rushed up to rescue us, retrieved our luggage, quickly had our passports stamped, and a car whisked us away towards the lights of Bucharest. In perfect English they identified themselves -- a welcome committee from the Ministry of Culture.

Once settled into the Athenee Palace Hotel we breathed a sigh of relief; we were safe and sound. Though worn and shabby, the hotel still bore signs of an elegant past -- red damask walls, huge ornate mirrors, dazzling crystal chandeliers, and wide curving stairways. Yes, our guides told us, this hotel was once famous for its gambling tables and marvelous cuisine, but, they added, that was before the revolution. That evening as I dined in the hotel's gracious garden restaurant, soothed by the excellent food and the old world manners of the elderly waiter, I almost forgot I was in Socialist Roumania. Suddenly, I was jarred back to the present:

no tipping allowed. Nevertheless, a pack of cigarettes was gratefully received. An instant later I regretted my generosity; there was no super-market around the corner with endless supplies of cigarettes.

I stretched out on the comfortable bed, my eyes already half-closed. But no, I was not to sleep that night, for until dawn jukebox music from a nearby nightclub blared forth endless streams of "continental" music, that banal European stew of watered-down Caribbean rhythm, American pop, and Viennese schmaltz.

At six the next morning, groggy from lack of sleep, we were on our way to Sinaia, the conference site, where we were to spend a week or so. "There are three palaces here," said our guide, as the first came into view, "one for each of the three kings who ruled here since the end of the Turkish occupation in the last century. The one we're passing right now was built for our first king, Carol I, a German prince, and as you see, it's a pretty dark and gloomy place, but how do you like the gardens? They were designed by French and Italians. "

Up, up, the road twisted into the wooded palace grounds. Finally, Pelisor House, the palace of the second Roumanian king, Ferdinand and his glamorous queen Maria, came into view, our home for the week. Unlike Carol I's palace, it was an enormous gingerbread house, an elegant imitation of peasant architecture. We walked through the enormous foyer to my own room. For a folklorist used to sleeping bags sometimes invaded by unwelcome insects, this was sheer heaven. The room was furnished with peasant handicrafts, blue and white rugs, embroidered curtains and bedspreads; thick white towels were warming on hot metal pipes in the bathroom.

My room, as it turned out, had a special history; it had been

287

King Ferdinand's own private quarters. In order to avoid being observed by guards stationed in the foyer when visiting the queen, the shy King had a stairway built in the bathroom. This led directly to the queen's quarters on the floor above. Now, this bathroom was no ordinary place: the bathtub was reputed to be of pure silver! During the conference, all the delegates came to see it. "Was it really silver?" they asked, tapping the sides. Some said, yes, others, said no, I among the no-sayers.

The next morning the conference began in earnest. Up the hill we went after breakfast to Foisor Palace, the third palace and once home of the deposed Carol II and his mistress, Magda Lupescu. This palace, our headquarters, had a decided lower-middle class look, the blue velour sofas and chairs looked like the kind found in bargain basements. The main meeting room, however, except for spindly gold-leafed chairs, was definitely 20th century efficiency; typewriters, mimeograph machines, tape recorders, movie and slide projectors were everywhere. Entangling earphone wires connected to five translations booths -- English, French, Russian, German, and Roumanian -- made walking around the room hazardous.

Since this was my first international conference, I was intrigued by the prospect of meeting so many people; there were more than a hundred people from thirty different countries. I wondered whether political enemies would bury their differences even for a while. Would the Israeli delegates be friendly to the Egyptian lady, and would the East Germans talk to the West Germans? On the surface there was plenty of good will to go around. The Roumanians supplied the proper atmosphere for budding friendships. Every day we were whisked around to special dinners, receptions, excursions; we had excellent food, and a bar to while away leisure hours drinking Turkish coffee and enjoying informal concerts. The pastry cook, for instance, formerly employed by the royal family, was nothing short of a genius; and who thought about calories and cholesterol in those days?

Then, one day, we were plummeted into reality. My companion on this trip, Ruth Rubin, a distinguished Yiddish folklorist, before leaving New York had received permission from the Roumanians to interview a Jewish folklorist, a survivor of the Holocaust. At the appointed time she appeared with a few interested Israeli colleagues to find not only her Roumanian colleague there but a government representative as well. First came words of welcome, then, to our complete surprise, he laid down rules; the interview would be conducted only in English and Roumanian; Yiddish, though the common language, was forbidden. Dismay was written on everyone's face, there were loud protests, and the meeting ended with bad feelings all around. Anti-Semitism was alive and well under Socialism; the Jewish folklorist was not even permitted to be a delegate to the conference.

But there was more to come. The keynote address by Mihai Pop, head of the Roumanian Folklore Institute, spelled out the prevailing theory on folklore. Under Socialism, he claimed, a new optimistic music was being created which reflected "a collective society engaged in the building of Socialism." Under capitalism, he expounded, "folk music reflected the unity of the popular masses in their struggle against the ruling classes." Heavens, I thought, who can belief such nonsense? Most of the delegates took these official pronouncements with a grain of salt. Given the enormous variety of folk music, and performance styles around the world, we knew it was a big, politically motivated lie. As for Pop's claim about new "Socialist" music, well, we would see if it existed in reality, or just theory at the forthcoming dance and music festival.

When we returned to Bucharest the competition was in full

swing. A veteran of many folk festivals, I now witnessed the biggest and most extravagant of my life. More than 3,000 singers, instrumentalists, and dancers in brilliant costumes were in the city from every province, the semi-finalists of an original 700,000. Imagine 700,000 in a country of 16 million! When not in the theater performing before judges or on outdoor stages, they sang, danced and traded songs on the street with each other far into the night. Gypsy bands (*lautari*) played an astounding variety of instruments. One orchestra consisted of fifteen kinds of shepherd pipes, and still another of alpenhorns and flutes -- and, of course, bagpipes and singers galore. I was also captivated by the dissonant polyphony practiced here long before the advent of Christianity. But nothing turned me on more than the oriental-like *doina*. Like the Blues and Flamenco, the *doina* is soul music, and its singers are stars like our own Bessie Smith or Billie Holiday.

Then there was the dance. Roumania, situated between East and West, has an endless variety -- primitive round dances like the *hora* and the *sirba*, high leaping shepherd dances, peasant adaptations of court dances, and recent imports from Hungary and Germany. To see them all together as we did in 1959 was like a review of history, a who's who of the peoples who settled there over millennia.

Finally, we heard some of the heralded "New Music". What a disappointment! It struggled toward mediocrity. Day after day we listened to lusty performances by mammoth-size factory and peasant-cooperative choruses. Unfortunately, the heavy Russian-style arrangements buried the charm and lightness of the original songs, as inappropriate as arranging the blues for a concert choir. Worst yet were the sanitized folk dances performed by Roumania's trained ballet corp with sticky coyness. But the bottom of the cultural pit were the so-called "Artistic Brigades", which like our own "agit-prop" of the Depression, were high in propaganda and low in art.

The festival over, the Roumanians organized a tour of the villages. That was more to our liking. Festivals were great occasions to see the most talented and most imaginative performances, but I preferred to see them in their natural setting. As our bus rolled along the highway, we passed fields of white poppies and stalks of green corn grown high, the small wooden houses painted in beautiful abstract designs. Everywhere we saw exquisitely embroidered clothes and household items. But -- the village streets were unpaved, only partially electrified, and looked as if nothing had changed in centuries.

The peasants opened their hearts to us. At each stop we were greeted by the entire village, everyone dressed in holiday finery. Our initial awkwardness and shyness disappeared as we joined them in the dance -- from which no one was excused. We whirled around at breakneck speed, linking arms or waists, were spun around by our partners until breathless, our hearts pounding from the effort; only strong male arms kept me from losing my balance and landing on the ground.

A peasant dance is fun and recreation but it is also a courtship game. The older women, busy matchmakers, made sure every man paired off with a female partner. They are right; nothing stirs the sexual juices more than close contact of a dance. However, our own popular dances like the frug, the twist, even the old Charleston, though not couple dances, never deterred our kids from finding sexual partners.

Only one incident marred our excursion. When our bus stopped at a hamlet for a short rest, we were greeted by peasants obviously waiting to talk to us. When our Roumanian-born member engaged them in conversation, a moment later, a Roumanian official stood at our side offering assistance. "We don't need your help, " we told him. "I'm sorry," he said. "You are not allowed to talk to strangers. We want to protect you." Despite our protests, he shooed the villagers away, and led us back to the bus.

Back in Bucharest I was about to experience Soviet censorship personally. Gathering facts for a *New York Times* article, I arranged an interview with a Roumanian composer I had met in Sinaia. The next morning I went to the appointed place, but he never appeared. Instead I found Bert Lloyd, an English folklorist, waiting for me. "Come along," he said, "the Composers Union wants to talk to you." "I don't want to talk to an organization," I complained, "just one person, that's all. Besides I have a date." "That's been canceled," he said firmly.

Bert led me to the Union's headquarters, an elegant old house, once the home of the late George Enescu, Roumania's greatest composer. In a spacious wood-paneled conference room fifteen men were gathered around a huge table waiting for me. Coffee and pastries were served and after a few pleasantries, we settled down to talk.

On my question about government funding, they had this to say: Yes, the government purchases works in three categories, art music, popular music, and one called "mass" music, the price established according to musical value. "What determines the musical value of a work?" I asked. The answer -- "It must be in keeping with the philosophy of Socialist realism." With further probing, the meaning became clear -- "We write music that will not offend our new Socialist listeners who know nothing about classical music." "After all," they said, "why should we play to an empty hall, or offend our listeners with too much dissonance?" "But," I asked. " what about your more educated listeners, is there anything more challenging for them?" In a moment of candor they confessed that a composer who used a text could write more experimental music! "How's that? " I asked, completely mystified. "Don't you see," he replied with a sly smile, "then people are listening to the words, and less to the music! " Pure hypocrisy, I thought to myself.

Then the talk turned to music in the United States, a jumble of misinformation. First, they postulated that workers are not <u>allowed</u> to attend concerts of classical music. Then they claimed no classical music is permitted on radio stations. Finally, came the crucial complaint, "Your popular music is corrupting our youth." I threw up my hands in dismay. "You can't blame us," I said, "no one is forcing them to listen to it. They listen because they like it." Then I added to myself, "You think Socialism is changing the world? Oh no, it's communications that does it." No wonder they were angry. They were helpless. How can you stop the kids from turning on their short-wave radio, or smuggling recordings from the West? A hopeless task!

Afterwards as I walked back to my hotel, I mulled over what I had just heard. Composers in the West would certainly envy the perks given to artists, but would they accept the price, the loss of artistic freedom? In hindsight, with the collapse of Soviet power, we know they, like the Nazis, produced nothing but dreary, conventional art. Yes, the Roumanian composers rightly criticized our commercially-driven musical world but, with all its wrinkles, it does not stifle creativity, nor imprison, banish, or commit artists to psychiatric wards for defying government dictums on the arts.

For years I had heard about ancient tribal rivalries in the Balkans. Under the Soviets they were kept at bay, remarkably so. However, at the end of our conference, an incident occurred that proved that though hidden, tribalism was still alive and well. When we asked our Hungarian delegate, a Catholic priest, to give a speech honoring the secretary of the ICTM at our final banquet, he was shocked at the request. "What," he said, "you ask me, a Hungarian, to give a formal speech in Roumania? I cannot do that." Years have passed since that visit, but the Balkans continue their intertribal wars to this very day.

Once again I flew in the same antique plane that brought me to Bucharest. Soon the Carpathian Mountains were below us, black and menacing as before. I drew the curtains to shut them out and prayed that rain would not force us to land in some remote clearing in the forest. I closed my eyes trying to get some sleep at last. Why did I think the airport was gloomy? It was so bright and bustling when we left. They even held the plane for me while, at the last minute, I bought a beautiful embroidered peasant blouse.

But sleep was impossible as my mind wandered from recollection to recollection. How lovely, those cool evenings under the stars in Sinaia as we listened to peasants singing ancient epic sagas on the terrace, the camaraderie in the bar, the friendships newly formed. Oh yes, the Egyptian lady did make friends with the Israelis. And the East Germans -- they were not Communists, the West Germans were -- and there was no love lost between them. Marxist theory in folk music? Well, the people march to their own tune, and theorists march to theirs.

Vienna, after oppressive Roumania, was a breath of fresh air. I floated around the city, indulged my passion for coffee with schlag, and gazed longingly at shop windows with goods too costly for my slender purse. I stayed at a third-class hotel in a district known for its cheap prostitutes, and was mistaken for one of them. But one night, I had a taste of life among the rich and privileged: Edith Harich-Schneider, the great harpsichordist I had met in Sinaia, invited me to dine with her at the sumptuous garden restaurant of the Schoenbrunn Palace. The soft glow of lights illuminated the sparkling glasses and fine china at our table, and red-jacketed waiters served us food and wine fit for a king (or two queens). "Yes," said Edith, "I agree with you. It is better for the artist to starve a little than be a lackey to some ignorant commissar."

Edith lived in a tiny apartment cluttered with books and musical scores. She had an extraordinary musical ear, could read an orchestral score and hear every instrument in her head. A true free spirit, caught in Japan during World War II, she remained there to give courses in Western music to Japanese musicians.

That was the last time I saw Edith. I flew to Geneva, picked up Peter who was spending the summer at a children's camp at the Lake, went on to Rapallo on the Italian Rivera, and then to Venice. We swam, basked in the sun, and like every one else, bought Venetian glass and spent hours at the Piazza di Signoria in full sight of the Grand Canal and Miguelangelo's David (the copy). One night we watched the commemoration of the Battle of Lepanto, when the Venetians defeated the Turks in the 16th century. From our seats high on the rafters overlooking the canal we saw the gondolas lit with multi-colored lamps glide along the black waters, listened to the music of the period, and laughed at the lunatic antics of *Il Teatro Piccolo di Milano*.

But nothing matched the pleasure of days spent with my young son; and that I cannot express in words.

295

Czechoslovakia

1962

"Terribly superstitious, the Slovaks," Czech friends in New York had warned me, "I tell you, Henrietta, those peasants haven't changed their ways in a thousand years. Ah, but Prague," they sighed, their voices tinged with nostalgia, "that was another world, beautiful, cultured, with theater, music, ballet, everything, and the best food in Europe."

Alas and alack, my friends would have been sorely disappointed in the Prague I saw in 1962. It was no longer the pre-World War II city they remembered. Yes, Prague was magnificent, but an oppressive air hung like a black cloud. With colleagues I explored the city, admired its medieval plazas, paused at the Charles Bridge to follow the gentle flow of the Moldau, the river that inspired Smetana's evocative orchestral work. We climbed the hill to the Hradcany, Prague's medieval castle, admired Jan Hus' Protestant church. Then one day, we stumbled on that other side of medieval Prague, not its official architecture, but the humble "Golden Lane". This narrow little street lined with miniature houses, as if built for midgets, had once been home to crafty alchemists who fooled a gullible monarch into believing base metal could be turned into gold; all they asked for was a little gold to start the process.

I looked for signs of the old Prague that once had been a literary and musical Mecca. The composers Smetana, Dvorak, and Janacek were long gone, and there was no sign of new ones to replace them. A hunt in Wenceslaus Square bookstores was also disappointing; there were no fine editions for which the Czechs were justly famous, only cheap, mediocre publications.

But we were not tourists, we hadn't come to bask in Prague's beauty, nor weep for its glorious past, we had come on a cultural mission. As in Roumania, we quickly learned that culture did not exist without politics. However, unlike the passive Roumanians, the Czechs grumbled, told anti-government jokes, and complained under their breath, sometimes out loud.

Our first awareness of Soviet-style control occurred shortly after arrival. Ruth Rubin, the Yiddish folklorist, also with me in Roumania, invited me to an interview she had arranged with a Yiddish writer at his apartment in one of the "Karl Marx Houses". I remembered they had been hailed by left-wingers back home as "model" working-class housing; actually, they looked like prisons. Gray and dreary blocks of concrete, not a single decoration relieved their ugliness. Only the little gardens tended by ground floor tenants relieved the monotony.

Our host, ever gracious, offered us little salads and cakes. "I apologize for this poor fare," he said, "but there is little to buy these days that's worth eating." Thanking him for his kindness, we talked the rest of the afternoon. "It was worse before," he told us, "but now the authorities are allowing me to publish in Yiddish. For years it was forbidden."

Just then we noticed a man walking back and forth in front of the apartment window. He would stop now and then to look inside and stare at us. "Who's that?" we asked in alarm. "Don't be frightened," the writer said, "he's the Party cell captain. He pretends to tend the garden, but he's really spying on me because I am entertaining foreigners." Ruth and I took the bus back to our hotel, depressed and not encouraged by the news of loosening restrictions on Jewish writing.

But the next day something occurred that is engraved in my memory forever. We visited the ancient 13th century synagogue, still in use in the 1960s, a curious wooden building with deep eaves and ancient fittings, so like the primitive peasant architecture seen later in the countryside. Across the street was the cemetery; since Jewish law forbids the removal of corpses, over centuries bodies were buried in layers, one on top of the other. In time the tombstones toppled over, or like misshapen teeth, leaned over in strange positions.

Then, led by a guide, we entered the nearby Pincus Chapel, a baroque synagogue, now a museum. Its elegance suggested that by the 17th century Jews had acquired wealth and position in the community. Soon we filed into a large empty room, its beige walls covered with neat rows of little black and red swiggles. The guide said, "Those marks on the wall are the names of hundreds of Czech Jews who died in German concentration camps." For a long minute not a sound was heard. Then, like me, many began to sob uncontrollably. Each name had once been a living person, flesh and blood, and now they were all dead, only their names left as a memorial. Finally, we filed out in silence, the guide jangling coins in his pocket to remind us to leave a little money in the till. Once in the fresh air, we breathed deeply; the sky was blue, and the sun shone brightly high in the heavens. Ah, beautiful Prague!

After several days we left by train for Gottwaldov in the province of Moravia to attend the International Folk Music Council conference. We settled into our seats gingerly, not daring to lean against the back rests: they were filthy, and the windows covered with soot. Even the uniforms of the ticket takers, all women, were dirt-incrusted, probably unwashed for a decade. It was with relief that we arrived at Gottwaldov.

Unlike the royal attentions in Roumania, we were merely tolerated by Czech officials; there were no banquets, and few receptions. Nevertheless, the Czech delegates eagerly awaited our arrival, hoping to re-establish contact with the West, broken under Soviet rule. We Americans were immediately sought out; they plied us with questions, and were openly critical of their government. "You see those men standing around the room," they said, "they are all government agents, here to spy on us, not you. We're not supposed to talk to you, but we don't care, we'll do it anyway even though we pay for it later."

By the end of the conference we knew folk music research followed the same path observed in Roumania; the Czechs had excellent folk music archives, and dedicated research workers, but their limited approach to their folk music left us baffled. Like Roumanians, they interpreted the words of their songs -- political, social, or personal -- according to Marxist theory, or ignored them altogether, concentrating mainly on musical analysis. Years later, just before the collapse of the Soviet Union, I was to understand the reasons for this approach. On a lecture tour of the United States, Doris Stockmann of East Berlin, and Oskar Elschek, director of the Slovak folk archives, gave their last talks in New York. Dr. Stockmann's lecture at Hunter College was so abstract, so buried in obtuse technical jargon, we understood nothing. The following week, Dr. Elschek spoke to the same audience. Descriptive and coherent, it sounded familiar. Yes, I remembered, it was the same talk I heard him give in Gottwaldov in 1962!

The next day, Oscar came to breakfast at my apartment. "Please," I said, "explain Doris' talk." "You don't understand," he answered with a note of sorrow in his voice, "under our system you avoid controversy. You have two paths: give a talk so abstract no one can accuse you of betraying socialist principles, or repeat what you have done before." There it was, a plausible explanation of how scholars survive under "Socialism". Unfortunately, even the best minds bend under political pressure.

While in Gottwaldov, Czech authorities invited us to visit the world famous Bata shoe factory. As champions of the people's music we welcomed the idea, a chance to know how people work as well as sing and dance. First we were taken through the small museum to see shoe styles over the centuries. Then we were herded into a small room, and as our guide gave us a run-down of Bata's history, the room lifted; it was an elevator. We jumped off (there were no doors) on the top floor and gradually worked our way down. Like Henry Ford's belt-line system, each worker performed a single task; one nailed the heel to the shoe, another painted it, and someone else glued on the sole, etc. They did the same thing day after day, month after month. After the tour, our guide delivered a lengthy speech about working class "dignity" under Socialism. The workers, he said, reach their full potential under our system. We snickered, and walked back to the convention hall. That black smoke, it was still pouring out of the Bata towers. And how come nobody smiled or talked to us while we were in the factory?

The highlight of the congress was a week-long bus tour of Slovak villages. We rolled merrily along the countryside in sight of the Tatra Mountains looming in the distance. One day we lunched at a quaint Swiss-style chalet, once the refuge of wealthy TB patients, and now open to bikers and hikers. After several days on the road, we were an unkempt lot, our clothes wrinkled, hair disheveled, and the men with three day-old beards. Although a momentary respite for us Westerners, the chalet was manna from heaven. Although the chalet was modest on the outside, inside there were dining room windows in pale grey velvet drapes, beige velvet chairs, sparkling crystal chandeliers, and tables set with fine crystal and china. In the center were long buffet tables piled high with fruit pastries, aromatic cheeses, liqueurs and mellow Turkish coffee.

Afterwards, as we continued the journey, the road led along fields of golden grain, with fruit orchards, and white poppies blooming in profusion. And the geese -- more geese than people. No wonder all the hotels had down-filled pillows and quilts! At each stop, our guide delivered lengthy speeches on the benefits of Socialism, but the villagers had their own ideas of how to entertain and feed us. We feasted on freshly baked dark breads, ripe red currants, pitchers of clabbered milk, and poppy seed pastries, like my own mother's.

I was also reminded of my mother's descriptions of her Ukrainian village in the early 20th century; no pavements, no sidewalks, wood- burning stoves, sparsely electrified, and mud up to one's ankles after the rain. And here I was fifty years later, in a Slovak hamlet, and nothing had changed. When I asked an eighty-year-old peasant how life had been under the Turks, she shook her head, sighed and said, "Terrible." Then I asked, "And under the Nazis? " "Terrible" she answered. "The Russians? " I persisted. Again the same answer. Finally I said, "But with your own people here, how is it now? " "Terrible," she said, closing the inquiry. Her town brothers, both in their seventies, standing at her side, echoed her words, "Yes," they said, "that's the way it's always been."

Then the villagers entertained us; we heard the curious sound of a shepherd's double pipe, the *fujara*, watched a wedding ceremony, listened to weird funeral laments, and medieval ballads. We marveled as two shepherds sang to each other across the hills, the way mountaineers communicated long before cellular phones. These Slavs, descendants of 6th-century sheep and goat herders from the Asian steppes, still performed the same seasonal rituals as their ancestors, 13 centuries before!

The costumes were brilliant, the women in long skirts billowing out like Chinese fans, loose embroidered blouses, tight waist-length vests, and lace caps; and the men in broad-brimmed hats, embroidered vests, knee-length pants, and boots. Years later at the Topkapi Museum in Istanbul, I was amazed to see the ancestor of the women's costume. The exquisite statuette of the pre-Islamic snake goddess, bare-breasted and holding two snakes aloft in her hands, wears a long skirt and tight little vest, just like the peasant dress seen everywhere in the Balkans -- only no bare breasts and no snakes.

One day, our bus made a stop at a remote primitive village. As we walked through the dusty unpaved main street lined with little wooden houses, I noticed a couple in the distance, who, by their clothes, I guessed to be Americans. I walked over to talk to them. "Yes," the man confirmed, "we live in the States but I was born here." Recently married, he had brought his bride to Czechoslovakia for their honeymoon. "Some things have changed here," he said," but old superstitions are still around." "By the way," I said, pointing to the nearby poppy fields, "do people here use poppies for anything besides pastries?" He laughed and said, "This village was famous because no one ever heard babies cry. The old ladies used to give them a weak tea made from the poppies to keep them quiet!"

Hooked from infancy, I thought. On the other hand, maybe

those peasants have found the practice beneficial, and harmless as well. In the last years I have been hearing about Mexican doctors' experiments with plants and other cures that Indians have used successfully for eons. And come to think of it, the logo of the medical profession consists of two intertwined snakes. I have read somewhere that the ancient Greeks had a formula to transform the poison into effective medication. A few years ago on a tour of the Turkish island of Ephesus, where the temple to the god of medicine is located, I asked our Turkish guide about it. "Yes," he said, "I was told in school that the ancients used snake poison to cure certain maladies, but we don't use it now."

The tour ended in Bratislava. There we visited the Folklore Institute where the Bela Bartok archive of folk songs is stored. Of both Slovak and Hungarian parents, Bartok was one of the first to actually make recordings of folk music (1904); the Institute not only preserves the originals but all the machines he used during the years of research.

On all our visits to the villages we were honored guests, the visiting authorities come to see their ancient dances and instruments, and hear them sing ancient ritual songs. One day, however, we had a surprise awaiting us. After the village jamboree, we Americans were surrounded by the eager youngsters. "Teach us how to do the "Twist", they begged, and we dutifully obliged. "Why do you want to dance our stuff?" I asked, playing the devil's advocate, "you have your own dances." "We're sick and tired of them," they said, "always doing the same thing. And, we like your music, too." So, I thought, even in these little hamlets, away from cities, far from the blandishments of the West, these youngsters are finding ways to connect with other teenagers in the world outside.

Later on back in Prague, at a private session, I heard a jazz

303

band, all conservatory students. They did wonders with early New Orleans style and 1930s Swing. "How did you learn to play?" I asked. "Sometimes they permit jazz and American protest songs on our only radio station," they said. "But mostly we learned from recordings our friends smuggle into the country. We don't have your instruments but manage pretty well with the ones we have."

I am reminded of another example of youngsters in the Soviet block reaching out beyond their own borders. In 1984 I spent a week in a charming Serbian village with Yugoslavia's senior ethnomusicologist. The young people there not only dressed like our own teenagers, jeans and tee shirts, but also listened to the latest rock music and watched Hollywood films. My friend considered this intolerable, a betrayal of their own culture, and called them together for a meeting. "What is the matter with you?" she said angrily, "our music is beautiful, admired everywhere in the world, yet you listen to this American junk." The youngsters listened to her, but made no comment. The next day, I again heard the familiar strains of rock blaring forth from their cassette players. Besides, in the 1960s there were already local rock bands in Yugoslavia, regularly featured on local radio stations.

On our last day in Prague I walked with my colleagues, Radmila Petrovic of Yugoslavia, Hannah Laudova, a Czech, and Raina Katzarova of Bulgaria, up the hill to see Prague's crown jewel, Hradcany castle, the site of the Gothic St. Vitus cathedral and the tomb of St. Wenceslaus. Suddenly, an enormous statue of Stalin loomed into view. Astonished, I stopped to stare at it; it towered above the entire city. "What in hell is that doing here?" I yelled. "Stalin's dead, isn't he?" Without losing a step, Hannah pushed me up the hill. "Oh come, Henrietta," she said impatiently, "don't let it bother you. We're sick of it too; we don't even look at it anymore. Besides, it's to be pulled down pretty soon."

We smiled at each other, held hands, and walked up the hill to the castle.

***

Germany and Austria
1987, 1988-89

It was with a heavy heart that I went to the 1987 meetings of the International Council for Traditional Music in East Berlin (ICTM), the new name for the International Folk Music Council (IFMC). The murder of my mother's family, her brothers, sisters, spouses and children was still fresh in my memory. Early in 1942 they had been lined up on a street in Rovno, Poland, tortured and shot to death. Even as the plane landed in Hamburg on the North Sea my apprehensive mood persisted. My first sight of the city was jolting! Was this light, airy city the place where storm troopers once marched, their arms raised on high shouting "Heil Hitler"? It was hard to believe.

A few hours later I boarded the train for West Berlin and was met at the railroad station by Susanne Zeigler, our German host, and Marcia Herndon, my American colleague. Two years before, at ICTM meetings in Stockholm and Helsinki, we had formed a group to study gender issues in music. Now we were meeting to formalize it as a sub-group within ICTM. Women, as well as men, from the four corners of the globe -- Africa, Egypt, Europe, East and West, and the States -- assembled at a modest *pension* of West Berlin to exchange views, and formulate a program. Hour

305

after hour we argued over the exact wording. However, on one point we all agreed: the time had come to recognize and publicize women's accomplishments in popular culture, ignored or belittled for ages. Happy with our proposal, we retired for the night. The next morning the atmosphere around the breakfast table was chilly, the German women silent and distant. Finally, they spoke up. "We can't sign such a document," they said, "we're afraid to lose our jobs." True or not, their fears were genuine, so we hammered out a softer, more conciliatory statement. We learned an important lesson; not everybody agreed on goals, or methods, no matter how noble the cause. I was reminded of a recent TV program I had seen in New York, an international panel discussion on women's liberation; to the American it meant access to the executive bathroom; to the Middle Eastern woman, the end of beatings by her husband.

Finally, we prepared to leave for the conference in East Berlin. On the advice of our West Berlin colleagues we bought East German marks at the railroad station. What a bargain! We got five marks for our dollar, better than one to one, the official rate of exchange. To avoid discovery we stashed the illegal marks in our shoes, my first act as a smuggler. Nervously we waited at Checkpoint Charlie. "Ah," said the guards cheerfully," so you are going to the ICTM Conference. Welcome, comrades, we wish you success." And they bowed us in.

Within minutes we arrived at our hotel and conference headquarters. So, here I was in East Berlin, again behind the Iron Curtain. But where was the proletarian austerity I had been warned about? The hotel rooms, the dining area, the pool and health club, and breakfast the next morning were the equal of any five-star hotel in the West. We feasted on a staggering menu of cured meats, smoked fish, gelatins, fruits, pastries, breads, salads, etc.

The hotel, however, fully aware of the illegal money exchange in the West, refused our marks accepting only dollars, as payment of our hotel bill. Still, in the shops we got real bargains, like opera glasses, and paid for them with our illegal marks.

Our first walk beyond the hotel revealed a dirty and neglected city. The row of 19th century Greek classical-style art museums, once their pride, and the ugly, forbidding Reichstag, had not been cleaned since the start of Communist rule. Even the people had the same shabby look, dressed in what looked like hand-me-downs, the kind sold in 14th Street bargain basements.

But inside the conference hall there was good feeling everywhere and an open exchange of views. Unlike the Balkans, the East German Communists did not publicly lecture us, over coffee and pastry the great progress under socialism, the lack of anti-Semitism (!), etc., were enthusiastically recited.

The conference highlight was the ovation I received for my own paper on Bessie Smith, the great blues singer. Bessie, like other jazz and blues singers, was admired throughout Europe for her magnificent voice and powerful delivery. My paper, however, focused not on her musicianship, but on her frank and stinging opinions about life -- her hostility toward whites, debilitating alcoholism, and her distrust of men. I'm sure what they admired most of all was her obvious enjoyment of sex. These were not the usual romantic love songs, but, frank talk about sexual pleasure. Her plain but salty language drew laughter and applause from the audience. Bessie was the celebrity of the meeting. Here are a few sample stanzas, the first from "I'm Wild About That Thing":

Give it to me, papa, I'm wild about that thing.
Do it easy, honey, don't get rough;

From you, papa, I can't get enough,
I'm wild about that thing, sweet joy it always brings.

The second is from "Black Mountain Blues", a tough and unforgiving song about a two-timing man whom she threatens with violence:

Had a man in Black Mountain,
The sweetest man in town,
He met a city gal and he throwed me down.
I'm bound for Black Mountain
Me and my razor and my gun.
I'm gonna shoot him if he stands still,
Cut him if he runs.

But finally the serious part of the conference was over, and the partying began. Since Berlin had no folk song or dance groups, we were entertained with chamber music concerts. I probably never would have remembered such routine affairs but for one non-musical reason. The concert was held at the elegant Sans Souci Palace at Potsdam in East Germany, where the Allies in 1945 hammered out the agreement that ended the war. Leisurely, we walked down long pebble paths, carefully tended green lawns and vast gardens of multi-hued flowers. Once in the palace, we were led upstairs to an exquisite concert room, and after the usual wine reception, were seated. As the string quartet began to play, my gaze wandered around the room. What a shock! In a series of recessed niches were statues of nude men, their genitals prominently displayed. Strange, the sight of a single male nude, like Michelangelo's David in Florence, hardly causes a ripple, but a roomful of them, well, that is another matter!

The conference over, we explored the city, had coffee and

pastries at cafes, sunned ourselves in the parks, and visited museums, saw abstract art forbidden under the Nazis, Lembruck's magnificent 19th century masterpiece "The Kneeling Woman", Kathi Kollewitz' realistic paintings of the poor, and Georg Grosz' biting satirical drawings of post-World War I Germany.

They even showed Nazi era art, insipid paintings of buxom blond blue-eyed women, and stalwart, muscular men, just as banal as the joyous peasants of Soviet art under Stalin. A few years later, on a return visit to Berlin, the Nazi exhibit had disappeared, "verboten", I was told, banished by the authorities. Certainly, my young German friends never mentioned it, or anything else about the Nazi era; it was better forgotten, buried under the rug.

Yes, parts of East Berlin were lovely: on elegant Unter den Linden; people were enjoying the warm air, wheeling babies in elegant carriages, boys flirting with the girls, and drinking coffee at outdoor cafes. Then one day I had a piercing reminder of a brutal past. Richard Campbell, an American musicologist long resident in Berlin, invited me and Jane Mink, a fellow ICTM member, on a tour of the old Jewish sector, where Jews had lived before the war. Richard led us down a little side street and stopped in front of a building with an imposing facade. "This is the synagogue," he said, "where Jews worshiped before the war, it was built in the 19th century." It was in a most deplorable state, in disuse and disrepair. I looked at it for a long time, couldn't talk, couldn't say a word -- and then burst into sobs. Though Richard and Jane tried to console me, I couldn't stop crying. Finally, they led me away and we walked to the nearby Jewish residential area. "This is where Jews used to live," said Richard, "you see the holes in those buildings? They were made by Soviet bullets when they liberated the city. Nobody lives there now; you see them exactly as they were in 1942. Nothing has changed." Then we walked to the cemetery.

That, too, showed signs of desecration and neglect, not even a placard to mark it as a Jewish burial site.

When I returned to Berlin several years later the Wall was down, Checkpoint Charlie was gone, and buses ran regularly through the Brandenburg Gate. Although East Berlin was still in a dilapidated state, the Old Synagogue had been renovated to its former glory. The cupola, now covered in gold leaf, shone brightly even on that cloudy day, a guided tour of the restored interior was available, and pamphlets on the synagogue's history were on sale. There was even a commemorative plaque marking the nearby Old People's Home where in 1938, thousands of Jews had sought refuge during *Kristallnacht*, and were sent off to their deaths in concentration camps.

In 1988 our gender group returned to Germany invited by "Women in Music", an international organization, to participate in a music festival at Heidelberg. This ancient university town, situated within vineyards and orchards, has been since the 14th century an imposing intellectual center. Still a beautiful town, it has hardly changed over the centuries. We wandered down medieval alleyways, paused at the River Neckar to gaze upon distant and tranquil valleys, and were almost transported to a distant past.

The festival jolted us back to the immediate present. For the next few days we listened to concerts of the latest trends in modern classical music. Since my years at WNYC in the 1940s I have championed experimentation, but these unmusical, hybrid products left me cold; they were techno-driven and lacked any semblance of emotion. On the other hand, the popular and folk music part of the festival was the best I ever attended. There were women, as well as men from every continent; we spent the days together, breakfasted, lunched and dined together. We heard music from women of different races, different religions, from agricultural areas, mining areas, from shops and industrial plants, each with its own musical language, each with its own story to tell. It was a historic meeting, the first of its kind to focus on women's contribution to popular culture, so long neglected and denied.

While there was harmony and tolerance within our small circle, on the streets of Heidelberg we saw evidence that Nazism, though out of power, was still alive. One day a dinner party attended by women from several countries, speaking English as their common language, was interrupted by several German youth, "You are in Germany, speak German," they said, belligerently. Afterwards, we had to comfort our German colleagues because they were even more distressed by this senseless hostility than the rest of us.

***

A year later we were again reminded of the Nazi past, this time in Schladming Austria, a ski-resort where the ICTM held meetings in 1989. When I learned Kurt Waldheim, the president of Austria, ex-Secretary of United Nations, and ex-Nazi, was scheduled to inaugurate our meeting, I informed our president, Eric Stockmann, of East Germany, and Wolfgang Suppan, the Austrian program director, that I would boycott the opening ceremony. Arriving the night before the opening, and assigned to a small guesthouse I could only organize the dozen or so stationed there. The next morning, with tension running high, the conference was called to order. Mr. Waldheim was introduced, and as he stepped to the podium poised for his speech, we walked out. A moment later a group of young German colleagues walked out too: they had organized their own protest. Later I found out that others had stayed away, too, an invisible and therefore ineffective protest. The meetings proceeded as usual, papers read, followed by

311

discussions. Here, as in Germany, unlike the Balkan states visited in previous years, there were no local folk singers or dancers, only the nightly oom-pah-pah band concert, certainly ranking as the world's dullest music.

Then came the finale, the business meeting, usually a tiresome session conducted without incident. This time, however, we had the first upheaval ever experienced at an ICTM meeting. When a young Brazilian woman asked why Mr. Waldheim, a known Nazi, had been invited to inaugurate the meeting, pandemonium broke out. Our president was flustered, and our general secretary made lame excuses, even offering to resign (which he had no intention of doing), and Mr. Suppan sat out the turmoil outside, and was heard to say, "It is finished, I have everything I wanted from this meeting." I've often wondered what he wanted, and what he got as a reward from Waldheim. Who knows, but he remains persona non-grata in our organization.

The conference over, and all the goodbyes said, we left this dull and dreary resort town as fast as we could. A few of us spent our last day together in nearby Salzburg, where the annual Mozart festival was in full swing. Photos of James Levine and Jessye Norman were plastered all over town. Salzburg is a beautiful town, Mozart, its commercial drawing card; his image everywhere, even on boxes of chocolate.

But during the festival Salzburg belongs to the rich and privileged, though not limited to the nobility, as it did in Mozart's time. (He himself had a low opinion of them, clearly expressed in his numerous letters). In our walks through town we were amazed at the sight of the luxurious gowns worn by the women, each one surely costing thousands of dollars. Sure enough, when I priced them at several boutiques, my suspicions were confirmed. Tickets were selling at $200 a seat, out of my range entirely. What the hell, I thought, I'll hear Mozart in New York at the Metropolitan Opera House for much less and just as good, if not better.

Happily, I returned to New York and as soon as possible and visited my family. Come to think of it, my grandson Nicholas plays a mean Mozart!

P.S. If my readers think my reports of repression in Soviet-controlled countries were isolated or insignificant incidents, they were in fact only the tip of the iceberg. A lead article in the *New York Times* of November 29th, 1999 states that domestic spying was typical everywhere in the Soviet world. The East German secret police, the *Stasi*, for instance, boasted 95,000 full time agents and as many as 160,000 unofficial informers spying on a population of 17 million. As for Nazism -- anti-Semitism, anti-gypsy, and anti-immigrant incidents are presently on the rise all over Europe, and no one knows if there is an end in sight.

And sad to report, in the United States there are now hundreds of Neo-Nazi Web sites. Many videos of concerts and numerous CDs with hundreds of hate songs can be bought on the Internet. The targets are not only Jews, but also blacks, Latinos, Asians, lesbians, gays, and even Christians, a throwback to Nazi worship of Norse gods; they are calls to kill.

***

48-Two peasant women. Galicia, Spain. *Photo: Neva Wartel, 1989.*

49-Henrietta Yurchenco. Galicia,
Spain. *Photo: Neva Wartel, 1989.*

50-Henrietta Yurchenco at her apartment at dinner with friends (left to right) Allen Cooper, Doris Dyen, and Deane Root. New York, 1999.

51-Henrietta Yurchenco at her apartment playing 4-hand piano with Allen Cooper. New York, 1999.

52-Henrietta Yurchenco at her apartment with best friend Dasha, a designer. New York, 1991.

(Left) 53-Akin Euba and Henrietta Yurchenco during the International Council of Traditional Music (ICTM) Conference, Berlin, Germany, 1987.

(Right) 54-Jane Mink Rosen, Cynthia Tse Kimberlin, and Henrietta Yurchenco during the ICTM Conference. Berlin, Germany, 1993.

55-Henrietta Yurchenco at her New York apartment. *Photo: Cynthia Tse Kimberlin, 2001.*

*P*ostscript

Memory is tricky, unreliable, and sometimes downright deceptive. I have written much about my life in these pages, but not everything. As I reread the completed manuscript a torrent of other memories I had thought long forgotten, flooded my consciousness. For instance, have I told you anything about my trips to India, Japan, Korea, Argentina or Ireland? Almost nothing. Also, what did I tell you about my love life? Practically nothing. I know it is fashionable these days for memoirs to dwell on sexual scandals and turbulent relationships. I would gladly have reported them had I ever committed anything out of the ordinary, like incest or sado-masochism, or affairs with presidents, kings or dictators. Alas, I never had experiences of that kind; recollections of the passions and fury of my intimate life have faded away, leaving me with the fuzzy feeling that they happened to someone else.

I have another reason for my reluctance to tell everything: to protect my reputation as a storyteller. When family and friends visit me afternoons at my apartment, we relax over tea and homemade cakes and muffins. From my window overlooking the Hudson River we watch the sun slowly sink behind the Jersey hills, the sky in streaks of red, orange and purple. The conversation turns to the latest political scandal, the new films, and plays on Broadway; everything is aired in the waning hours of the day. Often I interrupt the conversation with a story: "Have I ever told you," I begin, "about the time in Madras when I saw them pour yogurt over the elephant god?" Imagine how crushed I will feel if I am greeted with, "Yeah, yeah, we already read that in your memoirs!" As I said, I have to protect my reputation as a storyteller.

I should mention here that despite my advanced age I continue to lecture, give radio programs, produce CDs, write and travel, the last with difficultly, but I do it. I am also a happy homemaker; a gourmet cook and pastry maker, qualities enjoyed by friends and family. In addition I am a model grandmother to Helen, a budding musician, and Nicholas with both musical and literary talents. When they were children they admired me -- not because of my bizarre adventures in distant and unknown lands but because I had once killed a deadly scorpion with my own hands. Now, I offer them advice and help them in every way possible.

But, I also have other strong ties: to my son Peter, who gives me nothing but joy, his lovely wife Ingrid, and my entire family, principally my loving sister Ruth, and then my nieces, nephews and sister-in-law. I honor the memory of my brother, Nathaniel, my brother-in-law David Lester, and lastly, my nephew James, whose life ended too soon, and my unforgettable parents, Rebecca and Edward Weiss.

I also thank my friends and colleagues for their help in preparing this memoir: Sandra Hernandez and Neva Wartel.

***

Works in Various Media by Henrietta Yurchenco

Field Collections

Yurchenco's field recordings made between 1942 and 1992 are housed in the Folk Archives of the Library of Congress. Copies of individual collections are available at the:

Fonoteca of the Hebrew University, Jerusalem, Israel
Arias Montana Institute of Madrid, Spain
National Indian Institute, Mexico City, Mexico
Sephardic Foundation, New York, USA

Mexico and Guatemala
1942-46   Over 2,000 items from 14 different Indian tribes and folk communities.

Spain and Morocco
1953-56   Western and Central provinces of Spain, the Balearic Islands (Ibiza, Menorca), Tangier and Tetuan, Morocco among the Sephardic Jews.

Mexico
1964-66, 1971-72, 1981, 1988, 1992.
-Purepecha (Tarascan) Indians. 1942 and resumed in the 1960s. About 500 items. Many mestizo songs and instrumental pieces.
-Isthmus of Tehuantepec. 1942 and 1945, resumed in 1971-72 and 1992 among Zapotec Indians
-1988 Yucatan.   Ritual music in the community of Yaxcaba.

Puerto Rico
1967, 1969 Traditional music in mountain communities and in Loiza Aldea, one of coastal Puerto Rico's black towns.

John's Island, South Carolina
1970-71   Traditional music--children's game songs, gospel music in church and at home, prayers, preaching and testimonials, and blues.

Ireland
1973-74   Traditional music--ballads, dance music on instruments such as the fiddle, tin whistle, bagpipes, and concertina.

Colombia and Ecuador
1975-76   Black coastal communities of Colombia. Children's music in Ecuador.

Galicia, Spain
1990   Preliminary study of women's songs. Recordings and video.

Bibliography

Articles
1943   "La Musica Indigena en Chiapas", *America Indigena*, Mexico City, October.
1946   "Grabacion de Musica Indigena", *Nuestra Musica*, Mexico City, May.
1957   "Taping History in Morocco," *American Record Guide*, New York, December.
1958   "Taping History in Guatemala." *American Record Guide*, New York, December.
1959   "Roumanian Journal." *American Record Guide*, New York, December.
1960   "The Guided Muse" (on Roumania). *East Europe*, New York, September.
1961   "The Folk Music Craze." *Ingenue*, New York, July.
1962a   *Introduction to A Russian Song Book* (Random House), New York.

1962b "Fifteenth Conference of the International Folk Music Council in Czechoslovakia." *The World of Music* (UNESCO), Paris, October.

1962c "Primitive Music in Indian Mexico." *Hi-Fi/Stereo Review*, New York, October.

1963a "Survivals of Pre-Hispanic Music in Mexico." *Journal of the International Folk Music Council*, London, June.

1963b "The Folk Singing Generation." *Ingenue*, New York, March.

1963c "Investigacion Folklorico-Musical en Nayarit y Jalisco, Grupos Indigenas Coras y Huicholes." *Cuadernos de Bellas Artes*, Mexico City.

1964 "Sentimental Journey/Slovakian Style." *Folk Music*, New York, July.

1965 "In Defense of Bob Dylan." *Sounds and Fury*; reprinted 1966 in *The New Sound* (Scholastics), New York; in Bob Dylan's *Four Decades of Commentary*, 1998.

1966a Essay on "Folk Music" for the *Book of Knowledge*. New York.

1966b Essay on "Oriental Music" for the *Book of Knowledge*. New York.

1966c "Taping History in Mexico." *American Record Guide*, New York, September.

1982 "Styles of Performance and Multi-Part Music in Latin American Indian Music." South American Review.

1983 "Performing Styles in Mexican Indian Music with particular Reference to the Tarascan Pirecua." *Sabiduria Popular* (El Colegio de Michoacán).

1985 "El Rabinal Achí, a Prehispanic Dance-Drama of the Maya-Quiches of Guatemala." *Acta Musicologica*, Germany.

1987 "A Memoir: The Depression Years." *Sonneck Society Bulletin*, Summer.

1989   "Mexico's Unknown Composers" (In Spanish), *Mundo*, Mexico City, October.

1990   "Mean Mama Blues: Bessie Smith and theVaudeville Era". *Music, Gender, and Culture*, Berlin.

1991   "Trouble in the Mines: A History in Song and Story by Women of Appalachia." *American Music*, Summer.

1996a   "Blues Falling Down Like Hail." *American Music*, Winter.

1996b   "An Introduction to Music of Indian Mexico and Guatemala from Prehispanic Times to the Present". *Sonneck Society Bulletin*, Fall.

1998   "The Fiesta of Santiago in Loiza Aldea, Puerto Rico. A Caribbean Version of a 13th Century Spanish Pageant." *Sonneck Society Bulletin*, Fall.

Books
1966   *A Fiesta of Songs from Latin America and Spain*. New York: Putnam's Sons.

1970   *A Mighty Hard Road: The Woody Guthrie Story*. New York: McGraw-Hill.

1971   *Hablamos! Puerto Ricans Speak*. New York: Praeger.

In Manuscript
In Their Own Voices: Women in the Judeo-Hispanic Song and Story
La Vuelta al Mundo en 80 Años: Memorias

Discography

NOTE: Folkways listings are available at the Smithsonian Institution. For more information contact Smithsonian/Folkways, 955 L'Enfant Plaza Ste. 2600 – MRC 914, Washington, D.C. 20560. Phone: (202) 287-3262   E-mail: folkways@aol.com

Original Folkways albums are available by request on cassette or CD from Smithsonian Folkways, and from
Down Home Music, 10341 San Pablo Avenue, El Cerrito, CA 94530. Phone: (510) 525-2129. http//downhomemusic.com

1947 *Folk Music of Mexico*. Library of Congress Vol. 19.

1952 *Indian Music of Mexico: Tzotzil, Yaqui, Huichol, Seri, Cora*. Folkways F4413.

1966 *The Real Mexico*. Nonesuch H2009.

1968 *Latin American Children's Game Songs*. Recorded in Puerto Rico and Mexico. Folkways 7851.

1970a *Music of the Tarascan Indians of Mexico*. Folkways 4217.

1971b *Folk Songs of Puerto Rico*. Folkways 4412.

1973c *John's Island, South Carolina: Its People and Songs*. Folkways FS3840.

1975 *Anthology of Central and South American Indian Music*, Compiled by Alan Lazar. Folkways 04542. (Some of Yurchenco's recordings are included.)

1976 *Mexico South: Traditional Songs and Dances from the Isthmus of Tehuantepec*. Folkways FE4378.

1977 *Children's Games and Songs from Ecuador, Mexico and Puerto Rico*. Folkways FC7854.

1978 *Music of the Maya-Quiches of Guatemala: Rabinal Achí and Baile* de las Canastas. Folkways FE4226.

1983 *Ballads, Wedding Songs and Piyyutim, of the Sephardic Jews of Tetua and Tangier, Morocco*. Folkways FE4208.

1996 *The Bride's Joys and Sorrows. Songs and Ballads of the Moroccan Women of Tetuan, Morocco*. Global Village CD 148.

[1988] *El Lobo: Songs and Games of Latin America*. Rounder Kids 8078 © 1998.

2000 *Mexico: Rosa de Castilla and Other Love Songs*. Rounder CD 5158.

2001 *Musica de Michoacán*. Mexico.

2000   *La Vida Mexicana: Mariachis y Rancheros: Judith Reyes*.
Global Village.

Record Liner Notes

Provided liner notes on American, European and Latin American
folk music for record companies including Columbia, Vanguard,
Decca, Elektra, Folkways, Monitor, Artia, Parliament, Odyssey,
Mercury, Mercury-Phillips.

Criticism

1959-71	Folk Music Editor for the *American Record Guide*.
1962-65	Folk Music Editor for *Musical America*.
1961-69	Contributor to *Sing Out!*.
Ongoing	Contributor to *Yearbook for Traditional Music* (formerly *Journal of the International Folk Music Council*) and *Bulletin of the IFMC/ICTM*.
1971	*Library Notes*
Ongoing	*Ethnomusicology*
Ongoing	*American Music*
Ongoing	*Sonneck Society Bulletin*

Radio and Television

1939-41 Producer of Special Music Events for WNYC, 1939-41.
Pioneer broadcaster of folk music from all parts of the world.
Initiated the annual American Music Festival, an important
cultural event in New York City. Presented folk artists
including Woody Guthrie, Leadbelly, Pete Seeger, Aunt Molly
Jackson, Burl Ives, and Sarah Ogan Gunning.

1942   Series of broadcasts on Latin American music for the Inter-
American Indian Institute in Mexico and the Pan American
Union.

1960-62 Weekly broadcasts, "Music of Many Lands" for Heritage national network on FM stations.

1960-61 Weekly broadcasts, "Folk Music Abroad" on WBAI and other Pacifica stations.

1961-69 Weekly broadcasts, "Adventures in Folk Music" on WNYC, with and including Bob Dylan, Noble Sissle, Doc Watson, and Janis Ian.

1963 Yurchenco on television, interviewed by Willard Rhodes for Columbia University's series on Channel 5.

1995-2002 Numerous broadcasts over Mexican airways.

***

Index

— A —

Adorno, Theodor, 33
Alicia, 243, 247, 250, 253
- 254, 256
Angel, Miguel, 161
Anguiano, Lic, 96
Arevalo, Jose Luis, 150
Argentina, 24, 53, 83,
150, 315

Arguedas, Sol, 99, 188
Armistead, Sam, 247
Arqueada, Sr., 211
Arriaga, Agustin, 193
Arriola, Jorge Luis, 150
Ashkelon, 253
Ayala, Castor, 265 - 268,
273

— B —

Baez, Joan, 57, 64
Baja Verapaz, 151
Bali, 51, 102
Bartok, Bela, 33, 36, 304
Bateson, Gregory, 51
Becerri, Miss, 274
Belo, Jane, 51
Benamor, Flora, 244, 250
Benassayag, Alicia, 243,
247, 250
Benchimol, Ester, 242,
247, 251
Betanzas, Benjamin, 208
Bodet, Torres, 113
Bonilla, Sr., 126 129, 131

- 132, 134
Botkin, Benjamin, 114
Bowles, Paul, 31, 238
Braden, Spruille, 53
Brant, Henry, 31
Bratislava, 303
Breuer, Marcel, 24, 115,
175
Brimberg, Isaac, 30
Brooklyn College, 56
Browne, Byron, 29
Bucharest, 285 - 286, 290,
292, 294
Burgos, Antonio, 139, 232

— C —

Cambridge, 137, 175

Camille, 176, 190

— D —

Harris, Roy, 31

Hassan, Iacobo, 248, 252 - 253

Hawes, Ellen, 280

Hawes, Pete, 45 - 46

Hays, Lee, 45

Heidelberg, 311 - 312

Helak, John, 69

Hermosillo, 137 - 138, 145, 177, 184 - 185

Herndon, Marcia, 306

Herzog, George, 36 - 37

Hillery, Mabel, 60, 68

Hodges, Johnny, 61

Houston, Elsie, 37

Hoyt, Edith, 155, 166

Hudnut, Richard, 175

Huerta, Josquin, 208

Huichol, 118, 124 - 126, 129 - 130, 134 - 135, 183

Huilotita, 127 - 129

Hunter, Janey, 69

— I —

Illsley, Bundy, 199

Illsley, Cathy, 199

Illsley, Walter, 24, 66, 115, 175, 199

India, 37, 65, 247, 315

Inti, 99

Ireland, 260, 315, 318

Isabel, 89, 212, 215 - 217

Israel, 3, 244, 246, 248, 250, 252 - 255, 317

Israel, Ester Cadoch, 244, 250

Istanbul, 233, 302

Isthmus of Techuantepec, 203

Italy, 222

Ixtepec, 102

— J —

Jackson, Aunt Molly, 37, 46, 323

Jalisco, 125, 189, 205, 319

Japan, 86, 88, 124, 247, 295, 315

Jaracuaro Island, 192, 196

Jefferson, Blind Lemon, 48

Jenkins, Esau, 68

Jesus Maria, 119, 123

Jody, 195

John Reed Club, 23 - 24

Juchitan, 204, 208 - 209

— K —

— L —

— M —

— N —

— O —

— P —

— Q —

— R —

— S —

— T —

— U —

— V —

— W —

— Y —

— Z —